CAMBRIDGE LIBI

Books of enduri

History

The books reissued in this series include accounts of historical events and movements by eye-witnesses and contemporaries, as well as landmark studies that assembled significant source materials or developed new historiographical methods. The series includes work in social, political and military history on a wide range of periods and regions, giving modern scholars ready access to influential publications of the past.

The Works of Thomas Carlyle

Thomas Carlyle (1795–1881) was one of the most influential authors of the nineteenth century. Eagerly studied at the highest level of intellectual society, his satirical essays and perceptive historical biographies caused him to be regarded for much of the Victorian period as a literary genius and eminent social philosopher. After graduating from Edinburgh University in 1814, he published his first scholarly work on German literature in 1824, before finding literary success with his ground-breaking history of the French Revolution in 1837. After falling from favour during the first part of the twentieth century, his work has more recently become the subject of scholarly re-examination. His introduction of German literature and philosophy into the British intellectual milieu profoundly influenced later philosophical ideas and literary studies. These volumes are reproduced from the 1896 Centenary Edition of his collected works. Volume 20 contains his controversial collection of essays, *Latter–Day Pamphlets*.

Cambridge University Press has long been a pioneer in the reissuing of out-of-print titles from its own backlist, producing digital reprints of books that are still sought after by scholars and students but could not be reprinted economically using traditional technology. The Cambridge Library Collection extends this activity to a wider range of books which are still of importance to researchers and professionals, either for the source material they contain, or as landmarks in the history of their academic discipline.

Drawing from the world-renowned collections in the Cambridge University Library, and guided by the advice of experts in each subject area, Cambridge University Press is using state-of-the-art scanning machines in its own Printing House to capture the content of each book selected for inclusion. The files are processed to give a consistently clear, crisp image, and the books finished to the high quality standard for which the Press is recognised around the world. The latest print-on-demand technology ensures that the books will remain available indefinitely, and that orders for single or multiple copies can quickly be supplied.

The Cambridge Library Collection will bring back to life books of enduring scholarly value (including out-of-copyright works originally issued by other publishers) across a wide range of disciplines in the humanities and social sciences and in science and technology.

The Works of Thomas Carlyle

Volume 20:
Latter-Day Pamphlets

Edited by Henry Duff Traill

Cambridge
University Press

CAMBRIDGE UNIVERSITY PRESS

Cambridge, New York, Melbourne, Madrid, Cape Town, Singapore,
São Paolo, Delhi, Dubai, Tokyo, Mexico City

Published in the United States of America by Cambridge University Press, New York

www.cambridge.org
Information on this title: www.cambridge.org/9781108022439

This edition first published 1898
This digitally printed version 2010

ISBN 978-1-108-02243-9 Paperback

CENTENARY EDITION

THE WORKS OF

THOMAS CARLYLE

IN THIRTY VOLUMES

VOL. XX

LATTER-DAY PAMPHLETS

Thomas Carlyle.

From the Millais portrait.

THOMAS CARLYLE

LATTER-DAY PAMPHLETS

But as yet struggles the twelfth hour of the Night. Birds of darkness are on the wing; spectres uproar; the dead walk; the living dream. Thou, Eternal Providence, wilt make the Day dawn!—JEAN PAUL.

Then said his Lordship, 'Well, God mend all!'—'Nay, by God, Donald, we must help him to mend it!' said the other.—RUSHWORTH (*Sir David Ramsay and Lord Rea, in* 1630.)

IN ONE VOLUME

LONDON
CHAPMAN AND HALL
LIMITED
1898

Originally published 1850

CONTENTS

INTRODUCTION

Of all Carlyle's works the *Latter-Day Pamphlets* are the most 'occasional,' and for that reason, no doubt, they have suffered most from the hand of time. In truth they are journalism—that and nothing else: glorified journalism if we like, but bearing such traces of their originating spirit as no drapery of imagination or rhetoric or humour can altogether conceal. And what is more, the glorification of this journalism by the genius of the temporary journalist does not hide the fact that *as* journalism they are ineffective. They are too long, too discursive, too unpractical. They deal at once too much in generalities and too little; and though largely denunciatory of those tendencies, moral and intellectual, which seemed to Carlyle to make for misgovernment in the England of 1850, they do not confine themselves wholly to that safe philosophic region, but condescend upon particulars to such an extent as to keep the reader in continual expectancy of some definite recommendations of legislative or administrative policy — which never come. For the counsels contained in 'The New Downing Street' with its fantastic proposals of reduction in the Foreign Office, the War Office, and the exterior departments of the State in general, and its visionary scheme of setting the Home Office to work in 'regimenting Pauper Banditti into Soldiers of Industry,' could hardly even then, and certainly cannot now, be seriously considered.

And even the safer Carlylean generalities—the tirades at large against Democracy, vigorous, eloquent, grimly comic as they often are, impress one less than usual. The note is forced; the prophet is too wildly excited; there is a suggestion of panic in his utterances; and we could almost guess, without examining dates, that these warnings were uttered while the events of 1848 were still fresh in the writer's mind. One sees that Carlyle's nerves had not yet recovered from the shock of that 'Year of Revolutions,' with its cyclonic wave of European revolt; and small blame to him that he should have misread a phenomenon which remains imperfectly explained even at the present day. But misread it he clearly did. He evidently regarded it as the beginning of the end of Popular Rule, and inferred from it that Democracy—which those among us who still believe it to be bound for the abyss must at least admit, eight-and-forty years afterwards, to be descending the slope in a very leisurely and decorous fashion—had suddenly 'put on the pace' of the Gadarene swine. Yet, with all the pessimism of his outlook upon the domestic future of popularly governed countries, it is curious to note how undoubtingly Carlyle shared the international optimism which was so prevalent in the year before the great "Exhibition of the Arts and Industries of All Nations." 'As to foreign peace,' he writes, 'really all Europe now, especially with so many railroads, public journals, printed books, penny post, bills of exchange, and continual intercourse and mutual dependence, is more and more becoming (so to speak) one Parish.' 'So to speak' indeed! Carlyle goes on to admit that the Czar of Russia, in the 'Eastern part of the Parish' may have less peaceful notions than the rest of the world, but he knows too well he must keep them to himself. So that 'in spite of editorial prophecy, the Czar of Russia does not disturb our night's rest.' Carlyle, it is true, was thinking of and deriding the idea of a Russian attack on Western Democracy, and not of a Russian intrigue against an effete Eastern despotism. But what a desperately unhappy forecast to have taken of an Europe which, little more than four years afterwards, saw three Great Powers at war; and ere the next decade of the century had run half its course, had entered—with the Austro-Prussian attack on Denmark — upon that long era of unrest which shows no prospect of closing with the century.

It is little to be wondered at that *Latter-Day Pamphlets* had a somewhat convulsive effect on Carlyle's Radical and revolutionary friends, and produced something like a positive enstrangement between him and such men as Mazzini and Mill. Perhaps in the latter case, and in the intensely 'Little England' temper of the Radicalism of that day, the alienation was as much due to what was sound, sensible, and patriotic in the *Pamphlets* as to what was exaggerated and overstrained. Anyhow, it is pleasant for the Imperialist admirer of Carlyle in these days to be able to set-off against the melancholy prophetic failure just quoted a passage of such shrewdness and foresight and manly English spirit as that which I am about to quote :—

'And yet an instinct deeper than the Gospel of M'Croudy teaches all men that Colonies are worth something to a country! That if, under the present Colonial Office, they are a vexation to us and themselves, some other Colonial Office can and must be contrived which shall render them a blessing; and that the remedy will be to contrive such a Colonial Office or method of administration, and by no means to cut the Colonies loose. Colonies are not to be picked off the street every day; not a Colony of them but has been bought dear, well purchased by the toil and blood of those we have the honour to be sons of; and we cannot just afford to cut them away because M'Croudy finds the present management of them cost money. The present management will indeed require to be cut away;—but as for the Colonies, we purpose through Heaven's blessing to retain them a while yet! Shame on us for unworthy sons of brave fathers if we do not. Brave fathers, by valiant blood and sweat, purchased for us, from the bounty of Heaven, rich possessions in all zones; and we, wretched imbeciles, cannot do the function of administering them? And because the accounts do not stand well in the ledger, our remedy is, not to take shame to ourselves, and repent in sackcloth and ashes, and amend our beggarly imbecilities and insincerities in that as in other departments of our business, but to fling the business overboard, and declare the business itself to be bad? We are a hopeful set of heirs to a big fortune! It does not suit our Manton gunneries, grouse-shootings, mousings in the City; and like spirited young gentlemen we will give it up, and let the attorneys take it?'

Strange language this for the year 1850, though it is familiar enough to-day, or rather it has only ceased to be so because the very success of its reproofs has now rendered them superfluous. It is not without a melancholy pleasure that one quotes it, if only as a relief from the general impression that the volume, with all its spirit and eloquence and caustic irony, leaves behind it—namely that the prophet's is one of the most perilous of all the professions, and that for turning the wisdom of the wise to foolishness there is nothing so disastrously effective as the attempt to predict the mysterious course of the future.

H. D. TRAILL.

No. I

THE PRESENT TIME

[1st February 1850]

The Present Time, youngest-born of Eternity, child and heir of all the Past Times with their good and evil, and parent of all the Future, is ever a 'New Era' to the thinking man; and comes with new questions and significance, however commonplace it look: to know *it*, and what it bids us do, is ever the sum of knowledge for all of us. This new Day, sent us out of Heaven, this also has its heavenly omens;—amid the bustling trivialities and loud empty noises, its silent monitions, which, if we cannot read and obey, it will not be well with us! No;—nor is there any sin more fearfully avenged on men and Nations than that same, which indeed includes and presupposes all manner of sins: the sin which our old pious fathers called 'judicial blindness';—which we, with our light habits, may still call misinterpretation of the Time that now is; disloyalty to its real meanings and monitions, stupid disregard of these, stupid adherence active or passive to the counterfeits and mere current semblances of these. This is true of all times and days.

But in the days that are now passing-over us, even fools are arrested to ask the meaning of them; few of the generations of men have seen more impressive days. Days of endless calamity, disruption, dislocation, confusion worse confounded: if they are not days of endless hope too, then they are days of utter despair. For it is not a small hope that will suffice, the ruin being clearly, either in action or in prospect, universal. There must be a new world, if there is to be any world at all! That human things in our

Europe can ever return to the old sorry routine, and proceed with any steadiness or continuance there; this small hope is not now a tenable one. These days of universal death must be days of universal newbirth, if the ruin is not to be total and final! It is a Time to make the dullest man consider; and ask himself, Whence *he* came? Whither he is bound? —A veritable 'New Era,' to the foolish as well as to the wise.

Not long ago, the world saw, with thoughtless joy which might have been very thoughtful joy, a real miracle not heretofore considered possible or conceivable in the world,—a Reforming Pope. A simple pious creature, a good country-priest, invested unexpectedly with the tiara, takes up the New Testament, declares that this henceforth shall be his rule of governing. No more finesse, chicanery, hypocrisy, or false or foul dealing of any kind: God's truth shall be spoken, God's justice shall be done, on the throne called of St. Peter: an honest Pope, Papa, or Father of Christendom, shall preside there. And such a throne of St. Peter; and such a Christendom, for an honest Papa to preside in! The European populations everywhere hailed the omen; with shouting and rejoicing, leading-articles and tar-barrels; thinking people listened with astonishment,—not with sorrow if they were faithful or wise; with awe rather as at the heralding of death, and with a joy as of victory beyond death! Something pious, grand and as if awful in that joy, revealing once more the Presence of a Divine Justice in this world. For, to such men it was very clear how this poor devoted Pope would prosper, with his New Testament in his hand. An alarming business, that of governing in the throne of St. Peter by the rule of veracity! By the rule of veracity, the so-called throne of St. Peter was openly declared, above three-hundred years ago, to be a falsity, a huge mistake, a pestilent dead carcass, which this Sun was weary of. More than three hundred years ago, the throne of

St. Peter received peremptory judicial notice to quit; authentic order, registered in Heaven's chancery and since legible in the hearts of all brave men, to take itself away,—to begone, and let us have no more to do with *it* and its delusions and impious deliriums;—and it has been sitting every day since, it may depend upon it, at its own peril withal, and will have to pay exact damages yet for every day it has so sat. Law of veracity? What this Popedom had to do by the law of veracity, was to give-up its own foul galvanic life, an offence to gods and men; honestly to die, and get itself buried!

Far from this was the thing the poor Pope undertook in regard to it;—and yet, on the whole, it was essentially this too. "Reforming Pope?" said one of our acquaintance, often in those weeks, "Was there ever such a miracle? About to break-up that hugh imposthume too, by 'curing' it? Turgot and Necker were nothing to this. God is great; and when a scandal is to end, brings some devoted man to take charge of it in hope, not in despair!"—But cannot he reform? asked many simple persons;—to whom our friend in grim banter would reply: "Reform a Popedom,—hardly. A wretched old kettle, ruined from top to bottom, and consisting mainly now of foul *grime* and *rust:* stop the holes of it, as your antecessors have been doing, with temporary putty, it may hang-together yet a while; begin to hammer at it, solder at it, to what you call mend and rectify it,—it will fall to sherds, as sure as rust is rust; go all into nameless dissolution,—and the fat in the fire will be a thing worth looking at, poor Pope!"— —So accordingly it has proved. The poor Pope, amid felicitations and tar-barrels of various kinds, went on joyfully for a season: but he had awakened, he as no other man could do, the sleeping elements; mothers of the whirlwinds, conflagrations, earthquakes. Questions not very soluble at present, were even sages and heroes set to solve them, began everywhere with new emphasis to be asked. Questions which all official men wished, and almost hoped, to postpone till Doomsday. Doomsday itself *had* come; that was the terrible truth!—

For, sure enough, if once the law of veracity be acknowledged as the rule for human things, there will not anywhere be want of work for the reformer; in very few places do human things adhere quite closely to that law! Here was the Papa of Christendom proclaiming that such was actually the case;—whereupon all over Christendom such results as we have seen. The Sicilians, I think, were the first notable body that set-about applying this new strange rule sanctioned by the general Father; they said to themselves, We do not by the law of veracity belong to Naples and these Neapolitan Officials; we will, by favour of Heaven and the Pope, be free of these. Fighting ensued; insurrection, fiercely maintained in the Sicilian Cities; with much bloodshed, much tumult and loud noise, vociferation extending through all newspapers and countries. The effect of this, carried abroad by newspapers and rumour, was great in all places; greatest perhaps in Paris, which for sixty years past has been the City of Insurrections. The French People had plumed themselves on being, whatever else they were not, at least the chosen 'soldiers of liberty,' who took the lead of all creatures in that pursuit, at least; and had become, as their orators, editors and litterateurs diligently taught them, a People whose bayonets were sacred, a kind of Messiah People, saving a blind world in its own despite, and earning for themselves a terrestrial and even celestial glory very considerable indeed. And here were the wretched downtrodden populations of Sicily risen to rival them, and threatening to take the trade out of their hand.

No doubt of it, this hearing continually of the very Pope's glory as a Reformer, of the very Sicilians fighting divinely for liberty behind barricades,—must have bitterly aggravated the feeling of every Frenchman, as he looked around him, at home, on a Louis-Philippism which had became the scorn of all the world. "*Ichabod;* is the glory departing from us?

Under the sun is nothing baser, by all accounts and evidences, than the system of repression and corruption, of shameless dishonesty and unbelief in anything but human baseness, that we now live under. The Italians, the very Pope, have become apostles of liberty, and France is— —what is France!"—We know what France suddenly became in the end of February next; and by a clear enough genealogy, we can trace a considerable share in that event to the good simple Pope with the New Testament in his hand. An outbreak, or at least a radical change and even inversion of affairs hardly to be achieved without an outbreak, everybody felt was inevitable in France: but it had been universally expected that France would as usual take the initiative in that matter; and had there been no reforming Pope, no insurrectionary Sicily, France had certainly not broken-out then and so, but only afterwards and otherwise. The French explosion, not anticipated by the cunningest men there on the spot scrutinising it, burst-up unlimited, complete, defying computation or control.

Close following which, as if by sympathetic subterranean electricities, all Europe exploded, boundless, uncontrollable; and we had the year 1848, one of the most singular, disastrous, amazing, and, on the whole, humiliating years the European world ever saw. Not since the irruption of the Northern Barbarians has there been the like. Everywhere immeasurable Democracy rose monstrous, loud, blatant, inarticulate as the voice of Chaos. Everywhere the Official holy-of-holies was scandalously laid bare to dogs and the profane:—Enter, all the world, see what kind of Official holy it is. Kings everywhere, and reigning persons, stared in sudden horror, the voice of the whole world bellowing in their ear, "Begone, ye imbecile hypocrites, histrios not heroes! Off with you, off!" —and, what was peculiar and notable in this year for the first time, the Kings all made haste to go, as if exclaiming, "We *are* poor histrios, we sure enough;—did you want heroes? Don't kill us; we couldn't help it!" Not one of them turned round, and stood upon his Kingship, as upon a right he could afford to die for, or to risk his skin upon; by no manner of means. That, I say, is the alarming peculiarity at present. Democracy, on this new occasion, finds all Kings *conscious* that they are but Playactors. The miserable mortals, enacting their High Life Below Stairs, with faith only that this Universe may perhaps be all a phantasm and hypocrisis,—the truculent Constable of the Destinies suddenly enters: "Scandalous Phantasms, what do *you* here? Are 'solemnly constituted Impostors' the proper Kings of men? Did you think the Life of Man was a grimacing dance of apes? To be led always by the squeak of your paltry fiddle? Ye miserable, this Universe is not an upholstery Puppet-play, but a terrible God's Fact; and you, I think,—had not you better begone!" They fled precipitately, some of them with what we may call an exquisite ignominy,—in terror of the treadmill or worse. And everywhere the people, or the populace, take their own government upon themselves; and open 'kinglessness,' what we call *anarchy*,—how happy if it be anarchy *plus* a street-constable!—is everywhere the order of the day. Such was the history, from Baltic to Mediterranean, in Italy, France, Prussia, Austria, from end to end of Europe, in those March days of 1848. Since the destruction of the old Roman Empire by inroad of the Northern Barbarians, I have known nothing similar.

And so, then, there remained no King in Europe; no King except the Public Haranguer, haranguing on barrel-head, in leading-article; or getting himself aggregated into a National Parliament to harangue. And for about four months all France, and to a great degree all Europe, rough-ridden by every species of delirium, except happily the murderous for most part, was a weltering mob, presided over by M. de Lamartine at the Hôtel-de-Ville; a most eloquent fair-spoken literary gentleman, whom thoughtless persons took for a prophet, priest and heaven-sent evangelist, and whom a wise Yankee-friend of mine discerned to be properly 'the first stump-orator in the world, standing too on the highest stump,—for the time.' A sorrowful spectacle to men of reflection, during the time he lasted, that poor M. de Lamartine; with nothing in him but melodious wind and *soft sowder*, which he and others took for something divine and not diabolic! Sad enough: the eloquent latest impersonation of Chaos-come-again; able to talk for itself, and declare persuasively that *it* is Cosmos! However, you have but to wait a little, in such cases; all balloons do and must give-up their gas in the pressure of things, and are collapsed in a sufficiently wretched manner before long.

And so in City after City, street-barricades are piled, and truculent, more or less murderous insurrection begins; populace after populace rises, King after King capitulates or absconds; and from end to end of Europe Democracy has blazed-up explosive, much higher, more irresistible and less resisted than ever before; testifying too sadly on what a bottomless volcano, or universal powder-mine of most inflammable mutinous chaotic elements, separated from us by a thin earth-rind, Society with all its arrangements and acquirements everywhere, in the present epoch, rests! The kind of persons who excite or give signal to such revolutions,—students, young men of letters, advocates, editors, hot inexperienced enthusiasts, or fierce and justly bankrupt desperadoes, acting everywhere on the discontent of the millions and blowing it into flame,—might give rise to reflections as to the character of our epoch. Never till now did young men, and almost children, take such a command in human affairs. A changed time since the word *Senior* (Seigneur, or *Elder*) was first devised to signify 'lord,' or superior;—as in all languages of men we find it to have been! Not an honourable document this either, as to the spiritual condition of our epoch. In times when men love wisdom, the old man will ever be venerable, and be venerated, and reckoned noble: in times that love something else than wisdom, and indeed have little or no wisdom, and see little or none to love, the old man will cease to be venerated;—and looking more closely, also, you will find that in fact he has ceased to be venerable, and has begun to be contemptible; a foolish *boy* still, a boy without the graces, generosities, and opulent strength of young boys. In these days, what of *lordship* or leadership is still to be done, the youth must do it, not the mature or aged man; the mature man, hardened into sceptical egoism, knows no monition but that of his own frigid cautions, avarices, mean timidities; and can lead nowhither towards an object that even seems noble. But to return.

This mad state of matters will of course before long allay itself, as it has everywhere begun to do; the ordinary necessities of men's daily existence cannot comport with it, and these, whatever else is cast aside, will have their way. Some remounting,—very temporary remounting,—of the old machine, under new colours and altered forms, will probably ensue soon in most countries: the old histrionic Kings will be admitted back under conditions, under 'Constitutions,' with national Parliaments, or the like fashionable adjuncts; and everywhere the old daily life will try to begin again. But there is now no hope that such arrangements can be permanent; that they can be other than poor temporary makeshifts, which, if they try to fancy and make themselves permanent, will be displaced by new explosions, recurring more speedily than last time. In such baleful oscillation, afloat as amid raging bottomless eddies and conflicting sea-currents, not steadfast as on fixed foundations, must European Society continue swaying, now disastrously tumbling, then painfully readjusting itself, at ever shorter intervals,—till once the *new* rock-basis does come to light, and the weltering deluges of mutiny, and of need to mutiny, abate again!

For universal *Democracy*, whatever we may think of it, has declared itself as an inevitable fact of the days in which we live; and he who has any chance to instruct, or lead, in his days, must begin by admitting that: new street-barricades, and new anarchies, still more scandalous if still less sanguinary, must return and again return, till governing persons everywhere know and admit that. Democracy, it may be said everywhere, is here:—for sixty years now, ever since the grand or *First* French Revolution, that fact has been terribly announced to all the world; in message after message, some of them very terrible indeed; and now at last all the world ought really to believe it. That the world does believe it; that even Kings now as good as believe it, and know, or with just terror surmise, that they are but temporary phantasm Playactors, and that Democracy is the grand, alarming, imminent and indisputable Reality: this, among the scandalous phases we witnessed in the last two years, is a phasis full of hope: a sign that we are advancing closer and closer to the very Problem itself, which it will behove us to solve or die;—that all fighting and campaigning and coalitioning in regard to the *existence* of the Problem, is hopeless and superfluous henceforth. The gods have appointed it *so*; no Pitt, nor body of Pitts or mortal creatures can appoint it otherwise. Democracy, sure enough, is here: one knows not how long it will keep hidden underground even in Russia;—and here in England, though we object to it resolutely in the form of street-barricades and insurrectionary pikes, and decidedly will not open doors to it on those terms, the tramp of its million feet is on all streets and thoroughfares, the sound of its bewildered thousandfold voice is in all writings and speakings, in all thinkings and modes and activities of men: the soul that does not now, with hope or terror, discern *it*, is not the one we address on this occasion.

What *is* Democracy; this huge inevitable Product of the Destinies, which is everywhere the portion of our Europe in these latter days? There lies the question for us. Whence comes it, this universal big black Democracy; whither tends it; what is the meaning of it? A meaning it must have, or it would not be here. If we can find the right meaning of it, we may, wisely submitting or wisely resisting and controlling, still hope to live in the midst of it; if we cannot find the right meaning, if we find only the wrong or no meaning in it, to live will not be possible!—The whole social wisdom of the Present Time is summoned, in the name of the Giver of Wisdom, to make clear to itself, and lay deeply to heart with an eye to strenuous valiant practice and effort, what the meaning of this universal revolt of the European Populations, which calls itself Democracy, and decides to continue permanent, may be.

Certainly it is a drama full of action, event fast following event; in which curiosity finds endless scope, and there are interests at stake, enough to rivet the attention of all men, simple and wise. Whereat the idle multitude lift-up their voices, gratulating, celebrating sky-high; in rhyme and prose announcement, more than plentiful, that *now* the New Era, and long-expected Year One of Perfect Human Felicity has come. Glorious and immortal people, sublime French citizens, heroic barricades; triumph of civil and religious liberty—O Heaven! one of the inevitablest private miseries, to an earnest man in such circumstances, is this multitudinous efflux of oratory and psalmody, from the universal foolish human throat; drowning for the moment all reflection whatsoever, except the sorrowful one that you are fallen in an evil, heavy-laden, long-eared age, and must resignedly bear your part in the same. The front wall of your wretched old crazy dwelling, long denounced by you to no purpose, having at last fairly folded itself over, and fallen prostrate into the street, the floors, as may happen, will still hang-on by the mere beam-ends, and coherency of old carpentry, though in a sloping direction, and depend there till certain poor rusty nails and wormeaten dovetailings give way:—but is it cheering, in such circumstances, that the whole household burst-forth into celebrating the new joys of light and ventilation, liberty and picturesqueness of position, and thank God that now they have got a house to their mind? My dear household, cease singing and psalmodying; lay aside your fiddles, take out your work-implements, if you have any; for I can say with confidence the laws of gravitation are still active, and rusty nails, wormeaten dovetailings, and secret coherency of old carpentry, are not the best basis for a household!—In the lanes of Irish cities, I have heard say, the wretched people are sometimes found living, and perilously boiling their potatoes, on such swing-floors and inclined planes hanging-on by the joist-ends; but I did not hear that they sang very much in celebration of such lodging. No, they slid gently about, sat near the back wall, and perilously boiled their potatoes, in silence for most part!—

High shouts of exultation, in every dialect, by every vehicle of speech and writing, rise from far and near over this last avatar of Democracy in 1848: and yet, to wise minds, the first aspect it presents seems rather to be one of boundless misery and sorrow. What can be more miserable than this universal hunting-out of the high dignitaries, solemn functionaries, and potent, grave and reverend signiors of the world; this stormful rising-up of the inarticulate dumb masses everywhere, against those who pretended to be speaking for them and guiding them? These guides, then, were mere blind men only pretending to see? These rulers were not ruling at all; they had merely got-on the attributes and clothes of rulers, and were surreptitiously drawing the wages, while the work remained undone? The Kings were Sham-Kings, playacting as at Drury Lane;—and what were the people withal that took them for real?

It is probably the hugest disclosure of *falsity* in human things that was ever at one time made. These reverend Dignitaries that sat amid their far-shining symbols and long-sounding long-admitted professions, were mere Impostors, then? Not a true thing they were doing, but a false thing. The story they told men was a cunningly-devised fable; the gospels they preached to them were *not* an account of man's real position in this world, but an incoherent fabrication, of dead ghosts and unborn shadows, of traditions, cants, indolences, cowardices,—a falsity of falsities, which at last *ceases* to stick together. Wilfully and against their will, these high units of mankind were cheats, then; and the low millions who believed in them were dupes,—a kind of *inverse* cheats, too, or they would not have believed in them so long. A universal *Bankruptcy of Imposture*; that may be the brief definition of it. Imposture everywhere declared once more to be contrary to Nature; nobody will change its word into an act any farther:—fallen insolvent; unable to keep its head up by these false pretences, or make its pot boil any more for the present! A more scandalous phenomenon, wide as Europe, never afflicted the face of the sun. Bankruptcy everywhere; foul ignominy, and the abomination of desolation, in all high places: odious to look upon, as the carnage of a battle-field on the morrow morning;—a massacre not of the innocents; we cannot call it a massacre of the innocents; but a universal tumbling of Impostors and of Impostures into the street!—

Such a spectacle, can we call it joyful? There is a joy in it, to the wise man too; yes, but a joy full of awe, and as it were sadder than any sorrow,—like the vision of immortality, unattainable except through death and the grave! And yet who would not, in his heart of hearts, feel piously thankful that Imposture has fallen bankrupt? By all means let it fall bankrupt; in the name of God let it do so, with whatever misery to itself and to all of us. Imposture, be it known then,—known it must and shall be,—is hateful, unendurable to God and man. Let it understand this everywhere; and swiftly make ready for departure, wherever it yet lingers; and let it learn never to return, if possible! The eternal voices, very audibly again, are speaking to proclaim this message, from side to side of the world. Not a very cheering message, but a very indispensable one.

Alas, it is sad enough that Anarchy is here; that we are not permitted to regret its being here,—for who that had, for this divine Universe, an eye which was human at all, could wish that Shams of any kind, especially that Sham-Kings should continue? No: at all costs, it is to be prayed by all men that Shams may *cease*. Good Heavens, to what depths have we got, when this to many a man seems strange! Yet strange to many a man it does seem; and to many a solid Englishman, wholesomely digesting his pudding among what are called the cultivated classes, it seems strange exceedingly; a mad ignorant notion, quite heterodox, and big with mere ruin. He has been used to decent forms long since fallen empty of meaning, to plausible modes, solemnities grown ceremonial,—what you in your iconoclast humour call shams,—all his life long; never heard that there was any harm in them, that there was any getting-on without them. Did not cotton spin itself, beef grow, and groceries and spiceries come in from the East and the West, quite comfortably by the side of shams? Kings reigned, what they were pleased to call reigning; lawyers pleaded, bishops preached, and honourable members perorated; and to crown the whole, as if it were all real and no sham there, did not scrip continue saleable, and the banker pay in bullion, or paper with a metallic basis? "The greatest sham, I have always thought, is he that would destroy shams."

Even so. To such depth have *I*, the poor knowing person of this epoch, got;—almost below the level of lowest humanity, and down towards the state of apehood and oxhood! For never till in quite recent generations was such a scandalous blasphemy quietly set forth among the sons of Adam; never before did the creature called man believe generally in his heart that lies were the rule in this Earth; that in deliberate long-established lying could there be help or salvation for him, could there be at length other than hindrance and destruction for him. O Heavyside, my solid friend, this is the sorrow of sorrows: what on earth can become of us till this accursed enchantment, the general summary and consecration of delusions, be cast forth from the heart and life of one and all! Cast forth it will be; it must, or we are tending at all moments,—whitherward I do not like to name. Alas, and the casting of it out, to what heights and what depths will it lead us, in the sad universe mostly of lies and shams and hollow phantasms (grown very ghastly now), in which, as in a safe home, we have lived this century or two! To heights and depths of social and individual *divorce* from delusions,—of 'reform' in right sacred earnest, of indispensable amendment, and stern sorrowful abrogation and order to depart,—such as cannot well be spoken at present; as dare scarcely be thought at present; which nevertheless are very inevitable, and perhaps rather imminent several of them! Truly we have a heavy task of work before us; and there is a pressing call that we should seriously begin upon it, before it tumble into an inextricable mass, in which there will be no working, but only suffering and hopelessly perishing!—

Or perhaps Democracy, which we announce as now come, will itself manage it? Democracy, once modelled into suffrages, furnished with ballot-boxes and suchlike, will itself accomplish the salutary universal change from Delusive to Real, and make a new blessed world of us by and by?—To the great mass of men, I am aware, the matter presents itself quite on this hopeful side. Democracy they consider to *be* a kind of 'Government.' The old model, formed long since, and brought to perfection in England now two hundred years ago, has proclaimed itself to all Nations as the new healing for every woe: "Set-up a Parliament," the Nations everywhere say, when the old King is detected to be a Sham-King, and hunted out or not; "set-up a Parliament; let us have suffrages, universal suffrages; and all either at once or by due degrees will be right, and a real Millennium come!" Such is their way of construing the matter.

Such, alas, is by no means my way of construing the matter; if it were, I should have had the happiness of remaining silent, and been without call to speak here. It is because the contrary of all this is deeply manifest to me, and appears to be forgotten by multitudes of my contemporaries, that I have had to undertake addressing a word to them. The contrary of all this;—and the farther I look into the roots of all this, the more hateful, ruinous and dismal does the state of mind all this could have originated in appear to me. To examine this recipe of a Parliament, how fit it is for governing Nations, nay, how fit it may now be, in these new times, for governing England itself where we are used to it so long: this, too, is an alarming inquiry, to which all thinking men, and good citizens of their country, who have an ear for the small still voices and eternal intimations, across the temporary clamours and loud blaring proclamations, are now solemnly invited. Invited by the rigorous fact itself; which will one day, and that perhaps soon, demand practical decision or redecision of it from us,—with enormous penalty if we decide it wrong! I think we shall all have to consider this question, one day; better perhaps now than later, when the leisure may be less. If a Parliament, with suffrages and universal or any conceivable kind of suffrages, *is* the method, then certainly let us set about discovering the kind of suffrages, and rest no moment till we have got them. But it is possible a Parliament may not be the method! Possible the inveterate notions of the English People may have settled it as the method, and the Everlasting Laws of Nature may have settled it as not the method! Not the whole method; nor the method at all, if taken as the whole? If a Parliament with never such suffrages is *not* the method settled by this latter authority, then it will urgently behove us to become aware of that fact, and to quit such method;—we may depend upon it, however unanimous *we* be, every step taken in that direction will, by the Eternal Law of things, be a step *from* improvement, not towards it.

Not towards it, I say, if so! Unanimity of voting,—that will do nothing for us if *so*. Your ship cannot double Cape

Horn by its excellent plans of voting. The ship may vote this and that, above decks and below, in the most harmonious exquisitely constitutional manner: the ship, to get round Cape Horn, will find a set of conditions already voted for, and fixed with adamantine rigour by the ancient Elemental Powers, who are entirely careless how you vote. If you can, by voting or without voting, ascertain these conditions, and valiantly conform to them, you will get round the Cape: if you cannot,—the ruffian Winds will blow you ever back again; the inexorable Icebergs, dumb privy-councillors from Chaos, will nudge you with most chaotic 'admonition'; you will be flung half-frozen on the Patagonian cliffs, or admonished into shivers by your iceberg councillors, and sent sheer down to Davy Jones, and will never get round Cape Horn at all! Unanimity on board ship;—yes, indeed, the ship's crew may be very unanimous, which doubtless, for the time being, will be very comfortable to the ship's crew, and to their Phantasm Captain if they have one: but if the tack they unanimously steer upon is guiding them into the belly of the Abyss, it will not profit them much!—Ships accordingly do not use the ballot-box at all; and they reject the Phantasm species of Captains: one wishes much some other Entities,—since all entities lie under the same rigorous set of laws,—could be brought to show as much wisdom, and sense at least of self-preservation, the *first* command of Nature. Phantasm Captains with unanimous votings: this is considered to be all the law and all the prophets, at present.

If a man could shake-out of his mind the universal noise of political doctors in this generation and in the last generation or two, and consider the matter face to face, with his own sincere intelligence looking at it, I venture to say he would find this a very extraordinary method of navigating, whether in the Straits of Magellan or the undiscovered Sea of Time. To prosper in this world, to gain felicity, victory and improvement, either for a man or a nation, there is but one thing requisite, That the man or nation can discern what the true regulations of the Universe are in regard to him and his pursuit, and can faithfully and steadfastly follow these. These will lead him to victory; whoever it may be that sets him in the way of these,—were it Russian Autocrat, Chartist Parliament, Grand Lama, Force of Public Opinion, Archbishop of Canterbury, M'Croudy the Seraphic Doctor with his Last-evangel of Political Economy,—sets him in the sure way to please the Author of this Universe, and is his friend of friends. And again, whoever does the contrary is, for a like reason, his enemy of enemies. This may be taken as fixed.

And now by what method ascertain the monition of the gods in regard to our affairs? How decipher, with best fidelity, the eternal regulation of the Universe; and read, from amid such confused embroilments of human clamour and folly, what the real Divine Message to us is? A divine message, or eternal regulation of the Universe, there verily is, in regard to every conceivable procedure and affair of man: faithfully following this, said procedure or affair will prosper, and have the whole Universe to second it, and carry it, across the fluctuating contradictions, towards a victorious goal; not following this, mistaking this, disregarding this, destruction and wreck are certain for every affair. How find it? All the world answers me, "Count heads; ask Universal Suffrage, by the ballot-boxes, and that will tell." Universal Suffrage, ballot-boxes, count of heads? Well,—I perceive we have got into strange spiritual latitudes indeed. Within the last half century or so, either the Universe or else the heads of men must have altered very much. Half a century ago, and down from Father Adam's time till then, the Universe, wherever I could hear tell of it, was wont to be of somewhat abstruse nature; by no means carrying its secret written on its face, legible to every passer-by; on the contrary, obstinately hiding its secret from all foolish, slavish, wicked, insincere persons, and partially disclosing it to the wise and noble-minded alone, whose number was not the majority in my time!

Or perhaps the chief end of man being now, in these improved epochs, to make money and spend it, his interests in the Universe have become amazingly simplified of late; capable of being voted-on with effect by almost anybody? 'To buy in the cheapest market, and sell in the dearest': truly if that is the summary of his social duties, and the final divine-message he has to follow, we may trust him extensively to vote upon that. But if it is *not*, and never was, or can be? If the Universe will not carry on its divine bosom any commonwealth of mortals that have no higher aim,—being still 'a Temple and Hall of Doom,' not a mere Weaving-shop and Cattle-pen? If the unfathomable Universe has decided to *reject* Human Beavers pretending to be Men; and will abolish, pretty rapidly perhaps, in hideous mud-deluges, their 'markets' and them, unless they think of it?—In that case it were better to think of it: and the Democracies and Universal Suffrages, I can observe, will require to modify themselves a good deal!

Historically speaking, I believe there was no Nation that could subsist upon Democracy. Of ancient Republics, and *Demoi* and *Populi*, we have heard much; but it is now pretty well admitted to be nothing to our purpose;—a universal-suffrage republic, or a general-suffrage one, or any but a most-limited-suffrage one, never came to light, or dreamed of doing so, in ancient times. When the mass of the population were slaves, and the voters intrinsically a kind of *kings*, or men born to rule others; when the voters were *real* 'aristocrats' and manageable dependents of such,—then doubtless voting, and confused jumbling of talk and intrigue, might, without immediate destruction, or the need of a Cavaignac to intervene with cannon and sweep the streets clear of it, go on; and beautiful developments of manhood might be possible beside it, for a season. Beside it; or even, if you will, by means of it, and in virtue of it, though that is by no means so certain as is often supposed. Alas, no: the reflective constitutional mind has misgivings as to the origin of old

Greek and Roman nobleness; and indeed knows not how this or any other human nobleness could well be 'originated,' or brought to pass, by voting or without voting, in this world, except by the grace of God very mainly;—and remembers, with a sigh, that of the Seven Sages themselves no fewer than three were bits of Despotic Kings, *Τύραννοι*, 'Tyrants' so-called (such being greatly wanted there); and that the other four were very far from Red Republicans, if of any political faith whatever! We may quit the Ancient Classical concern, and leave it to College-clubs and speculative debating-societies, in these late days.

Of the various French Republics that have been tried, or that are still on trial,—of these also it is not needful to say any word. But there is one modern instance of Democracy nearly perfect, the Republic of the United States, which has actually subsisted for threescore years or more, with immense success as is affirmed; to which many still appeal, as to a sign of hope for all nations, and a 'Model Republic.' Is not America an instance in point? Why should not all Nations subsist and flourish on Democracy, as America does?

Of America it would ill beseem any Englishman, and me perhaps as little as another, to speak unkindly, to speak *unpatriotically*, if any of us even felt so. Sure enough, America is a great, and in many respects a blessed and hopeful phenomenon. Sure enough, these hardy millions of Anglo-saxon men prove themselves worthy of their genealogy; and, with the axe and plough and hammer, if not yet with any much finer kind of implements, are triumphantly clearing-out wide spaces, seedfields for the sustenance and refuge of mankind, arenas for the future history of the world; doing, in their day and generation, a creditable and cheering feat under the sun. But as to a Model Republic, or a model anything, the wise among themselves know too well that there is nothing to be said. Nay, the title hitherto to be a Commonwealth or Nation at all, among the ἔθνη of the world, is, strictly considered, still a thing they are but striving for, and indeed have not yet done much towards attaining. Their Constitution, such as it may be, was made here, not there; went over with them from the Old-Puritan English workshop ready-made. Deduct what they carried with them from England ready-made,—their common English Language, and that same Constitution, or rather elixir of constitutions, their inveterate and now, as it were, inborn reverence for the Constable's Staff; two quite immense attainments, which England had to spend much blood, and valiant sweat of brow and brain, for centuries long, in achieving;—and what new elements of polity or nationhood, what noble new phasis of human arrangement, or social device worthy of Prometheus or of Epimetheus, yet comes to light in America? Cotton-crops and Indian-corn and dollars come to light; and half a world of untilled land, where populations that respect the constable can live, for the present *without* Government: this comes to light; and the profound sorrow of all nobler hearts, here uttering itself as silent patient unspeakable ennui, there coming out as vague elegiac wailings, that there is still next to nothing more. 'Anarchy *plus* a street-constable': that also is anarchic to me, and other than quite lovely!

I foresee, too, that, long before the waste lands are full, the very street-constable, on these poor terms, will have become impossible: without the waste lands, as here in our Europe, I do not see how he could continue possible many weeks. Cease to brag to me of America, and its model institutions and constitutions. To men in their sleep there is nothing granted in this world: nothing, or as good as nothing, to men that sit idly *caucusing* and ballot-boxing on the graves of their heroic ancestors, saying, 'It is well, it is well!' Corn and bacon are granted: not a very sublime boon, on such conditions; a boon moreover which, on such conditions, cannot last! No: America too will have to strain its energies, in quite other fashion than this; to crack its sinews, and all-but break its heart, as the rest of us have had to do, in thousandfold wrestle with the Pythons and mud-demons, before it can become a habitation for the gods. America's battle is yet to fight; and we, sorrowful though nothing doubting, will wish her strength for it. New Spiritual Pythons, plenty of them; enormous Megatherions, as ugly as were ever born of mud, loom huge and hideous out of the twilight Future on America; and she will have her own agony, and her own victory, but on other terms than she is yet quite aware of. Hitherto she but ploughs and hammers, in a very successful manner; hitherto, in spite of her 'roast-goose with apple-sauce,' she is not much. 'Roast-goose with apple-sauce for the poorest working-man': well, surely that is something,—thanks to your respect for the street-constable, and to your continents of fertile waste land;—but that, even if it could continue, is by no means enough; that is not even an instalment towards what will be required of you. My friend, brag not yet of our American cousins! Their quantity of cotton, dollars, industry and resources, I believe to be almost unspeakable; but I can by no means worship the like of these. What great human soul, what great thought, what great noble thing that one could worship, or loyally admire, has yet been produced there? None: the American cousins have yet done none of these things. "What they have done?" growls Smelfungus, tired of the subject: "They have doubled their population every twenty years. They have begotten, with a rapidity beyond recorded example, Eighteen Millions of the greatest *bores* ever seen in this world before,—that hitherto is their feat in History!"—And so we leave them, for the present; and cannot predict the success of Democracy, on this side of the Atlantic, from their example.

Alas, on this side of the Atlantic and on that, Democracy, we apprehend, is forever impossible! So much, with certainty of loud astonished contradiction from all manner of men at present, but with sure appeal to the Law of Nature and the ever-abiding Fact, may be suggested and asserted once more. The Universe itself is a Monarchy and Hierarchy; large liberty of 'voting' there, all manner of choice, utmost free-will, but with conditions inexorable and immeasurable annexed to every exercise of the same. A most free commonwealth of 'voters'; but with Eternal Justice to preside over it, Eternal Justice enforced by Almighty Power! This is the model of 'constitutions'; this: nor in any Nation where there has not yet (in some supportable and withal some constantly-increasing degree) been confided to the *Noblest*, with his select series of *Nobler*, the divine everlasting duty of directing and controlling the Ignoble, has the 'Kingdom of God,' which we all pray for, 'come,' nor can 'His will' even *tend* to be 'done on Earth as it is in Heaven' till then. My Christian friends, and indeed my Sham-Christian and Anti-Christian, and all manner of men, are invited to reflect on this. They will find it to be the truth of the case. The Noble in the high place, the Ignoble in the low; that is, in all times and in all countries, the Almighty Maker's Law.

To raise the Sham-Noblest, and solemnly consecrate *him* by whatever method, new-devised, or slavishly adhered to from old wont, this, little as we may regard it, is, in all times and countries, a practical blasphemy, and Nature will in no wise forget it. Alas, there lies the origin, the fatal necessity, of modern Democracy everywhere. It is the Noblest, not the Sham-Noblest; it is God-Almighty's Noble, not the Court-Tailor's Noble, nor the Able-Editor's Noble, that must in some approximate degree, be raised to the supreme place; he and not a counterfeit,—under penalties! Penalties deep as death, and at length terrible as hell-on-earth, my constitutional friend!—Will the ballot-box raise the Noblest to the chief place; does any sane man deliberately believe such a thing? That nevertheless is the indispensable result, attain it how we may: if that is attained, all is attained; if not that, nothing. He that cannot believe the ballot-box to be attaining it, will be comparatively indifferent to the ballot-box. Excellent for keeping the ship's crew at peace under their Phantasm Captain; but unserviceable, under such, for getting round Cape Horn. Alas, that there should be human beings requiring to have these things argued of, at this late time of day!

I say, it is the everlasting privilege of the foolish to be governed by the wise; to be guided in the right path by those who know it better than they. This is the first 'right of man'; compared with which all other rights are as nothing,—mere superfluities, corollaries which will follow of their own accord out of this; if they be not contradictions to this, and less than nothing! To the wise it is not a privilege; far other indeed. Doubtless, as bringing preservation to their country, it implies preservation of themselves withal; but intrinsically it is the harshest duty a wise man, if he be indeed wise, has laid to his hand. A duty which he would fain enough shirk; which accordingly, in these sad times of doubt and cowardly sloth, he has long everywhere been endeavouring to reduce to its minimum, and has in fact in most cases nearly escaped altogether. It is an ungoverned world; a world which we flatter ourselves will henceforth need no governing. On the dust of our heroic ancestors we too sit ballot-boxing, saying to one another, It is well, it is well! By inheritance of their noble struggles, we have been permitted to sit slothful so long. By noble toil, not by shallow laughter and vain talk, they made this English Existence from a savage forest into an arable inhabitable field for us; and we, idly dreaming it would grow spontaneous crops forever,—find it now in a too questionable state; peremptorily requiring real labour and agriculture again. Real 'agriculture' is not pleasant; much pleasanter to reap and winnow (with ballot-box or otherwise) than to plough!

Who would govern that can get along without governing? He that is fittest for it, is of all men the unwillingest unless constrained. By multifarious devices we have been endeavouring to dispense with governing; and by very superficial speculations, of *laissez-faire*, supply-and-demand, etc. etc. to persuade ourselves that it is best so. The Real Captain, unless it be some Captain of mechanical Industry hired by Mammon, where is he in these days? Most likely, in silence, in sad isolation somewhere, in remote obscurity; trying if, in an evil ungoverned time, he cannot at least govern himself. The Real Captain undiscoverable; the Phantasm Captain everywhere very conspicuous:—it is thought Phantasm Captains, aided by ballot-boxes, are the true method, after all. They are much the pleasantest for the time being! And so no *Dux* or Duke of any sort, in any province of our affairs, now *leads*: the Duke's Bailiff *leads*, what little leading is required for getting-in the rents; and the Duke merely rides in the state-coach. It is everywhere so: and now at last we see a world all rushing towards strange consummations, because it is and has long been so!

I do not suppose any reader of mine, or many persons in England at all, have much faith in Fraternity, Equality and the Revolutionary Millenniums preached by the French Prophets in this age: but there are many movements here too which tend inevitably in the like direction; and good men, who would stand aghast at Red Republic and its adjuncts, seem to me travelling at full speed towards that or a similar goal! Certainly the notion everywhere prevails among us too, and preaches itself abroad in every dialect, uncontradicted anywhere so far as I can hear, That the grand panacea for social woes is what we call 'enfranchisement,' 'emancipation'; or, translated into practical language, the cutting asunder of human relations, wherever they are found grievous, as is like to be pretty universally the case at the rate we have been going for some generations past. Let us all be 'free' of one another; we shall then be happy. Free, without bond or connection except that of cash payment; fair day's wages for the fair day's work; bargained for by voluntary contract, and law of supply-and-demand: this is thought to be the true solution of all difficulties and injustices that have occurred between man and man.

To rectify the relation that exists between two men, is there no method, then, but that of ending it? The old relation has become unsuitable, obsolete, perhaps unjust; it imperatively requires to be amended; and the remedy is, Abolish it, let there henceforth be no relation at all. From the 'Sacrament of Marriage' downwards, human beings used to be manifoldly related, one to another, and each to all; and there was no relation among human beings, just or unjust, that had not its grievances and difficulties, its necessities on both sides to bear and forbear. But henceforth, be it known, we have changed all that, by favour of Heaven: 'the voluntary principle' has come-up, which will itself do the business for us; and now let a new Sacrament, that of *Divorce*, which we call emancipation, and spout-of on our platforms, be universally the order of the day!—Have men considered whither all this is tending, and what it certainly enough betokens? Cut every human relation which has anywhere grown uneasy sheer asunder; reduce whatsoever was compulsory to voluntary, whatsoever was permanent among us to the condition of nomadic:—in other words, loosen by assiduous wedges in every joint, the whole fabric of social existence, stone from stone; till at last, all now being loose enough, it can, as we already see in most countries, be overset by sudden outburst of revolutionary rage; and, lying as mere mountains of anarchic rubbish, solicit you to sing Fraternity etc. over it, and to rejoice in the new remarkable era of human progress we have arrived at.

Certainly Emancipation proceeds with rapid strides among us, this good while; and has got to such a length as might give rise to reflections in men of a serious turn. West-Indian Blacks are emancipated, and it appears refuse to work: Irish Whites have long been entirely emancipated; and nobody asks them to work, or on condition of finding them potatoes (which, of course, is indispensable), permits them to work.—Among speculative persons, a question has sometimes risen: In the progress of Emancipation, are we to look for a time when all the Horses also are to be emancipated, and brought to the supply-and-demand principle? Horses too have 'motives'; are acted-on by hunger, fear, hope, love of oats, terror of platted leather; nay, they have vanity, ambition, emulation, thankfulness, vindictiveness; some rude outline of all our human spiritualities,—a rude resemblance to us in mind and intelligence, even as they have in bodily frame. The Horse, poor dumb four-footed fellow, he too has his private feelings, his affections, gratitudes; and deserves good usage; no human master, without crime, shall treat him unjustly either, or recklessly lay-on the whip where it is not needed:—I am sure if I could make him 'happy,' I should be willing to grant a small vote (in addition to the late twenty millions) for that object!

Him too you occasionally tyrannise over; and with bad result to yourselves, among others; using the leather in a tyrannous unnecessary manner; withholding, or scantily furnishing, the oats and ventilated stabling that are due. Rugged horse-subduers, one fears they are a little tyrannous at times. 'Am I not a horse, and *half*-brother?'—To remedy which, so far as remediable, fancy—the horses all 'emancipated'; restored to their primeval right of property in the grass of this Globe: turned-out to graze in an independent supply-and-demand manner! So long as grass lasts, I dare say they are very happy, or think themselves so. And Farmer Hodge sallying forth, on a dry spring morning, with a sieve of oats in his hand, and agony of eager expectation in his heart, is he happy? Help me to plough this day, Black Dobbin: oats in full measure if thou wilt. 'Hlunh, No—thank!' snorts Black Dobbin; he prefers glorious liberty and the grass. Bay Darby, wilt not thou perhaps? 'Hlunh!' Gray Joan, then, my beautiful broad-bottomed mare,—O Heaven, she too answers Hlunh! Not a quadruped of them will plough a stroke for me. Corn-crops are *ended* in this world!—For the sake, if not of Hodge, then of Hodge's horses, one prays this benevolent practice might now cease, and a new and better one try to begin. Small kindness to Hodge's horses to emancipate them! The fate of all emancipated horses is, sooner or later, inevitable. To have in this habitable Earth no grass to eat,—in Black Jamaica gradually none, as in White Connemara already none;—to roam aimless, wasting the seed-fields of the world; and be hunted home to Chaos, by the due watch-dogs and due hell-dogs, with such horrors of forsaken wretchedness as were never seen before! These things are not sport; they are terribly true, in this country at this hour.

Between our Black West Indies and our White Ireland, between these two extremes of lazy refusal to work, and of famishing inability to find any work, what a world have we made of it, with our fierce Mammon-worships, and our benevolent philanderings, and idle godless nonsenses of one kind and another! Supply-and-demand, Leave-it-alone, Voluntary Principle, Time will mend it:—till British industrial existence seems fast becoming one huge poison-swamp of reeking pestilence physical and moral; a hideous *living* Golgotha of souls and bodies buried alive; such a Curtius' gulf, communicating with the Nether Deeps, as the Sun never saw till now. These scenes, which the *Morning Chronicle* is bringing home to all minds of men,—thanks to it for a service such as Newspapers have seldom done,—ought to excite unspeakable reflections in every mind. Thirty-thousand outcast Needlewomen working themselves swiftly to death; three-million Paupers rotting in forced idleness, *helping* said Needlewomen to die: these are but items in the sad ledger of despair.

Thirty-thousand wretched women, sunk in that putrefying well of abominations; they have oozed-in upon London, from the universal Stygian quagmire of British industrial life; are accumulated in the *well* of the concern, to that extent.

British charity is smitten to the heart, at the laying-bare of such a scene; passionately undertakes, by enormous subscription of money, or by other enormous effort, to redress that individual horror; as I and all men hope it may. But, alas, what next? This general well and cesspool once baled clean out today, will begin before night to fill itself anew. The universal Stygian quagmire is still there; opulent in women ready to be ruined, and in men ready. Towards the same sad cesspool will these waste currents of human ruin ooze and gravitate as heretofore; except in draining the universal quagmire itself there is no remedy. "And for that, what is the method?" cry many in an angry manner. To whom, for the present, I answer only, "Not 'emancipation,' it would seem, my friends; not the cutting-loose of human ties, something far the reverse of that!"

Many things have been written about shirtmaking; but here perhaps is the saddest thing of all, not written anywhere till now, that I know of. Shirts by the thirty-thousand are made at twopence-halfpenny each;—and in the mean while no needlewoman, distressed or other, can be procured in London by any housewife to give, for fair wages, fair help in sewing. Ask any thrifty house-mother, high or low, and she will answer. In high houses and in low, there is the same answer: no *real* needlewoman, 'distressed' or other, has been found attainable in any of the houses I frequent. Imaginary needlewomen, who demand considerable wages, and have a deepish appetite for beer and viands, I hear of everywhere; but their sewing proves too often a distracted puckering and botching; not sewing, only the fallacious hope of it, a fond imagination of the mind. Good sempstresses are to be hired in every village; and in London, with its famishing thirty-thousand, not at all, or hardly.—Is not No-government beautiful in human business? To such length has the Leave-alone principle carried it, by way of organising labour, in this affair of shirtmaking. Let us hope the Leave-alone principle has now got its apotheosis; and taken wing towards higher regions than ours, to deal henceforth with a class of affairs more appropriate for it!

Reader, did you ever hear of 'Constituted Anarchy'? Anarchy; the choking, sweltering, deadly and killing rule of No-rule; the consecration of cupidity, and braying folly, and dim stupidity and baseness, in most of the affairs of men? Slopshirts attainable three-halfpence cheaper, by the ruin of living bodies and immortal souls? Solemn Bishops and high Dignitaries, *our* divine 'Pillars of Fire by night,' debating meanwhile, with their largest wigs and gravest look, upon something they call 'prevenient grace'? Alas, our noble men of genius, Heaven's *real* messengers to us, they also rendered nearly futile by the wasteful time;—preappointed they everywhere, and assiduously trained by all their pedagogues and monitors, to 'rise in Parliament,' to compose orations, write books, or in short speak *words*, for the approval of reviewers; instead of doing real kingly *work* to be approved of by the gods! Our 'Government,' a highly 'responsible' one; responsible to no God that I can hear of, but to the twenty-seven million *gods* of the shilling gallery. A Government tumbling and drifting on the whirlpools and mud-deluges, floating atop in a conspicuous manner, no-whither,—like the carcass of a drowned ass. Authentic *Chaos* come up into this sunny Cosmos again; and all men singing *Gloria in excelsis* to it. In spirituals and temporals, in field and workshop, from Manchester to Dorsetshire, from Lambeth Palace to the Lanes of Whitechapel, wherever men meet and toil and traffic together,—Anarchy, Anarchy; and only the street-constable (though with ever-increasing difficulty) still maintaining himself in the middle of it; that so, for one thing, this blessed exchange of slop-shirts for the souls of women may transact itself in a peaceable manner!—I, for my part, do profess myself in eternal opposition to this, and discern well that universal Ruin has us in the wind, unless we can get out of this. My friend Crabbe, in a late number of his *Intermittent Radiator*, pertinently enough exclaims:

'When shall we have done with all this of British Liberty, Voluntary Principle, Dangers of Centralisation, and the like? It is really getting too bad. For British Liberty, it seems, the people cannot be taught to read. British Liberty, shuddering to interfere with the rights of capital, takes six or eight millions of money annually to feed the idle labourer whom it dare not employ. For British Liberty we live over poisonous cesspools, gully-drains, and detestable abominations; and omnipotent London cannot sweep the dirt out of itself. British Liberty produces—what? Floods of Hansard Debates every year, and apparently little else at present. If these are the results of British Liberty, I, for one, move we should lay it on the shelf a little, and look-out for something other and farther. We have achieved British Liberty hundreds of years ago; and are fast growing, on the strength of it, one of the most absurd populations the Sun, among his great Museum of Absurdities, looks down upon at present.'

Curious enough: the model of the world just now is England and her Constitution; all Nations striving towards it: poor France swimming these last sixty years in seas of horrid dissolution and confusion, resolute to attain this blessedness of free voting, or to die in chase of it. Prussia too, solid Germany itself, has all broken out into crackling of musketry, loud pamphleteering and Frankfort parliamenting and palavering; Germany too will scale the sacred mountains, how steep soever, and, by talisman of ballot-box, inhabit a political Elysium henceforth. All the Nations have that one hope. Very notable, and rather sad to the humane onlooker. For it is sadly conjectured, all the Nations labour somewhat under a mistake as to England, and the causes of her freedom and her prosperous cotton-spinning; and have much misread the nature of her Parliament, and the effect of ballot-boxes and universal-suffrages there.

What if it were because the English Parliament was from

the first, and is only just now ceasing to be, a Council of actual Rulers, real Governing Persons (called Peers, Mitred Abbots, Lords, Knights of the Shire, or howsoever called), actually *ruling* each his section of the country,—and possessing (it must be said) in the lump, or when assembled as a Council, uncommon patience, devoutness, probity, discretion and good fortune,—that the said Parliament ever came to be good for much? In that case it will not be easy to 'imitate' the English Parliament; and the ballot-box and suffrage will be the mere bow of Robin Hood, which it is given to very few to bend, or shoot with to any perfection. And if the Peers become mere big Capitalists, Railway Directors, gigantic Hucksters, Kings of Scrip, *without* lordly quality, or other virtue except cash; and the Mitred Abbots change to mere Able-Editors, masters of Parliamentary Eloquence, Doctors of Political Economy, and suchlike; and all *have* to be elected by a universal-suffrage ballot-box,—I do not see how the English Parliament itself will long continue sea-worthy! Nay, I find England in her own big dumb heart, wherever you come upon her in a silent meditative hour, begins to have dreadful misgivings about it.

The model of the world, then, is at once unattainable by the world, and not much worth attaining? England, as I read the omens, is now called a second time to 'show the Nations how to live'; for by her Parliament, as chief governing entity, I fear she is not long for this world! Poor England must herself again, in these new strange times, the old methods being quite worn out, 'learn how to live.' That now is the terrible problem for England, as for all the Nations; and she alone of all, not *yet* sunk into open Anarchy, but left with time for repentance and amendment; she, wealthiest of all in material resource, in spiritual energy, in ancient loyalty to law, and in the qualities that yield such loyalty,—she perhaps alone of all may be able, with huge travail, and the strain of all her faculties, to accomplish some solution. She will have to try it, she has now to try it; she must accomplish it, or perish from her place in the world!

England, as I persuade myself, still contains in it many *kings*; possesses, as Old Rome did, many men not needing 'election' to command, but eternally elected for it by the Maker Himself. England's one hope is in these, just now. They are among the silent, I believe; mostly far away from platforms and public palaverings; not speaking forth the image of their nobleness in transitory words, but imprinting it, each on his own little section of the world, in silent facts, in modest valiant actions, that will endure forevermore. They must sit silent no longer. They are summoned to assert themselves; to act forth, and articulately vindicate, in the teeth of howling multitudes, of a world too justly *maddened* into all manner of delirious clamours, what of wisdom they derive from God. England, and the Eternal Voices, summon them; poor England never so needed them as now. Up, be doing everywhere: the hour of crisis has verily come! In all sections of English life, the god-made *king* is needed; is pressingly demanded in most; in some, cannot longer, without peril as of conflagration, be dispensed with. He, wheresoever he finds himself, can say, "Here too am I wanted; here is the kingdom I have to subjugate, and introduce God's Laws into,—God's Laws, instead of Mammon's and M'Croudy's and the Old Anarch's! Here is my work, here or nowhere."— —Are there many such, who will answer to the call, in England? It turns on that, whether England, rapidly crumbling in these very years and months, shall go down to the Abyss as her neighbours have all done, or survive to new grander destinies *without* solution of continuity! Probably the chief question of the world at present.

The true 'commander' and king; he who knows for himself the divine Appointments of this Universe, the Eternal Laws ordained by God the Maker, in conforming to which lies victory and felicity, in departing from which lies, and forever must lie, sorrow and defeat, for each and all of the

Posterity of Adam in every time and every place; he who has sworn fealty to these, and dare alone against the world assert these, and dare not with the whole world at his back deflect from these;—he, I know too well, is a rare man. Difficult to discover; not quite discoverable, I apprehend, by manœuvring of ballot-boxes, and riddling of the popular clamour according to the most approved methods. He is not sold at any shop I know of,—though sometimes, as at the sign of the Ballot-box, he is advertised for sale. Difficult indeed to discover: and not very much assisted, or encouraged in late times, to discover *himself*;—which, I think, might be a kind of help? Encouraged rather, and commanded in all ways, if he be wise, to *hide* himself, and give place to the windy Counterfeit of himself; such as the universal-suffrages can recognise, such as loves the most sweet voices of the universal-suffrages!—O Peter, what becomes of such a People; what can become?

Did you never hear, with the mind's ear as well, that fateful Hebrew Prophecy, I think the fatefulest of all, which sounds daily through the streets, "Ou' clo'! Ou' clo'!"—A certain People, once upon a time, clamorously voted by overwhelming majority, "Not *he*; Barabbas, not he! *Him*, and what he is, and what he deserves, we know well enough: a reviler of the Chief Priests and sacred Chancery wigs; a seditious Heretic, physical-force Chartist, and enemy of his country and mankind: To the gallows and the cross with him! Barabbas is our man; Barabbas, we are for Barabbas!" They got Barabbas:—have you well considered what a fund of purblind obduracy, of opaque *flunkyism* grown truculent and transcendent; what an eye for the phylacteries, and want of eye for the eternal noblenesses; sordid loyalty to the prosperous Semblances, and high-treason against the Supreme Fact, such a vote betokens in these natures? For it was the consummation of a long series of such; they and their fathers had long kept voting so. A singular People; who could both produce such divine men, and then could so stone and crucify them; a People terrible from the beginning!—Well, they got Barabbas; and they got, of course, such guidance as Barabbas and the like of him could give them; and, of course, they stumbled ever downwards and devilwards, in their truculent stiffnecked way; and—and, at this hour, after eighteen centuries of sad fortune, they prophetically sing "Ou' clo'!" in all the cities of the world. Might the world, at this late hour, but take note of them, and understand their song a little!

Yes, there are some things the universal-suffrage can decide,—and about these it will be exceedingly useful to consult the universal-suffrage: but in regard to most things of importance, and in regard to the choice of men especially, there is (astonishing as it may seem) next to no capability on the part of universal-suffrage.—I request all candid persons, who have never so little originality of mind, and every man has a little, to consider this. If true, it involves such a change in our now-fashionable modes of procedure as fills me with astonishment and alarm. *If* popular suffrage is not the way of ascertaining what the Laws of the Universe are, and who it is that will best guide us in the way of these,—then woe is to us if we do not take another method. Delolme on the British Constitution will not save us; deaf will the Parcæ be to votes of the House, to leading-articles, constitutional philosophies. The other method—alas, it involves a stopping short, or vital change of direction, in the glorious career which all Europe, with shouts heaven-high, is now galloping along: and that, happen when it may, will, to many of us, be probably a rather surprising business!

One thing I do know, and can again assert with great confidence, supported by the whole Universe, and by some Two-hundred generations of men, who have left us some record of themselves there, That the few Wise will have, by one method or another, to take command of the innumerable Foolish; that they must be got to take it;—and that, in fact, since Wisdom, which means also Valour and heroic

Nobleness, is alone strong in this world, and one wise man is stronger than all men unwise, they can be got. That they must take it; and having taken, must keep it, and do their God's-Message in it, and defend the same, at their life's peril, against all men and devils. This I do clearly believe to be the backbone of all Future Society, as it has been of all Past; and that without it, there is no Society possible in the world. And what a business *this* will be, before it end in some degree of victory again, and whether the time for shouts of triumph and tremendous cheers upon it is yet come, or not yet by a great way, I perceive too well! A business to make us all very serious indeed. A business not to be accomplished but by noble manhood, and devout all-daring, all-enduring loyalty to Heaven, such as fatally *sleeps* at present,—such as is not *dead* at present either, unless the gods have doomed this world of theirs to die! A business which long centuries of faithful travail and heroic agony, on the part of all the noble that are born to us, will not end; and which to us, of this 'tremendous cheering' century, it were blessedness very great to see successfully begun. Begun, tried by all manner of methods, if there is one wise Statesman or man left among us, it verily must be;—begun, successfully or unsuccessfully, we do hope to see it!

In all European countries, especially in England, one class of Captains and commanders of men, recognisable as the beginning of a new real and not imaginary 'Aristocracy,' has already in some measure developed itself: the Captains of Industry;—happily the class who above all, or at least first of all, are wanted in this time. In the doing of material work, we have already men among us that can command bodies of men. And surely, on the other hand, there is no lack of men needing to be commanded: the sad class of brother-men whom we had to describe as 'Hodge's emancipated horses,' reduced to roving famine,—this too has in all countries developed itself; and, in fatal geometrical progression, is ever more developing itself, with a rapidity which alarms every one. On this ground, if not on all manner of other grounds, it may be truly said, the 'Organisation of Labour' (*not* organisable by the mad methods tried hitherto) is the universal vital Problem of the world.

To bring these hordes of outcast captainless soldiers under due captaincy? This is really the question of questions; on the answer to which turns, among other things, the fate of all Governments, constitutional and other,—the possibility of their continuing to exist, or the impossibility. Captainless, uncommanded, these wretched outcast 'soldiers,' since they cannot starve, must needs become banditti, street-barricaders,—destroyers of every Government that *cannot* put them under captains, and send them upon enterprises, and in short render life human to them. Our English plan of Poor Laws, which we once piqued ourselves upon as sovereign, is evidently fast breaking down. Ireland, now admitted into the Idle Workhouse, is rapidly bursting it in pieces. That never was a 'human' destiny for any honest son of Adam; nowhere but in England could it have lasted at all; and now, with Ireland sharer in it, and the fulness of time come, it is as good as ended. Alas, yes. Here in Connemara, your crazy Ship of the State, otherwise dreadfully rotten in many of its timbers I believe, has sprung a leak: spite of all hands at the pump, the water is rising; the Ship, I perceive, will founder, if you cannot stop this leak!

To bring these Captainless under due captaincy? The anxious thoughts of all men that do think are turned upon that question; and their efforts, though as yet blindly and to no purpose, under the multifarious impediments and obscurations, all point thitherward. Isolated men, and their vague efforts, cannot do it. Government everywhere is called upon,—in England as loudly as elsewhere,—to give the initiative. A new strange task of these new epochs; which no Government, never so 'constitutional,' can escape from undertaking.

For it is vitally necessary to the existence of Society itself; it must be undertaken, and succeeded in too, or worse will follow,—and, as we already see in Irish Connaught and some other places, will follow soon. To whatever thing still calls itself by the name of Government, were it never so constitutional and impeded by official impossibilities, all men will naturally look for help, and direction what to do, in this extremity. If help or direction is not given; if the thing called Government merely drift and tumble to and fro, nowhither, on the popular vortexes, like some carcass of a drowned ass, constitutionally put 'at the top of affairs,—popular indignation will infallibly accumulate upon it; one day, the popular lightning, descending forked and horrible from the black air, will annihilate said supreme carcass, and smite *it* home to its native ooze again!—Your Lordship, this is too true, though irreverently spoken: indeed one knows not how to speak of it; and to me it is infinitely sad and miserable, spoken or not!—Unless perhaps the Voluntary Principle will still help us through? Perhaps this Irish leak, in such a rotten distressed condition of the Ship, with all the crew so anxious about it, will be kind enough to stop of itself?—

Dismiss that hope, your Lordship! Let all real and imaginary Governors of England, at the pass we have arrived at, dismiss forever that fallacious fatal solace to their do-nothingism: of itself, too clearly, the leak will never stop; by human skill and energy it must be stopped, or there is nothing but the sea-bottom for us all! A Chief Governor of England really ought to recognise his situation; to discern that, doing nothing, and merely drifting to and fro, in however constitutional a manner, he is a squanderer of precious moments, moments that perhaps are priceless; a truly alarming Chief Governor. Surely, to a Chief Governor of England, worthy of that high name,—surely to him, as to every living man, in every conceivable situation short of the Kingdom of the Dead,—there is *something* possible; some plan of action other than that of standing mildly, with crossed arms, till he and we—sink? Complex as his situation is, he, of all Governors now extant among these distracted Nations, has, as I compute, by far the greatest possibilities. The Captains, actual or potential, are there, and the million Captainless: and such resources for bringing them together as no other has. To these outcast soldiers of his, unregimented roving banditti for the present, or unworking workhouse prisoners who are almost uglier than banditti; to these floods of Irish Beggars, Able-bodied Paupers, and nomadic Lackalls, now stagnating or roaming everywhere, drowning the face of the world (too truly) into an untenantable swamp and Stygian quagmire, has the Chief Governor of this country no word whatever to say? Nothing but "Rate in aid," "Time will mend it," "Necessary business of the Session"; and "After me the Deluge"? A Chief Governor that can front his Irish difficulty, and steadily contemplate the horoscope of Irish and British Pauperism, and whitherward it is leading him and us, in this humour, must be a—What shall we call such a Chief Governor? Alas, in spite of old use and wont,—little other than a tolerated Solecism, growing daily more intolerable! He decidedly ought to have some word to say on this matter, —to be incessantly occupied in getting something which he could practically say!—Perhaps to the following, or a much finer effect?

Speech of the British Prime-Minister to the floods of Irish and other Beggars, the able-bodied Lackalls, nomadic or stationary, and the general assembly, outdoor and indoor, of the Pauper Populations of these Realms

"Vagrant Lackalls, foolish most of you, criminal many of you, miserable all; the sight of you fills me with astonishment and despair. What to do with you I know not; long have I been meditating, and it is hard to tell. Here are some three millions of you, as I count: so many of you fallen sheer over into the abysses of open Beggary; and, fearful to think, every new unit that falls is *loading* so much more the chain that drags the others over. On the edge of the precipice hang uncounted millions; increasing, I am told, at the rate of 1200 a-day. They hang there on the giddy edge, poor souls, cramping themselves down, holding-on with all their strength; but falling, falling one after another; and the chain is getting *heavy*, so that ever more fall; and who at last will stand? What to do with you? The question, What to do with you? especially since the potato died, is like to break my heart!

"One thing, after much meditating, I have at last discovered, and now know for some time back: That you cannot be left to roam abroad in this unguided manner, stumbling over the precipices, and loading ever heavier the fatal *chain* upon those who might be able to stand; that this of locking you up in temporary Idle Workhouses, when you stumble, and subsisting you on Indian meal, till you can sally forth again on fresh roamings, and fresh stumblings, and ultimate descent to the devil;—that this is *not* the plan; and that it never was, or could out of England have been supposed to be, much as I have prided myself upon it!

"Vagrant Lackalls, I at last perceive, all this that has been sung and spoken, for a long while, about enfranchisement, emancipation, freedom, suffrage, civil and religious liberty over the world, is little other than sad temporary jargon, brought upon us by a stern necessity,—but now ordered by a sterner to take itself away again a little. Sad temporary jargon, I say: made-up of sense and nonsense,—sense in small quantities, and nonsense in very large;—and, if taken for the whole or permanent truth of human things, it is no better than fatal infinite nonsense eternally *untrue*. All men, I think, will soon have to quit this, to consider this as a thing pretty well achieved; and to look-out towards another thing much more needing achievement at the time that now is.

"All men will have to quit it, I believe. But to you, my indigent friends, the time for quitting it has palpably arrived! To talk of glorious self-government, of suffrages and hustings, and the fight of freedom and suchlike, is a vain thing in your case. By all human definitions and conceptions of the said fight of freedom, you for your part have lost it, and can fight no more. Glorious self-government is a glory not for you, —not for Hodge's emancipated horses, nor you. No; I say, No. You, for your part, have tried it, and *failed.* Left to walk your own road, the will-o'-wisps beguiled you, your short sight could not descry the pitfalls; the deadly tumult and press has whirled you hither and thither, regardless of your struggles and your shrieks; and here at last you lie; fallen flat into the ditch, drowning there and dying, unless the others that are still standing please to pick you up. The others that still stand have their own difficulties, I can tell you!—But you, by imperfect energy and redundant appetite, by doing too little work and drinking too much beer, you (I bid you observe) have proved that you cannot do it! You lie there plainly in the ditch. And I am to pick you up again, on these mad terms; help you ever again, as with our best heart's-blood, to do what, once for all, the gods have made impossible? To load the fatal *chain* with your perpetual staggerings and sprawlings; and ever again load it, till we all lie sprawling? My indigent, incompetent friends, I will not! Know that, whoever may be 'sons of freedom,' you for your part are not and cannot be such. Not 'free' you, I think, whoever may be free. You palpably are fallen captive,—*caitiff,* as they once named it:—you do, silently, but eloquently, demand, in the name of mercy itself, that some genuine command be taken of you.

"Yes, my indigent incompetent friends; some genuine practical command. Such,—if I rightly interpret those mad Chartisms, Repeal Agitations, Red Republics, and other delirious inarticulate howlings and bellowings which all the populations of the world now utter, evidently cries of pain on their and your part,—is the demand which you, Captives, make of all men that are not Captive, but are still Free. Free men,—alas, had you ever any notion who the free men were, who the not-free, the incapable of freedom! The free men, if you could have understood it, they are the wise men; the patient, self-denying, valiant; the Nobles of the World; who can discern the Law of this Universe, what it is, and piously *obey* it; these, in late sad times, having cast you loose, you are fallen captive to greedy sons of profit-and-loss; to bad and ever to worse; and at length to Beer and the Devil. Algiers, Brazil or Dahomey hold nothing in them so authentically *slave* as you are, my indigent incompetent friends!

"Good Heavens, and I have to raise some eight or nine millions annually, six for England itself, and to wreck the morals of my working population beyond all money's worth, to keep the life from going out of *you*: a small service to you, as I many times bitterly repeat! Alas, yes; before high Heaven I must declare it such. I think the old Spartans, who would have killed you instead, had shown more 'humanity,' more of manhood, than I thus do! More humanity, I say, more of *man*hood, and of sense for what the dignity of man demands imperatively of you and of me and of us all. We call it charity, beneficence, and other fine names, this brutish Workhouse Scheme of ours; and it is but sluggish heartlessness, and insincerity, and cowardly lowness of soul. Not 'humanity' or manhood, I think; perhaps *ape*hood rather,—paltry imitancy, from the teeth outward, of what our heart never felt nor *our* understanding ever saw; dim indolent adherence to extraneous hearsays and extinct traditions; traditions now really about extinct; not living now to almost any of us, and still haunting with their spectralities and gibbering *ghosts* (in a truly baleful manner) almost all of us! Making this our struggling 'Twelfth Hour of the Night' inexpressibly hideous!—

"But as for you, my indigent incompetent friends, I have

to repeat with sorrow, but with perfect clearness, what is plainly undeniable, and is even clamorous to get itself admitted, that you are of the nature of *slaves*,—or if you prefer the word, of *nomadic, and now even vagrant and vagabond, servants that can find no master on those terms;* which seems to me a much uglier word. Emancipation? You have been 'emancipated' with a vengeance! Foolish souls, I say the whole world cannot emancipate you. Fealty to ignorant Unruliness, to gluttonous sluggish Improvidence, to the Beerpot and the Devil, who is there that can emancipate a man in that predicament? Not a whole Reform Bill, a whole French Revolution executed for his behoof alone: nothing but God the Maker can emancipate him, by making him anew.

"To forward which glorious consummation, will it not be well, O indigent friends, that you, fallen flat there, shall henceforth learn to take advice of others as to the methods of standing? Plainly I let you know, and all the world and the worlds know, that I for my part mean it so. Not as glorious unfortunate sons of freedom, but as recognised captives, as unfortunate fallen brothers requiring that I should command you, and if need were, control and compel you, can there henceforth be a relation between us. Ask me not for Indian meal; you shall be compelled to earn it first; know that on other terms I will not give you any. Before Heaven and Earth, and God the Maker of us all, I declare it is a scandal to see *such* a life kept in you, by the sweat and heart's-blood of your brothers; and that, if we cannot mend it, death were preferable! Go to, we must get out of this unutterable coil of nonsenses, constitutional, philanthropical, etc., in which (surely without mutual hatred, if with less of 'love' than is supposed) we are all strangling one another! Your want of wants, I say, is that you be *commanded* in this world, not being able to command yourselves. Know therefore that it shall be so with you. Nomadism, I give you notice, has ended; needful permanency, soldier-like obedience, and the opportunity and the necessity of hard steady labour for your living, have begun. Know that the Idle Workhouse is shut against you henceforth; you cannot enter there at will, nor leave at will;—you shall enter a quite other Refuge, under conditions strict as soldiering, and not leave till I have done with you. He that prefers the glorious (or perhaps even the rebellious *in*glorious) 'career of freedom,' let him prove that he can travel there, and be the master of himself; and right good speed to him. He who has proved that he cannot travel there or be the master of himself,—let him, in the name of all the gods, become a servant, and accept the just rules of servitude!

"Arise, enlist in my Irish, my Scotch and English 'Regiments of the New Era,'—which I have been concocting, day and night, during these three Grouse-seasons (taking earnest incessant counsel, with all manner of Industrial Notabilities and men of insight, on the matter), and have now brought to a kind of preparation for incipiency, thank Heaven! Enlist there, ye poor wandering banditti; obey, work, suffer, abstain, as all of us have had to do: so shall you be useful in God's creation, so shall you be helped to gain a manful living for yourselves; not otherwise than so. Industrial Regiments"—[*Here numerous persons, with big wigs many of them, and austere aspect, whom I take to be Professors of the Dismal Science, start up in an agitated vehement manner: but the Premier resolutely beckons them down again*]—"Regiments not to fight the French or others, who are peaceable enough towards us; but to fight the Bogs and Wildernesses at home and abroad, and to chain the Devils of the Pit which are walking too openly among us.

"Work, for you? Work, surely, is not quite undiscoverable in an Earth so wide as ours, if we will take the right methods for it! Indigent friends, we will adopt this new relation (which is *old* as the world); this will lead us towards such. Rigorous conditions, not to be violated on either side, lie in this relation; conditions planted there by God Himself;

which woe will betide us if we do not discover, gradually more and more discover, and conform to! Industrial Colonels, Workmasters, Taskmasters, Life-commanders, equitable as Rhadamanthus and inflexible as he: such, I perceive, you do need; and such, you being once put under law as soldiers are, will be discoverable for you. I perceive, with boundless alarm, that I shall have to set about discovering such,—I, since I am at the top of affairs, with all men looking to me. Alas, it is my new task in this New Era; and God knows, I too, little other than a redtape Talking-machine, and unhappy Bag of Parliamentary Eloquence hitherto, am far behind with it! But street-barricades rise everywhere: the hour of Fate has come. In Connemara there has sprung a leak, since the potato died; Connaught, if it were not for Treasury-grants and rates-in-aid, would have to recur to Cannibalism even now, and Human Society would cease to pretend that it existed there. Done this thing must be. Alas, I perceive that if I cannot do it, then surely I shall die, and perhaps shall not have Christian burial! But I already raise near upon Ten Millions for feeding you in idleness, my nomadic friends; work, under due regulations, I really might try to get of"—[*Here arises indescribable uproar, no longer repressible, from all manner of Economists, Emancipationists, Constitutionalists, and miscellaneous Professors of the Dismal Science, pretty numerously scattered about; and cries of "Private Enterprise," "Rights of Capital," "Voluntary Principle," "Doctrines of the British Constitution," swollen by the general assenting hum of all the world, quite drown the Chief Minister for a while. He, with invincible resolution, persists*; *obtains hearing again*:]

"Respectable Professors of the Dismal Science, soft you a little. Alas, I know what you would say. For my sins, I have read much in those inimitable volumes of yours,—really I should think, some barrowfuls of them in my time,—and, in these last forty years of theory and practice, have pretty well seized what of Divine Message you were sent with to me.

Perhaps as small a message, give me leave to say, as ever there was such a noise made about before. Trust me, I have not forgotten it, shall never forget it. Those Laws of the Shop-till are indisputable to me; and practically useful in certain departments of the Universe, as the multiplication-table itself. Once I even tried to sail through the Immensities with them, and to front the big coming Eternities with them; but I found it would not do. As the Supreme Rule of Statesmanship, or Government of Men,—since this Universe is not wholly a Shop,—no. You rejoice in my improved tariffs, free-trade movements and the like, on every hand; for which be thankful, and even sing litanies if you choose. But here at last, in the Idle-Workhouse movement,—unexampled yet on Earth or in the waters under the Earth,—I am fairly brought to a stand; and have had to make reflections, of the most alarming, and indeed awful, and as it were religious nature! Professors of the Dismal Science, I perceive that the length of your tether is now pretty well run; and that I must request you to talk a little lower in future. By the side of the shop-till,—see, your small 'Law of God' is hung up, along with the multiplication-table itself. But beyond and above the shop-till, allow me to say, you shall as good as hold your peace. Respectable Professors, I perceive it is not now the Gigantic Hucksters, but it is the Immortal Gods, yes, they, in their terror and their beauty, in their wrath and their beneficence, that are coming into play in the affairs of this world! Soft you a little. Do not you interrupt me, but try to understand and help me!—

—"Work, was I saying? My indigent unguided friends, I should think some work might be discoverable for you. Enlist, stand drill; become, from a nomadic Banditti of Idleness, Soldiers of Industry! I will lead you to the Irish Bogs, to the vacant desolations of Connaught now falling into Cannibalism, to mistilled Connaught, to ditto Munster, Leinster, Ulster, I will lead you: to the English fox-covers, furze-grown Commons, New Forests, Salisbury Plains: likewise to the Scotch Hill-sides, and bare rushy slopes, which as yet feed only sheep,—moist uplands, thousands of square miles in extent, which are destined yet to grow green crops, and fresh butter and milk and beef without limit (wherein no 'Foreigner can compete with us'), were the Glasgow sewers once opened on them, and you with your Colonels carried thither. In the Three Kingdoms, or in the Forty Colonies, depend upon it, you shall be led to your work!

"To each of you I will then say: Here is work for you; strike into it with manlike, soldierlike obedience and heartiness, according to the methods here prescribed,—wages follow for you without difficulty; all manner of just remuneration, and at length emancipation itself follows. Refuse to strike into it; shirk the heavy labour, disobey the rules,—I will admonish and endeavour to incite you; if in vain, I will flog you; if still in vain, I will at last shoot you,—and make God's Earth, and the forlorn-hope in God's Battle, free of you. Understand it, I advise you! The Organisation of Labour" — —[*Left speaking*, says our reporter.]

'Left speaking': alas, that he should have to 'speak' so much! There are things that should be done, not spoken; that till the doing of them is begun, cannot well be spoken. He may have to 'speak' seven years yet, before a spade be struck into the Bog of Allen; and then perhaps it will be too late!—

You perceive, my friends, we have actually got into the 'New Era' there has been such prophesying of: here we all are, arrived at last;—and it is by no means the land flowing with milk and honey we were led to expect! Very much the reverse. A terrible *new* country this: no neighbours in it yet, that I can see, but irrational flabby monsters (philanthropic and other) of the giant species; hyænas, laughing hyænas, predatory wolves; probably *devils*, blue (or perhaps blue-and-yellow) devils, as St. Guthlac found in Croyland long ago. A huge untrodden haggard country, the 'chaotic battle-field of Frost and Fire'; a country of savage glaciers, granite mountains, of foul jungles, unhewed forests, quaking bogs;—which we shall have our own ados to make arable and habitable, I think! We must stick by it, however;—of all enterprises the impossiblest is that of getting out of *it*, and shifting into another. To work, then, one and all; hands to work!

No. II

MODEL PRISONS

[1st March 1850]

The deranged condition of our affairs is a universal topic among men at present; and the heavy miseries pressing, in their rudest shape, on the great dumb inarticulate class, and from this, by a sure law, spreading upwards, in a less palpable but not less certain and perhaps still more fatal shape on all classes to the very highest, are admitted everywhere to be great, increasing and now almost unendurable. How to diminish them,—this is every man's question. For in fact they do imperatively need diminution; and unless they can be diminished, there are many other things that cannot very long continue to exist beside them. A serious question indeed, How to diminish them!

Among the articulate classes, as they may be called, there are two ways of proceeding in regard to this. One large body of the intelligent and influential, busied mainly in personal affairs, accepts the social iniquities, or whatever you may call them, and the miseries consequent thereupon; accepts them, admits them to be extremely miserable, pronounces them entirely inevitable, incurable except by Heaven, and eats its pudding with as little thought of them as possible. Not a very noble class of citizens these; not a very hopeful or salutary method of dealing with social iniquities this of theirs, however it may answer in respect to themselves and their personal affairs! But now there is the select small minority in whom some sentiment of public spirit and human pity still survives, among whom, or not anywhere, the good Cause may expect to find soldiers and servants: their method of proceeding, in these times, is also very strange. They embark in the 'philanthropic movement'; they calculate that the miseries of the world can be cured by bringing the philanthropic movement to bear on them. To universal public misery, and universal neglect of the clearest public duties, let private charity superadd itself: there will thus be some balance restored, and maintained again; thus,—or by what conceivable method? On these terms they, for their part, embark in the sacred cause; resolute to cure a world's woes by rose-water; desperately bent on trying to the uttermost that mild method. It seems not to have struck these good men that no world, or thing here below, ever fell into misery, without having first fallen into folly, into sin against the Supreme Ruler of it, by adopting as a law of conduct what was not a law, but the reverse of one; and that, till its folly, till its sin be cast out of it, there is not the smallest hope of its misery going,—that not for all the charity and rose-water in the world will its misery try to go till then!

This is a sad error; all the sadder as it is the error chiefly of the more humane and noble-minded of our generation; among whom, as we said, or elsewhere not at all, the cause of real Reform must expect its servants. At present, and for a long while past, whatsoever young soul awoke in England with some disposition towards generosity and social heroism, or at lowest with some intimation of the beauty of such a disposition,—he, in whom the poor world might have looked for a Reformer, and valiant mender of its foul ways, was almost sure to become a Philanthropist, reforming merely by this rose-water method. To admit that the world's ways are foul, and not the ways of God the Maker, but of Satan the Destroyer, many of them, and that they must be mended or we all die; that if huge misery prevails, huge cowardice, falsity, disloyalty, universal Injustice high and low, have still longer prevailed, and must straightway try to cease prevailing: this is what no visible reformer has yet thought of doing. All so-called 'reforms' hitherto are grounded either on openly-admitted egoism (cheap bread to the cotton-spinner, voting to those that have no vote, and the like), which does not point towards very celestial developments of the Reform movement; or else upon this of remedying social injustices by indiscriminate contributions of philanthropy, a method surely still more unpromising. Such contributions, being indiscriminate, are but a new injustice; these will never lead to reform, or abolition of injustice, whatever else they lead to!

Not by that method shall we 'get round Cape Horn,' by never such unanimity of voting, under the most approved Phantasm Captains! It is miserable to see. Having, as it were, quite lost our way round Cape Horn, and being sorely 'admonished' by the Iceberg and other dumb councillors, the pilots,—instead of taking to their sextants, and asking with a seriousness unknown for a long while, What the Laws of wind and water, and of Earth and of Heaven are,—decide that now, in these new circumstances, they will, to the worthy and unworthy, serve-out a double allowance of grog. In this way they hope to do it,—by steering on the old wrong tack, and serving-out more and more copiously what little *aquavitæ* may be still on board! Philanthropy, emancipation, and pity for human calamity is very beautiful; but the deep oblivion of the Law of Right and Wrong; this 'indiscriminate mashing-up of Right and Wrong into a patent treacle' of the Philanthropic movement, is by no means beautiful; this, on the contrary, is altogether ugly and alarming.

Truly if there be not something inarticulate among us, not yet uttered but pressing towards utterance, which is much wiser than anything we have lately articulated or brought into word or action, our outlooks are rather lamentable. The great majority of the powerful and active-minded, sunk in egoistic scepticisms, busied in chase of lucre, pleasure, and mere vulgar objects, looking with indifference on the world's woes, and passing carelessly by on the other side; and the select minority, of whom better might have been expected, bending all their strength to cure them by methods which can only make bad worse, and in the end render cure hopeless. A blind loquacious pruriency of indiscriminate Philanthropism substituting itself, with much self-laudation, for the silent divinely awful sense of Right and Wrong;—testifying too clearly that here is no longer a divine sense of Right and Wrong; that, in the smoke of this universal, and alas inevitable and indispensable revolutionary fire, and burning-up of worn-out rags of which the world is full, our life-atmosphere has (for the time) become one vile London fog, and the eternal loadstars are gone out for us! Gone out;—yet very visible if you can get above the fog; still there in their place, and quite the same as they always were! To whoever does still know of loadstars, the proceedings, which expand themselves daily, of these sublime philanthropic associations, and 'universal sluggard-and-scoundrel protection-societies,' are a perpetual affliction. With their emancipations and abolition-principles, and reigns of brotherhood and new methods of love, they have done great things in the White and in the Black World, during late years; and are preparing for greater.

In the interest of human reform, if there is ever to be any reform, and return to prosperity or to the possibility of prospering, it is urgent that the nonsense of all this (and it is mostly nonsense, but not quite) should be sent about its business straightway, and forbidden to deceive the well-meaning souls among us any more. Reform, if we will understand that divine word, cannot begin till then. One day, I do know, this, as is the doom of all nonsense, will be drummed-out of the world, with due placard stuck on its back, and the populace flinging dead cats at it: but whether soon or not, is by no means so certain. I rather guess, *not* at present, not quite soon. Fraternity, in other countries, has gone on, till it found itself unexpectedly manipulating guillotines by its chosen Robespierres, and become a fraternity like Cain's. Much to its amazement! For in fact it is not all nonsense; there is an infinitesimal fraction of sense in it withal; which is so difficult to disengage;—which must be disengaged, and laid hold of, before Fraternity can vanish.

But to our subject,—the Model Prison, and the strange theory of life now in action there. That, for the present, is my share in the wide adventure of Philanthropism; the world's share, and how and when it is to be liquidated and ended, rests with the Supreme Destinies.

Several months ago, some friends took me with them to see one of the London Prisons; a Prison of the exemplary or model kind. An immense circuit of buildings; cut-out, girt with a high ring-wall, from the lanes and streets of the quarter, which is a dim and crowded one. Gateway as to a fortified place; then a spacious court, like the square of a city; broad staircases, passages to interior courts; fronts of stately architecture all round. It lodges some Thousand or Twelve-hundred prisoners, besides the officers of the establishment. Surely one of the most perfect buildings, within the compass of London. We looked at the apartments, sleeping-cells, dining-rooms, working-rooms, general courts or special and private: excellent all, the ne-plus-ultra of human care and ingenuity; in my life I never saw so clean a building; probably no Duke in England lives in a mansion of such perfect and thorough cleanness.

The bread, the cocoa, soup, meat, all the various sorts of food, in their respective cooking-places, we tasted: found them of excellence superlative. The prisoners sat at work, light work, picking oakum, and the like, in airy apartments with glass roofs, of agreeable temperature and perfect ventilation; silent, or at least conversing only by secret signs: others were out, taking their hour of promenade in clean flagged courts: methodic composure, cleanliness, peace, substantial wholesome comfort reigned everywhere supreme. The women in other apartments, some notable murderesses among them, all in the like state of methodic composure and substantial wholesome comfort, sat sewing: in long ranges of wash-houses, drying-houses and whatever pertains to the getting-up of clean linen, were certain others, with all conceivable mechanical furtherances, not too arduously working. The notable murderesses were, though with great precautions of privacy, pointed out to us; and we were requested not to look openly at them, or seem to notice them at all, as it was found to 'cherish their vanity' when visitors looked at them. Schools too were there; intelligent teachers of both sexes, studiously instructing the still ignorant of these thieves.

From an inner upper room or gallery, we looked down into a range of private courts, where certain Chartist Notabilities were undergoing their term. Chartist Notability First struck me very much: I had seen him about a year before, by involuntary accident and much to my disgust, magnetising a silly young person; and had noted well the unlovely voracious look of him, his thick oily skin, his heavy dull-burning eyes, his greedy mouth, the dusky potent insatiable *animalism* that looked out of every feature of him: a fellow adequate to animal-magnetise most things, I did suppose;—and here was the post I now found him arrived at. Next neighbour to him was Notability Second, a philosophic or literary Chartist; walking rapidly to and fro in his private court, a clean, high-walled place; the world and its cares quite excluded, for some months to come: master of his own time and spiritual resources to, as I supposed, a really enviable extent. What 'literary man' to an equal extent! I fancied I, for my own part, so left with paper and ink, and all taxes and botherations shut-out from me, could have written such a Book as no reader will here ever get of me. Never, O reader, never here in a mere house with taxes and botherations. Here, alas, one has to snatch one's poor Book, bit by bit, as from a conflagration; and to think and live, comparatively, as if the house were not one's own, but mainly the world's and the devil's. Notability Second might have filled one with envy.

The Captain of the place, a gentleman of ancient Military or Royal-Navy habits, was one of the most perfect governors; professionally and by nature zealous for cleanliness, punctuality, good order of every kind; a humane heart and yet a strong one; soft of speech and manner, yet with an inflexible rigour of command, so far as his limits went: 'iron hand in a velvet glove,' as Napoleon defined it. A man of real worth, challenging at once love and respect: the light of those mild bright eyes seemed to permeate the place as with an all-pervading vigilance, and kindly yet victorious illumination; in the soft definite voice it was as if Nature herself were promulgating her orders, gentlest mildest orders, which however, in the end, there would be no disobeying, which in the end there would be no living without fulfilment of. A true '*aristos*,' and commander of men. A man worthy to have commanded and guided forward, in good ways, Twelve-hundred of the best commonpeople in London or the world: he was here, for many years past, giving all his care and faculty to command, and guide forward in such ways as there were, Twelve-hundred of the worst. I looked with considerable admiration on this gentleman; and with considerable astonishment, the reverse of admiration, on the work he had here been set upon.

This excellent Captain was too old a Commander to complain of anything; indeed he struggled visibly the other way, to find in his own mind that all here was best; but I could sufficiently discern that, in his natural instincts, if not mounting up to the region of his thoughts, there was a continual protest going on against much of it; that nature and all his inarticulate persuasion (however much forbidden to articulate itself) taught him the futility and unfeasibility of the system followed here. The Visiting Magistrates, he gently regretted rather than complained, had lately taken his treadwheel from him, men were just now pulling it down; and how he was henceforth to enforce discipline on these bad subjects, was much a difficulty with him. "They cared for nothing but the treadwheel, and for having their rations cut short": of the two sole penalties, hard work and occasional hunger, there remained now only one, and that by no means the better one, as he thought. The 'sympathy' of visitors, too, their 'pity' for his interesting scoundrel-subjects, though he tried to like it, was evidently no joy to this practical mind. Pity, yes:—but pity for the scoundrel-species? For those who will not have pity on themselves, and will force the Universe and the Laws of Nature to have no 'pity' on them? Meseems I could discover fitter objects of pity!

In fact it too was clear, this excellent man had got a field for his faculties which, in several respects, was by no means the suitable one. To drill Twelve-hundred scoundrels by 'the method of kindness,' and of abolishing your very treadwheel, —how could any commander rejoice to have such a work cut-out for him? You had but to look in the faces of these Twelve-hundred, and despair, for most part, of ever 'commanding' them at all. Miserable distorted blockheads, the generality; ape-faces, imp-faces, angry dog-faces, heavy sullen ox-faces; degraded underfoot perverse creatures, sons of *in*-docility, greedy mutinous darkness, and in one word, of STUPIDITY, which is the general mother of such. Stupidity intellectual and stupidity moral (for the one always means the other, as you will, with surprise or not, discover if you look) had born this progeny: base-natured beings, on whom in the course of a maleficent subterranean life of London Scoundrelism, the Genius of Darkness (called Satan, Devil, and other names) had now visibly impressed his seal, and had marked them out as soldiers of Chaos and of him,—appointed to serve in *his* Regiments, First of the line, Second ditto, and so on in their order. Him, you could perceive, they would serve; but not easily another than him. These were the subjects whom our brave Captain and Prison-Governor was appointed to command, and reclaim to *other* service, by 'the method of love,' with a treadwheel abolished.

Hopeless forevermore such a project. These abject, ape, wolf, ox, imp and other diabolic-animal specimens of humanity, who of the very gods could ever have commanded them by love? A collar round the neck, and a cartwhip flourished over the back; these, in a just and steady human hand, were what the gods would have appointed them; and now when, by long misconduct and neglect, they had sworn themselves into the Devil's regiments of the line, and got the seal of Chaos impressed on their visage, it was very doubtful whether even these would be of avail for the unfortunate commander of Twelve-hundred men! By 'love,' without hope except of peaceably teasing oakum, or fear except of a temporary loss of dinner, he was to guide these men, and wisely constrain them,—whitherward? No-whither: that was his goal, if you will think well of it; that was a second fundamental falsity in his problem. False in the warp and false in the woof, thought one of us; about as false a problem as any I have seen a good man set upon lately! To guide scoundrels by 'love'; that is a false woof, I take it, a method that will not hold together; hardly for the flower of men will love alone do; and for the sediment and scoundrelism of men it has not even a chance to do. And then to guide any class of men, scoundrel or other, *No-whither*, which was this poor Captain's problem, in this Prison with oakum for its one element of hope or outlook, how can that prosper by 'love' or by any conceivable method? That is a warp wholly false. Out of which false warp, or originally false condition to start from, combined and daily woven into by your false woof, or methods of 'love' and suchlike, there arises for our poor Captain the falsest of problems, and for a man of his faculty the unfairest of situations. His problem was, not to command good men to do something, but bad men to do (with superficial disguises) nothing.

On the whole, what a beautiful Establishment here fitted-up for the accommodation of the scoundrel-world, male and female! As I said, no Duke in England is, for all rational purposes which a human being can or ought to aim at, lodged, fed, tended, taken care of, with such perfection. Of poor craftsmen that pay rates and taxes from their day's wages, of the dim millions that toil and moil continually under the sun, we know what is the lodging and the tending. Of the Johnsons, Goldsmiths, lodged in their squalid garrets; working often enough amid famine, darkness, tumult, dust and desolation, what work *they* have to do:—of these as of 'spiritual backwoodsmen,' understood to be preappointed to such a life, and like the pigs to killing, 'quite used to it,' I say nothing. But of Dukes, which Duke, I could ask, has cocoa, soup, meat, and food in general made ready, so fit for keeping him in health, in ability to do and to enjoy? Which Duke has a house so thoroughly clean, pure and airy; lives in an element so wholesome, and perfectly adapted to the uses of soul and body as this same, which is provided here for the Devil's regiments of the line? No Duke that I have ever known. Dukes are waited-on by deleterious French cooks, by perfunctory grooms of the chambers, and expensive crowds of eye-servants, more imaginary than real: while here, Science, Human Intellect and Beneficence have searched and sat studious, eager to do their very best; they have chosen a real Artist in Governing to see their best, in all details of it, done. Happy regiments of the line, what soldier to any earthly or celestial Power has such a lodging and attendance as you here? No soldier or servant direct or indirect of God or of man, in this England at present. Joy to you, regiments of the line. Your Master, I am told, has his Elect, and professes to be 'Prince of the Kingdoms of this World'; and truly I see he has power to do a good turn to those he loves, in England at least. Shall we say, May *he*, may the Devil give you good of it, ye Elect of Scoundrelism? I will rather pass by, uttering no prayer at all; musing rather in silence on the singular 'worship of God,' or practical 'reverence done to Human Worth' (which is the outcome and essence of all real 'worship' whatsoever) among the posterity of Adam at this day.

For all round this beautiful Establishment, or Oasis of Purity, intended for the Devil's regiments of the line, lay continents of dingy poor and dirty dwellings, where the unfortunate not *yet* enlisted into that Force were struggling manifoldly,—in their workshops, in their marble-yards and timber-yards and tan-yards, in their close cellars, cobbler-stalls, hungry garrets, and poor dark trade-shops with red-herrings and tobacco-pipes crossed in the window,—to keep the Devil out-of-doors, and *not* enlist with him. And it was by a tax on these that the Barracks for the regiments of the line were kept up. Visiting Magistrates, impelled by Exeter Hall, by Able-Editors, and the Philanthropic Movement of the Age, had given orders to that effect. Rates on the poor servant of God and of her Majesty, who still serves both in his way, painfully selling red-herrings; rates on him and his red-herrings to boil right soup for the Devil's declared Elect! Never in my travels, in any age or clime, had I fallen-in with such Visiting Magistrates before. Reserved they, I should suppose, for these ultimate or penultimate ages of the world, rich in all prodigies, political, spiritual,—ages surely with such a length of ears as was never paralleled before.

If I had a commonwealth to reform or to govern, certainly it should not be the Devil's regiments of the line that I would first of all concentrate my attention on! With them I should be apt to make rather brief work; to them one would apply the besom, try to sweep *them* with some rapidity into the dust-bin, and well out of one's road, I should rather say. Fill your thrashing-floor with docks, ragweeds, mugworths, and ply your flail upon them,—that is not the method to obtain sacks of wheat. Away, you; begone swiftly, *ye* regiments of the line: in the name of God and of His poor struggling servants, sore put to it to live in these bad days, I mean to rid myself of you with some degree of brevity. To feed you in palaces, to hire captains and schoolmasters and the choicest spiritual and material artificers to expend their industries on you,—No, by the Eternal! I have quite other work for that class of artists; Seven-and-twenty Millions of neglected mortals who have not yet quite declared for the Devil. Mark it, my diabolic friends, I mean to lay leather on the backs of you, collars round the necks of you; and will teach you, after the example of the gods, that this world is *not* your inheritance, or glad to see you in it. You, ye diabolic canaille, what has a Governor much to do with you? You, I think, he will rather swiftly dismiss from his thoughts,—which have the whole celestial and terrestrial for their scope, and not the subterranean of scoundreldom alone. You, I consider, he will sweep pretty rapidly into some Norfolk Island, into some special Convict Colony or remote domestic Moorland, into some stone-walled Silent-System, under hard drill-sergeants, just as Rhadamanthus, and inflexible as he, and there leave you to reap what you have sown; he meanwhile turning his endeavours to the thousandfold immeasurable interests of men and gods,—dismissing the one extremely contemptible interest of scoundrels; sweeping that into the cesspool, tumbling that over London Bridge, in a very brief manner, if needful! Who are you, ye thriftless sweepings of Creation, that we should forever be pestered with you? Have we no work to do but drilling Devil's regiments of the line?

If I had schoolmasters, my benevolent friend, do you imagine I would set them on teaching a set of unteachables, who as you perceive have already made up their mind that black *is* white,—that the Devil namely is the advantageous Master to serve in this world? My esteemed Benefactor of Humanity, it shall be far from me. Minds open to that particular conviction are not the material I like to work upon. When once my schoolmasters have gone over all the other classes of society from top to bottom; and have no other soul to try with teaching, all being thoroughly taught,

—I will then send them to operate on *these* regiments of the line: then, and, assure yourself, never till then. The truth is, I am sick of scoundreldom, my esteemed Benefactor; it always was detestable to me; and here where I find it lodged in palaces and waited on by the benevolent of the world, it is more detestable, not to say insufferable to me than ever.

Of Beneficence, Benevolence, and the people that come together to talk on platforms and subscribe five pounds, I will say nothing here; indeed there is not room here for the twentieth part of what were to be said of them. The beneficence, benevolence, and sublime virtue which issues in eloquent talk reported in the Newspapers, with the subscription of five pounds, and the feeling that one is a good citizen and ornament to society,—concerning this, there were a great many unexpected remarks to be made; but let this one, for the present occasion, suffice:

My sublime benevolent friends, don't you perceive, for one thing, that here is a shockingly unfruitful investment for your capital of Benevolence; precisely the *worst*, indeed, which human ingenuity could select for you? "Laws are unjust, temptations great," etc. etc.: alas, I know it, and mourn for it, and passionately call on all men to help in altering it. But according to every hypothesis as to the law, and the temptations and pressures towards vice, here are the individuals who, of all the society, have yielded to said pressure. These are of the worst substance for enduring pressure! The others yet stand and make resistance to temptation, to the law's injustice; under all the perversities and strangling impediments there are, the rest of the society still keep their feet, and struggle forward, marching under the banner of *Cosmos*, of God and Human Virtue; these select Few, as I explain to you, are they who have fallen to *Chaos*, and are sworn into certain regiments of the line. A superior proclivity to Chaos is declared in these, by the very fact of their being here! Of all the generation we live in, these are the worst stuff. These, I say, are the Elixir of the

Infatuated among living mortals: if you want the *worst* investment for your Benevolence, here you accurately have it. O my surprising friends! Nowhere so as here can you be certain that a given quantity of wise teaching bestowed, of benevolent trouble taken, will yield *zero*, or the net *minimum* of return. It is sowing of your wheat upon Irish quagmires; laboriously harrowing it in upon the sand of the sea-shore. O my astonishing benevolent friends!

Yonder, in those dingy habitations, and shops of red-herring and tobacco-pipes, where men have not yet quite declared for the Devil; there, I say, is land: here is mere sea-beach. Thither go with your benevolence, thither to those dingy caverns of the poor; and there instruct and drill and manage, there where some fruit may come from it. And, above all and inclusive of all, cannot you go to those Solemn human Shams, Phantasm Captains, and Supreme Quacks that ride prosperously in every thoroughfare; and with severe benevolence, ask them, What they are doing here? They are the men whom it would behove you to drill a little, and tie to the halberts in a benevolent manner, if you could! "We cannot," say you? Yes, my friends, to a certain extent you can. By many well-known active methods, and by all manner of passive methods, you can. Strive thitherward, I advise you; thither, with whatever social effort there may lie in you! The well-head and 'consecrated' thrice-accursed chief fountain of all those waters of bitterness,—it is they, those Solemn Shams and Supreme Quacks of yours, little as they or you imagine it! Them, with severe benevolence, put a stop to; them send to their Father, far from the sight of the true and just,—if you would ever see a just world here!

What sort of reformers and workers are you, that work only on the rotten material? That never think of meddling with the material while it continues sound; that stress it and strain it with new rates and assessments, till once it has given way and declared itself rotten; whereupon you snatch greedily at it, and say, Now let us try to do some good upon it! You mistake in every way, my friends: the fact is, you fancy yourselves men of virtue, benevolence, what not; and you are not even men of sincerity and honest sense. I grieve to say it; but it is true. Good from you, and your operations, is not to be expected. You may go down!

Howard is a beautiful Philanthropist, eulogised by Burke, and in most men's minds a sort of beatified individual. How glorious, having finished-off one's affairs in Bedfordshire, or in fact finding them very dull, inane, and worthy of being quitted and got away from, to set out on a cruise over the Jails first of Britain; then, finding that answer, over the Jails of the habitable Globe! 'A voyage of discovery, a circumnavigation of charity; to collate distresses, to gauge wretchedness, to take the dimensions of human misery':—really it is very fine. Captain Cook's voyage for the Terra Australis, Ross's, Franklin's for the ditto Borealis: men make various cruises and voyages in this world,—for want of money, want of work, and one or the other want,—which are attended with their difficulties too, and do *not* make the cruiser a demigod. On the whole, I have myself nothing but respect, comparatively speaking, for the dull solid Howard, and his 'benevolence,' and other impulses that set him cruising; Heaven had grown weary of Jail-fevers, and other the like *un*just penalties inflicted upon scoundrels,—for scoundrels too, and even the very Devil, should not have *more* than their due;—and Heaven, in its opulence, created a man to make an end of that. Created him; disgusted him with the grocer business; tried him with Calvinism, rural ennui, and sore bereavement in his Bedfordshire retreat;—and, in short, at last got him set to his work, and in a condition to achieve it. For which I am thankful to Heaven; and do also, with doffed hat, humbly salute John Howard. A practical solid man. if a dull and even dreary; 'carries his weighing-scales in his pocket': when your jailor answers, "The prisoner's allowance of food is so and so; and we observe it sacredly; here, for example, is a ration."—"Hey! a ration this?" and solid John suddenly produces his weighing-scales; weighs it, marks down in his tablets what the actual quantity of it is. That is the art and manner of the man. A man full of English accuracy; English veracity, solidity, simplicity; by whom this universal Jail-commission, not to be paid for in money but far otherwise, is set about, with all the slow energy, the patience, practicality, sedulity and sagacity common to the best English commissioners paid in money and not expressly otherwise.

For it is the glory of England that she has a turn for fidelity in practical work; that sham-workers, though very numerous, are rarer than elsewhere; that a man who undertakes work for you will still, in various provinces of our affairs, do it, instead of merely seeming to do it. John Howard, without pay in money, *did* this of the Jail-fever, as other Englishmen do work, in a truly workmanlike manner: his distinction was that he did it without money. He had not 500*l.* or 5,000*l.* a-year of salary for it; but lived merely on his Bedfordshire estates, and as Snigsby irreverently expresses it, 'by chewing his own cud.' And, sure enough, if any man might chew the cud of placid reflections, solid Howard, a mournful man otherwise, might at intervals indulge a little in that luxury. No money-salary had he for his work; he had merely the income of his properties, and what he could derive from within. Is this such a sublime distinction, then? Well, let it pass at its value. There have been benefactors of mankind who had more need of money than he, and got none too. Milton, it is known, did his *Paradise Lost* at the easy rate of five pounds. Kepler worked out the secret of the Heavenly Motions in a dreadfully painful manner; 'going over the calculations sixty times';—and having not only no public money, but no private either;

and, in fact, writing almanacs for his bread-and-water, while he did this of the Heavenly Motions; having no Bedfordshire estates; nothing but a pension of 18*l.* (which they would not pay him), the valuable faculty of writing almanacs, and at length the invaluable one of dying, when the Heavenly bodies were vanquished, and battle's conflagration had collapsed into cold dark ashes, and the starvation reached too high a pitch for the poor man.

Howard is not the only benefactor that has worked without money for us; there have been some more,—and will be, I hope! For the Destinies are opulent; and send here and there a man into the world to do work, for which they do not mean to pay him in money. And they smite him beneficently with sore afflictions, and blight his world all into grim frozen ruins round him,—and can make a wandering Exile of their Dante, and not a soft-bedded Podestà of Florence, if they wish to get a *Divine Comedy* out of him. Nay, that rather is their way, when they have worthy work for such a man; they scourge him manifoldly to the due pitch, sometimes nearly of despair, that he may search desperately for his work, and find it; they urge him on still with beneficent stripes when needful, as is constantly the case between whiles; and, in fact, have privately decided to reward him with beneficent death by and by, and not with money at all. O my benevolent friend, I honour Howard very much; but it is on this side idolatry a long way, not to an infinite, but to a decidedly finite extent! And you,—put not the modest noble Howard, a truly modest man, to the blush, by forcing these reflections on us!

Cholera Doctors, hired to dive into black dens of infection and despair, they, rushing about all day from lane to lane, with their life in their hand, are found to do their function; which is a much more rugged one than Howard's. Or what say we, Cholera Doctors? Ragged losels gathered by beat of drum from the overcrowded streets of cities, and drilled a little and dressed in red, do not they stand fire in an uncensurable manner; and handsomely give their life, if needful, at the rate of a shilling per day? Human virtue, if we went down to the roots of it, is not so rare. The materials of human virtue are everywhere abundant as the light of the sun: raw materials,—O woe, and loss, and scandal thrice and threefold, that they so seldom are elaborated, and built into a result! that they lie yet unelaborated, and stagnant in the souls of wide-spread dreary millions, fermenting, festering; and issue at last as energetic vice instead of strong practical virtue! A Mrs. Manning 'dying game,'—alas, is not that the foiled potentiality of a kind of heroine too? Not a heroic Judith, not a mother of the Gracchi now, but a hideous murderess, fit to be the mother of hyænas! To such extent can potentialities be foiled. Education, kingship, command,—where is it, whither has it fled? Woe a thousand times, that this, which is the task of all kings, captains, priests, public speakers, land-owners, book-writers, mill-owners, and persons possessing or pretending to possess authority among mankind,—is left neglected among them all; and instead of it so little done but protocolling, black-or-white surplicing, partridge-shooting, parliamentary eloquence and popular twaddle-literature; with such results as we see!—

Howard abated the Jail-fever; but it seems to me he has been the innocent cause of a far more distressing fever which rages high just now; what we may call the Benevolent-Platform Fever. Howard is to be regarded as the unlucky fountain of that tumultuous frothy ocean-tide of benevolent sentimentality, 'abolition of punishment,' all-absorbing 'prison-discipline,' and general morbid sympathy, instead of hearty hatred, for scoundrels; which is threatening to drown human society as in deluges, and leave, instead of an 'edifice of society' fit for the habitation of men, a continent of fetid ooze inhabitable only by mud-gods and creatures that walk upon their belly. Few things more distress a thinking soul at this time.

Most sick am I, O friends, of this sugary disastrous jargon of philanthropy, the reign of love, new era of universal brotherhood, and not Paradise to the Well-deserving but Paradise to All-and-sundry, which possesses the benighted minds of men and women in our day. My friends, I think you are much mistaken about Paradise! 'No Paradise for anybody: he that cannot do without Paradise, go his ways': suppose you tried that for a while! I reckon that the safer version.—Unhappy sugary brethren, this is all untrue, this other; contrary to the fact; not a tatter of it will hang together in the wind and weather of fact. In brotherhood with the base and foolish I, for one, do not mean to live. Not in brotherhood with them was life hitherto worth much to me; in pity, in hope not yet quite swallowed of disgust, —otherwise in enmity that must last through eternity, in unappeasable aversion shall I have to live with these! Brotherhood? No, be the thought far from me. They are Adam's children,—alas yes, I well remember that, and never shall forget it; hence this rage and sorrow. But they have gone over to the dragons; they have quitted the Father's house, and set-up with the Old Serpent: till they return, how can they be brothers? They are enemies, deadly to themselves and to me and to you, till then; till then, while hope yet lasts, I will treat them as brothers fallen insane;— when hope has ended, with tears grown sacred and wrath grown sacred, I will cut them off in the name of God! It is at my peril if I do not. With the servant of Satan I dare not continue in partnership. Him I must put away, resolutely and forever; 'lest,' as it is written, 'I become partaker of his plagues.'

Beautiful Black Peasantry, who have fallen idle and have got the Devil at your elbow; interesting White Felonry, who are not idle, but have enlisted into the Devil's regiments of the line,—know that my benevolence for you is comparatively trifling! What I have of that divine feeling is due to others, not to you. A 'universal Sluggard-and-Scoundrel

Protection Society' is not the one I mean to institute in these times, where so much wants protection, and is sinking to sad issues for want of it! The scoundrel needs no protection. The scoundrel that *will* hasten to the gallows, why not rather clear the way for him! Better he reach *his* goal and outgate by the natural proclivity, than be so expensively dammed-up and detained, poisoning everything as he stagnates and meanders along, to arrive at last a hundred times fouler, and swollen a hundred times bigger! Benevolent men should reflect on this.—And you Quashee, my pumpkin,—(not a bad fellow either, this poor Quashee, when tolerably guided!)—idle Quashee, I say you must get the Devil *sent away* from your elbow, my poor dark friend! In this world there will be no existence for you otherwise. No, not as the brother of your folly will I live beside you. Please to withdraw out of my way, if I am not to contradict your folly, and amend it, and put it in the stocks if it will not amend. By the Eternal Maker, it is on that footing alone that you and I can live together! And if you had respectable traditions dated from beyond Magna Charta, or from beyond the Deluge, to the contrary, and written sheepskins that would thatch the face of the world,—behold I, for one individual, do not believe said respectable traditions, nor regard said written sheepskins except as things which *you*, till you grow wiser, will believe. Adieu, Quashee; I will wish you better guidance than you have had of late.

On the whole, what a reflection it is that we cannot bestow on an unworthy man any particle of our benevolence, our patronage, or whatever resource is ours,—without withdrawing it, it and all that will grow of it, from one worthy, to whom it of right belongs! We cannot, I say; impossible; it is the eternal law of things. Incompetent Duncan M'Pastehorn, the hapless incompetent mortal to whom I give the cobbling of my boots,—and cannot find in my heart to refuse it, the poor drunken wretch having a wife and ten children; he *withdraws* the job from sober, plainly competent, and meritorous Mr. Sparrowbill, generally short of work too; discourages Sparrowbill; teaches him that he too may as well drink and loiter and bungle; that this is not a scene for merit and demerit at all, but for dupery, and whining flattery, and incompetent cobbling of every description;—clearly tending to the ruin of poor Sparrowbill! What harm had Sparrowbill done me that I should so help to ruin him? And I couldn't *save* the unsalvable M'Pastehorn; I merely yielded him, for insufficient work, here and there a half-crown,—which he oftenest drank. And now Sparrowbill also is drinking!

Justice, Justice: woe betides us everywhere when, for this reason or for that, we fail to do justice! No beneficence, benevolence, or other virtuous contribution will make good the want. And in what a rate of terrible geometrical progression, far beyond *our* poor computation, any act of Injustice once done by us grows; rooting itself ever anew, spreading ever anew, like a banyan-tree,—blasting all life under it, for it is a poison-tree! There is but one thing needed for the world; but that one is indispensable. Justice, Justice, in the name of Heaven; give us Justice, and we live; give us only counterfeits of it, or succedanea for it, and we die!

O this universal syllabub of philanthropic twaddle! My friend, it is very sad, now when Christianity is as good as extinct in all hearts, to meet this ghastly Phantasm of Christianity parading through almost all. "I will clean your foul thoroughfares, and make your Devil's-cloaca of a world into a garden of Heaven," jabbers this Phantasm, itself a phosphorescence and unclean! The worst, it is written, comes from corruption of the best:—Semitic forms now lying putrescent, dead and still unburied, this phosphorescence rises. I say sometimes, such a blockhead Idol, and miserable *White* Mumbojumbo, fashioned out of deciduous sticks and cast clothes, out of extinct cants and modern sentimentalisms, as that which they sing litanies to at Exeter Hall and extensively elsewhere, was perhaps never set-up by human folly before. Unhappy creatures, that is not the Maker of the Universe, not that,—look one moment at the Universe, and see! That is a paltry Phantasm, engendered in your own sick brain; whoever follows that as a Reality will fall into the ditch.

Reform, reform, all men see and feel, is imperatively needed. Reform must either be got, and speedily, or else we die: and nearly all the men that speak, instruct us, saying, "Have you quite done your interesting Negroes in the Sugar Islands? Rush to the Jails, then, O ye reformers; snatch-up the interesting scoundrel-population there, to them be nursing-fathers and nursing-mothers. And O wash, and dress, and teach, and recover to the service of Heaven, these poor lost souls; *so*, we assure you, will society attain the needful reform, and life be still possible in this world." Thus sing the oracles everywhere; nearly all the men that speak,—though we doubt not, there are, as usual, immense majorities consciously or unconsciously wiser who hold their tongue. But except this of whitewashing the scoundrel-population, one sees little 'reform' going on. There is perhaps some endeavour to do a little scavengering; and, as the all-including point, to cheapen the terrible cost of Government: but neither of these enterprises makes progress owing to impediments.

"Whitewash your scoundrel-population; sweep-out your abominable gutters (if not in the name of God, ye brutish slatterns, then in the name of Cholera and the Royal College of Surgeons): do these two things;—and observe, much cheaper if you please!"—Well, here surely is an Evangel of Freedom, and real Program of a new Era. What surliest misanthrope would not find this world lovely, were these things done; scoundrels whitewashed; some degree of scavengering upon the gutters; and at a cheap rate, thirdly? That surely is an occasion on which, if ever on any, the Genius of Reform may pipe all hands!—Poor old Genius of Reform; bedrid this good while; with little but broken ballot-boxes, and tattered stripes of Benthamee Constitutions lying round him; and on the walls mere shadows of clothing-colonels, rates-in-aid, poor-law unions, defunct potato and the Irish difficulty,—he does not seem long for this world, piping to that effect?

Not the least disgusting feature of this Gospel according to the Platform is its reference to religion, and even to the Christian Religion, as an authority and mandate for what it does. Christian Religion? Does the Christian or any religion prescribe love of scoundrels then? I hope it prescribes a healthy hatred of scoundrels;—otherwise what am I, in Heaven's name, to make of it? Me, for one, it will not serve as a religion on those strange terms. Just hatred of scoundrels, I say; fixed, irreconcilable, inexorable enmity to the enemies of God: this, and not love for them, and incessant whitewashing, and dressing and cockering of them, must, if you look into it, be the backbone of any human religion whatsoever. Christian Religion! In what words can I address you, ye unfortunates, sunk in the slushy ooze till the worship of mud-serpents, and unutterable Pythons and poisonous slimy monstrosities, seems to you the worship of God? This is the rotten carcass of Christianity; this malodorous phosphorescence of *post-mortem* sentimentalism. O Heavens, from the Christianity of Oliver Cromwell, wrestling in grim fight with Satan and his incarnate Blackguardisms, Hypocrisies, Injustices, and legion of human and infernal angels, to that of eloquent Mr. Hesperus Fiddlestring denouncing capital punishments, and inculcating the benevolences on platforms, what a road have we travelled!

A foolish stump-orator, perorating on his platform mere benevolences, seems a pleasant object to many persons; a harmless or insignificant one to almost all. Look at him, however; scan him till you discern the nature of him, he is not pleasant, but ugly and perilous. That beautiful speech of his takes captive every long ear, and kindles into quasi-sacred enthusiasm the minds of not a few; but it is quite in the teeth of the everlasting facts of this Universe, and will come only to mischief for every party concerned. Consider that little spouting wretch. Within the paltry skin of him, it is too probable, he holds few human virtues, beyond those essential for digesting victual: envious, cowardly, vain, splenetic hungry soul; what heroism, in word or thought or action, will you ever get from the like of him? He, in his necessity, has taken into the benevolent line; warms the cold vacuity of his inner man to some extent, in a comfortable manner, not by silently doing some virtue of his own, but by fiercely recommending hearsay pseudo-virtues and respectable benevolences to other people. Do you call that a good trade? Long-eared fellow-creatures, more or less resembling himself, answer, "Hear, hear! Live Fiddlestring forever!" Wherefrom follow Abolition Congresses, Odes to the Gallows;—perhaps some dirty little Bill, getting itself debated next Session in Parliament, to waste certain nights of our legislative Year, and cause skipping in our Morning Newspaper, till the abortion can be emptied out again and sent fairly floating down the gutters.

Not with entire approbation do I, for one, look on that eloquent individual. Wise benevolence, if it had authority, would order that individual, I believe, to find some other trade: "Eloquent individual, pleading here against the Laws of Nature,—for many reasons, I bid thee close that mouth of thine. Enough of balderdash these long-eared have now drunk. Depart thou; *do* some benevolent work; at lowest, be silent. Disappear, I say; away, and jargon no more in that manner, lest a worst thing befal thee." *Exeat* Fiddlestring!—Beneficent men are not they who appear on platforms, pleading against the Almighty Maker's Laws; these are the maleficent men, whose lips it is pity that some authority cannot straightway shut. Pandora's Box is not more baleful than the gifts these eloquent benefactors are pressing on us. Close your pedlar's-pack, my friend; swift, away with it! Pernicious, fraught with mere woe and sugary poison is that kind of benevolence and beneficence.

Truly, one of the saddest sights in these times is that of poor creatures, on platforms, in parliaments and other situations, making and unmaking 'Laws'; in whose soul, full of mere vacant hearsay and windy babble, is and was no image of Heaven's Law; whom it never struck that Heaven had a Law, or that the Earth—could not have what kind of Law you pleased! Human Statute-books, accordingly, are growing horrible to think of. An impiety and poisonous futility every Law of them that is so made; all Nature is against it; it will and can do nothing but mischief wheresoever it shows itself in Nature: and such Laws lie now like an incubus over this Earth, so innumerable are they. How long, O Lord, how long!—O ye Eternities, Divine Silences, do you dwell no more, then, in the hearts of the noble and the true; and is there no inspiration of the Almighty any more vouchsafed us? The inspiration of the Morning Newspapers—alas, we have had enough of that, and are arrived at the gates of death by means of that!

"Really, one of the most difficult questions this we have in these times, What to do with our criminals?" blandly observed a certain Law-dignitary, in my hearing once, taking the cigar from his mouth, and pensively smiling over a group of us under the summer beech-tree, as Favonius carried off the tobacco-smoke; and the group said nothing, only smiled and nodded, answering by new tobacco-clouds. "What to do with our criminals?" asked the official Law-dignitary again, as if entirely at a loss.—"I suppose," said one ancient figure not engaged in smoking, "the plan would be to treat them according to the real law of the case; to make the Law of England, in respect of them, correspond to the Law of the Universe. Criminals, I suppose, would prove manageable in that way: if we could do approximately as God Almighty does towards them; in a word, if we could try to do Justice towards them."—"I'll thank you for a definition of Justice?" sneered the official person in a cheerily scornful and triumphant manner, backed by a slight laugh from the honourable company; which irritated the other speaker.—"Well, I have no pocket-definition of Justice," said he, "to give your Lordship. It has not quite been my trade to look for such a definition; I could rather fancy it had been your Lordship's trade, sitting on your high place this long while. But one thing I can tell you: Justice always *is*, whether we define it or not. Everything done, suffered or proposed, in Parliament or out of it, *is* either just or else unjust; either is accepted by the gods and eternal facts, or is rejected by them. Your Lordship and I, with or without definition, do a little know Justice, I will hope; if we don't both know it and do it, we are hourly travelling down towards—Heavens, must I name such a place! That is the place we are bound to, with all our trading-pack, and the small or extensive budgets of human business laid on us; and there, if we *don't know* Justice, we, and all our budgets and Acts of Parliament, shall find lodging when the day is done!"—The official person, a polite man otherwise, grinned as he best could some semblance of a laugh, mirthful as that of the ass eating thistles, and ended in "Hah, oh, ah!"—

Indeed, it is wonderful to hear what account we at present give ourselves of the punishment of criminals. No 'revenge'—O Heavens, no; all preachers on Sunday strictly forbid that; and even (at least on Sundays) prescribe the contrary of that. It is for the sake of 'example,' that you punish; to 'protect society' and its purse and skin; to deter the innocent from falling into crime; and especially withal, for the purpose of improving the poor criminal himself,—or at lowest, of hanging and ending him, that he may not grow worse. For the poor criminal is to be 'improved' if possible: against him no 'revenge' even on weekdays; nothing but love for him, and pity and help; poor fellow, is he not miserable enough? Very miserable,—though much less so than the Master of him, called Satan, is understood (on Sundays) to have long deservedly been!

My friends, will you permit me to say that all this, to one poor judgment among your number, is the mournfulest twaddle that human tongues could shake from them; that it has no solid foundation in the nature of things; and to a healthy human heart no credibility whatever? Permit me to say, only to hearts long drowned in dead Tradition, and for themselves neither believing nor disbelieving, could this seem credible. Think, and ask yourselves, in spite of all this preaching and perorating from the teeth outward! Hearts that are quite strangers to eternal Fact, and acquainted only at all hours with temporary Semblances parading about in a prosperous and persuasive condition; hearts that from their first appearance in this world have breathed since birth, in all spiritual matters, which means in all matters not pecuniary, the poisonous atmosphere of universal Cant, could believe such a thing. Cant moral, Cant religious, Cant political; an atmosphere which envelops all things for us unfortunates, and has long done; which goes beyond the Zenith and below the Nadir for us, and has as good as choked the spiritual life out of all of us,—God pity such wretches, with little or nothing *real* about them but their purse and their abdominal department! Hearts, alas, which everywhere except in the metallurgic and cottonspinning provinces, have communed with no Reality, or awful Presence of a Fact, godlike or diabolic, in this Universe or this unfathomable Life at all. Hunger-stricken asphyxied hearts, which have nourished themselves on what they call religions, Christian religions. Good Heaven, once more fancy the Christian religion of Oliver Cromwell; or of some noble Christian man, whom you yourself may have been blessed enough, once, long since, in your life, to know! These are not *untrue* religions; they are the putrescences and foul residues of religions that are extinct, that have plainly to every honest nostril been dead some time, and the remains of which—O ye eternal Heavens, will the nostril never be delivered from them!—Such hearts, when they get upon platforms, and into questions not involving money, can 'believe' many things!—

I take the liberty of asserting that there is one valid reason, and only one, for either punishing a man or rewarding him in this world; one reason, which ancient piety could well define: That you may do the will and commandment of God with regard to him; that you may do justice to him. This is your one true aim in respect of him; aim thitherward, with all your heart and all your strength and all your soul; thitherward, and not elsewhither at all! This aim is true, and will carry you to all earthly heights and benefits, and beyond the stars and Heavens. All other aims are purblind, illegitimate, untrue; and will never carry you beyond the shop-counter, nay, very soon will prove themselves incapable of maintaining you even there. Find out what the Law of God is with regard to a man; make that your human law, or I say it will be ill with you, and not well! If you love your thief or murderer, if Nature and eternal Fact love him, then do as you are now doing. But if Nature and Fact do *not* love him? If they have set inexorable penalties upon him, and planted natural wrath against him in every god-created human heart,—then I advise you, cease, and change your hand.

Reward and punishment? Alas, alas, I must say you reward and punish pretty much alike! Your dignities, peerages, promotions, your kingships, your brazen statues erected in capital and county towns to our select demigods of *your* selecting, testify loudly enough what kind of heroes and hero-worshippers you are. Woe to the People that no longer venerates, as the emblem of God himself, the aspect of Human Worth; that no longer knows what human worth and unworth is! Sure as the Decrees of the Eternal, that People cannot come to good. By a course too clear, by a necessity too evident, that People will come into the hands of the unworthy; and either turn on its bad career, or stagger downwards to ruin and abolition. Does the Hebrew People prophetically sing "Ou' clo'!" in all thoroughfares, these eighteen hundred years in vain?

To reward men according to their worth: alas, the perfection of this, we know, amounts to the millennium! Neither is perfect punishment, according to the like rule, to be attained,—nor even, by a legislator of these chaotic days, to be too zealously attempted. But when he does attempt it, —yes, when he summons out the Society to sit deliberative on this matter, and consult the oracles upon it, and solemnly settle it in the name of God; then, if never before, he should try to be a little in the right in settling it!—In regard to reward of merit, I do not bethink me of any attempt whatever, worth calling an attempt, on the part of modern Governments; which surely is an immense oversight on their part, and will one day be seen to have been an altogether fatal one. But as to the punishment of crime, happily this cannot be quite neglected. When men have a purse and a skin, they seek salvation at least for these; and the Four Pleas of the Crown are a thing that must and will be attended to. By punishment, capital or other, by treadmilling and blind rigour, or by whitewashing and blind laxity, the extremely disagreeable offences of theft and murder must be kept down within limits.

And so you take criminal caitiffs, murderers, and the like, and hang them on gibbets 'for an example to deter others.' Whereupon arise friends of humanity, and object. With very great reason, as I consider, if *your* hypothesis be correct. What right have you to hang any poor creature 'for an example'? He can turn round upon you and say, "Why make 'an example' of me, a merely ill-situated, pitiable man? Have you no more respect for misfortune? Misfortune, I have been told, is sacred. And yet you hang me, now I am fallen into your hands; choke the life out of me, for an example! Again I ask, Why make an example of *me*, for your own convenience alone?"—All 'revenge' being out of the question, it seems to me the caitiff is unanswerable; and he and the philanthropic platforms have the logic all on their side.

The one answer to him is: "Caitiff, we hate thee; and discern for some six thousand years now, that we are called upon by the whole Universe to do it. Not with a diabolic but with a divine hatred. God himself, we have always understood, 'hates sin,' with a most authentic, celestial, and eternal hatred. A hatred, a hostility inexorable, unappeasable, which blasts the scoundrel, and all scoundrels ultimately, into black annihilation and disappearance from the sum of things. The path of it as the path of a flaming sword: he that has eyes may see it, walking inexorable, divinely beautiful and divinely terrible, through the chaotic gulf of Human History, and everywhere burning, as with unquenchable fire, the false and death-worthy from the true and life-worthy; making all Human History, and the Biography of every man, a God's Cosmos in place of a Devil's Chaos. So is it, in the end; even so, to every man who is a man, and not a mutinous beast, and has eyes to see. To thee, caitiff, these things were and are, quite incredible; to us they are too awfully certain,—the Eternal Law of this Universe, whether thou and others will believe it or disbelieve. We, not to be partakers in thy destructive adventure of *defying* God and all the Universe, dare not allow thee to continue longer among us. As a palpable deserter from the ranks where all men, at their eternal peril, are bound to be: palpable deserter, taken with the red hand fighting thus against the whole Universe and its Laws, we—send thee back into the whole Universe, solemnly expel thee from our community; and will, in the name of God, not with joy and exultation, but with sorrow stern as thy own, hang thee on Wednesday next, and so end."

Other ground on which to deliberately slay a disarmed fellow-man I can see none. Example, effects upon the public mind, effects upon this and upon that: all this is mere appendage and accident; of all this I make no attempt to keep account,—sensible that no arithmetic will or can keep account of it; that its 'effects,' on this hand and on that, transcend all calculation. One thing, if I can calculate it, will include all, and produce beneficial effects beyond calculation, and no ill effect at all, anywhere or at any time: What the Law of the Universe, or Law of God, *is* with regard to this caitiff? That, by all sacred research and consideration, I will try to find out; to that I will come as near as human means admit; that shall be my exemplar and 'example'; all men shall through me see that, and be profited *beyond* calculation by seeing it.

What this Law of the Universe, or Law made by God, is? Men at one time read it in their Bible. In many Bibles, Books, and authentic symbols and monitions of Nature and the Word (of Fact, that is, and of Human Speech, or Wise Interpretation of Fact), there are still clear indications towards it. Most important it is, for this and for some other reasons, that men do, in some way, get to see it a little! And if no man could now see it by any Bible, there is written in the heart of every man an authentic copy of it direct from Heaven itself: there, if he have learnt to decipher Heaven's writing, and can read the sacred oracles (a sad case for him if he altogether cannot), every born man may still find some copy of it.

'Revenge,' my friends! revenge, and the natural hatred of scoundrels, and the ineradicable tendency to *revancher* oneself upon them, and pay them what they have merited: this is forevermore intrinsically a correct, and even a divine feeling in the mind of every man. Only the excess of it is diabolic; the essence I say is manlike, and even godlike,—a monition sent to poor man by the Maker himself. Thou, poor reader, in spite of all this melancholy twaddle, and blotting-out of Heaven's sunlight by mountains of horsehair and officiality, hast still a human heart. If, in returning to thy poor peaceable dwelling-place, after an honest hard day's work, thou wert to find, for example, a brutal scoundrel who for lucre or other object of his, had slaughtered the life that was dearest to thee; thy true wife, for example, thy true old mother, swimming in her blood; the human scoundrel, or two-legged wolf, standing over such a tragedy: I hope a man would have so much divine rage in his heart as to snatch the nearest weapon, and put a conclusion upon said human wolf, for one! A palpable messenger of Satan, that one; accredited by all the Devils, to be put an end to by all the children of God. The soul of every god-created man flames wholly into one divine blaze of sacred wrath at sight of such a Devil's messenger; authentic first-hand monition from the Eternal Maker himself as to what is next to be done. Do it, or be thyself an ally of Devil's-messengers; a sheep for two-legged human wolves, well deserving to be eaten, as thou soon wilt be!

My humane friends, I perceive this same sacred glow of divine wrath, or authentic monition at first hand from God himself, to be the foundation for all Criminal Law, and Official horsehair-and-bombazeen procedure against Scoundrels in this world. This first-hand gospel from the Eternities, imparted to every mortal, this is still, and will forever be, your sanction and commission for the punishment of human scoundrels. See well how you will translate this message from Heaven and the Eternities into a form suitable to this World and its Times. Let not violence, haste, blind impetuous impulse, preside in executing it; the injured man, invincibly liable to fall into these, shall not himself execute it: the whole world, in person of a Minister appointed for that end, and surrounded with the due solemnities and caveats, with bailiffs, apparitors, advocates, and the hushed expectation of all men, shall do it, as under the eye of God who made all men. How it shall be done? this is ever a vast question, involving immense considerations. Thus Edmund Burke saw, in the Two Houses of Parliament, with King, Constitution, and all manner of Civil-Lists, and Chancellors' wigs and Exchequer budgets, only the 'method of getting twelve just men put into a jury-box': that, in Burke's view, was the summary of what they were all meant for. How the judge will do it? Yes, indeed:—but let him see well that he does do it; for it is a thing that must by no means be left undone! A sacred gospel from the Highest: not to be smothered under horsehair and bombazeen, or drowned in platform froth, or in anywise omitted or neglected, without the most alarming penalties to all concerned!

Neglect to treat the hero as hero, the penalties,—which are inevitable too, and terrible to think of, as your Hebrew friends can tell you,—may be some time in coming; they will only gradually come. Not all at once will your Thirty-thousand Needlewomen, your Three-million Paupers, your Connaught fallen into potential Cannibalism, and other fine consequences of the practice, come to light;—though come to light they will; and "Ou' clo'!" itself may be in store for you, if you persist steadily enough. But neglect to treat even your declared scoundrel as scoundrel, this is the last consummation of the process, the drop by which the cup runs over; the penalties of this, most alarming, extensive, and such as you little dream of, will straightway very rapidly come. Dim oblivion of Right and Wrong, among the masses of your population, will come; doubts as to Right and Wrong, indistinct notion that Right and Wrong are not eternal, but accidental, and settled by uncertain votings and talkings, will come. Prurient influenza of Platform Benevolence, and 'Paradise to All-and-sundry,' will come. In the general putrescence of your 'religions,' as you call them, a strange new religion, named of Universal Love, with Sacraments mainly of *Divorce*, with Balzac, Sue and Company for Evangelists, and Madame Sand for Virgin, will come,—and results fast following therefrom which will astonish you very much!

'The terrible anarchies of these years,' says Crabbe, in his *Radiator*, 'are brought upon us by a necessity too visible.

By the crime of Kings,—alas, yes; but by that of Peoples too. Not by the crime of one class, but by the fatal obscuration, and all but obliteration of the sense of Right and Wrong in the minds and practices of every class. What a scene in the drama of Universal History, this of ours! A world-wide loud bellow and bray of universal Misery; *lowing*, with crushed maddened heart, its inarticulate prayer to Heaven:—very pardonable to me, and in some of its transcendent developments, as in the grand French Revolution, most respectable and ever-memorable. For Injustice reigns everywhere; and this murderous struggle for what they call "Fraternity," and so forth, has a spice of eternal sense in it, though so terribly disfigured! Amalgam of sense and nonsense; eternal sense by the grain, and temporary nonsense by the square mile: as is the habit with poor sons of men. Which pardonable amalgam, however, if it be taken as the pure final sense, I must warn you and all creatures, is unpardonable, criminal, and fatal nonsense;—with which I, for one, will take care not to concern myself!

'*Dogs should not be taught to eat leather*, says the old adage: no;—and where, by general fault and error, and the inevitable nemesis of things, the universal kennel is set to diet upon *leather*; and from its keepers, its "Liberal Premiers," or whatever their title is, will accept or expect nothing else, and calls it by the pleasant name of progress, reform, emancipation, abolition-principles, and the like,—I consider the fate of said kennel and of said keepers to be a thing settled. Red republic in Phrygian nightcap, organisation of labour *à la* Louis Blanc; street-barricades, and then murderous cannon-volleys *à la* Cavaignac and Windischgrätz, follow out of one another, as grapes, must, new wine, and sour all-splitting vinegar do:—vinegar is but *vin-aigre*, or the selfsame "wine" grown *sharp*! If, moreover, I find the Worship of Human Nobleness abolished in any country, and a *new* astonishing Phallus-Worship, with universal Balzac-Sand melodies and litanies in treble and in bass, established in its stead, what can I compute but that Nature, in horrible throes, will repugn against such substitution,—that, in short, the astonishing new Phallus-Worship, with its finer sensibilities of the heart, and "great satisfying loves," with its sacred kiss of peace for scoundrel and hero alike, with its all-embracing Brotherhood, and universal Sacrament of Divorce, will have to take itself away again!'

The Ancient Germans, it appears, had no scruple about public executions; on the contrary, they thought the just gods themselves might fitly preside over these; that these were a solemn and highest act of worship, if justly done. When a German man had done a crime deserving death, they, in solemn general assembly of the tribe, doomed him, and considered that Fate and all Nature had from the beginning doomed him, to die with ignominy. Certain crimes there were of a supreme nature; him that had perpetrated one of these, they believed to have declared himself a prince of scoundrels. Him once convicted they laid hold of, nothing doubting;—bore him, after judgment, to the deepest convenient Peatbog; plunged him in there, drove an oaken frame down over him, solemnly in the name of gods and men: "There, prince of scoundrels, that is what we have had to think of thee, on clear acquaintance; our grim good-night to thee is that! In the name of all the gods, lie there, and be our partnership with thee dissolved henceforth. It will be better for us, we imagine!"

My friends, after all this beautiful whitewash and humanity and prison-discipline; and such blubbering and whimpering, and soft Litany to divine and also to quite other sorts of Pity, as we have had for a century now,—give me leave to admonish you that that of the Ancient Germans too was a thing inexpressibly necessary to keep in mind. If that is not kept in mind, the universal Litany to Pity is a mere universal nuisance, and torpid blasphemy against the gods. I do not much respect it, that purblind blubbering and litanying, as it is seen at present; and the litanying over scoundrels I go the length of disrespecting, and in some cases even of detesting. Yes, my friends, scoundrel is scoundrel: that remains for ever a fact; and there exists not in the earth whitewash that can make the scoundrel a friend of this Universe; he remains an enemy if you spent your life in whitewashing him. He won't whitewash; this one won't. The one method clearly is, That, after fair trial, you dissolve partnership with him; send him, in the name of Heaven, whither *he* is striving all this while, and have done with him. And, in a time like this, I would advise you, see likewise that you be speedy about it! For there is immense work, and of a far hopefuler sort, to be done *elsewhere*.

Alas, alas, to see once the 'prince of scoundrels,' the Supreme Scoundrel, him whom of all men the gods liked *worst*, solemnly laid hold of, and hung upon the gallows in sight of the people; what a lesson to all the people! Sermons might be preached; the Son of Thunder and the Mouth of Gold might turn their periods now with some hope; for here, in the most impressive way, is a divine sermon *acted*. Didactic as no spoken sermon could be. Didactic, devotional too;—in awed solemnity, a recognition that Eternal Justice rules the world; that at the call of this human pity shall fall silent, and man be stern as his Master and Mandatory is!—Understand too that except upon a basis of even such rigour, sorrowful, silent, inexorable as that of Destiny and Doom, there is no true pity possible. The pity that proves so possible and plentiful without that basis, is mere *ignavia* and cowardly effeminacy; maudlin laxity of heart, grounded on blinkard dimness of head—contemptible as a drunkard's tears.

To see our Supreme Scoundrel hung upon the gallows, alas, that is far from us just now! There is a *worst* man in England, too,—curious to think of,—whom it would be inexpressibly advantageous to lay hold of, and hang, the first of all. But we do not know him with the least certainty, the least approach even to a guess,—such buzzards and dullards and poor children of the Dusk are we, in spite of our Statistics, Unshackled Presses, and Torches of Knowledge;—not eagles soaring sunward, not brothers of the lightnings and the radiances we; a dim horn-eyed, owl-population, intent mainly on the catching of mice! Alas, the supreme scoundrel, alike with the supreme hero, is very far from being known. Nor have we the smallest apparatus for dealing with either of them, if he were known. Our supreme scoundrel sits, I conjecture, well-cushioned, in high places, at this time; rolls softly through the world, and lives a prosperous gentleman; instead of sinking him in peat-bogs, we mount the brazen image of him on high columns: such is the world's temporary judgment about its supreme scoundrels; a mad world, my masters. To get the supreme scoundrel always accurately the first hanged,—this, which presupposes that the supreme hero were always the first promoted, this were precisely the millennium itself, clear evidence that the millennium had come: alas, we must forbear hope of this. Much water will run-by before we see this.

And yet to quit all aim towards it; to go blindly floundering along, wrapt-up in clouds of horsehair, bombazeen, and sheepskin officiality, oblivious that there exists such an aim: this is indeed fatal. In every human law there must either exist such an aim, or else the law is not a human but a diabolic one. Diabolic, I say: no quantity of bombazeen, or lawyers' wigs, three-readings, and solemn trumpeting and bow-wowing in high places or in low, can hide from me its frightful infernal tendency;—bound, and sinking at all moments gradually to Gehenna, this 'law'; and dragging down much with it! 'To decree *injustice* by a *law*': inspired Prophets have long since seen, what every clear soul may still see, that of all Anarchies and Devil-worships there is none like this; that this is the 'Throne of Iniquity' set up in the name of the Highest, the human Apotheosis of Anarchy itself. "*Quiet* Anarchy," you exultingly say? Yes; quiet Anarchy, which the longer it sits 'quiet' will have the frightfuler account to settle at last. For every doit of the account, as I often say, will have to be settled one day, as sure as God lives. Principal, and compound interest rigorously computed; and the interest is at a terrible rate per cent. in these cases! Alas, the aspect of certain beatified Anarchies, sitting 'quiet'; and of others in a state of infernal explosion for sixty years back: this, the one view our Europe offers at present, makes these days very sad.—

My unfortunate philanthropic friends, it is this long-continued oblivion of the soul of law that has reduced the Criminal Question to such a pass among us. Many other things have come, and are coming, for the same sad reason, to a pass! Not the supreme scoundrel have our laws aimed at; but, in an uncertain fitful manner, at the inferior or lowest scoundrel, who robs shop-tills and puts the skin of mankind in danger. How can Parliament get through the Criminal Question? Parliament, oblivious of Heavenly Law, will find itself in hopeless *reductio ad absurdum* in regard to innumerable other questions,—in regard to all questions whatsoever by and by. There will be no existence possible for Parliament on these current terms. Parliament, in its law-makings, must really try to attain some vision again of what Heaven's Laws are. A thing not easy to do; a thing requiring sad sincerity of heart, reverence, pious earnestness, valiant manful wisdom;—qualities not overabundant in Parliament just now, nor out of it, I fear.

Adieu, my friends. My anger against you is gone; my sad reflections on you, and on the depths to which you and I and all of us are sunk in these strange times, are not to be uttered at present. You would have saved the Sarawak Pirates, then? The Almighty Maker is wroth that the Sarawak cutthroats, with their poisoned spears, are away?

What must his wrath be that the Thirty-thousand Needle-women are still here, and the question of 'prevenient grace' not yet settled! O my friends, in sad earnest, sad and deadly earnest, there much needs that God would mend all this, and that we should help him to mend it!—And don't you think, for one thing, 'Farmer Hodge's horses' in the Sugar Islands are pretty well 'emancipated' now? My clear opinion farther is, we had better quit the Scoundrel-province of Reform; better close that under hatches, in some rapid summary manner, and go elsewhither with our Reform efforts. A whole world, for want of Reform, is drowning and sinking; threatening to swamp itself into a Stygian quagmire, uninhabitable by any noble-minded man. Let us to the well-heads, I say; to the chief fountains of these waters of bitterness; and there strike home and dig! To puddle in the embouchures and drowned outskirts, and ulterior and ultimate *issues* and cloacas of the affair: what profit can there be in that? Nothing to be saved there; nothing to be fished-up there, except with endless peril and spread of pestilence, a miscellany of broken waifs and dead dogs! In the name of Heaven, quit that!

No. III

DOWNING STREET

[1st April 1850]

From all corners of the wide British Dominion there rises one complaint against the ineffectuality of what are nicknamed our 'redtape' establishments, our Government Offices, Colonial Office, Foreign Office and the others, in Downing Street and the neighbourhood. To me individually these branches of human business are little known; but every British citizen and reflective passer-by has occasion to wonder much, and inquire earnestly, concerning them. To all men it is evident that the social interests of One-hundred and fifty Millions of us depend on the mysterious industry there carried on; and likewise that the dissatisfaction with it is great, universal, and continually increasing in intensity,—in fact, mounting, we might say, to the pitch of settled despair.

Every colony, every agent for a matter colonial, has his tragic tale to tell you of his sad experiences in the Colonial Office; what blind obstructions, fatal indolences, pedantries, stupidities, on the right and on the left, he had to do battle with; what a world-wide jungle of redtape, inhabited by doleful creatures, deaf or nearly so to human reason or entreaty, he had entered on; and how he paused in amazement, almost in despair; passionately appealed now to this doleful creature, now to that, and to the dead redtape jungle, and to the living Universe itself, and to the Voices and to the Silences;—and, on the whole, found that it was an adventure, in sorrowful fact, equal to the fabulous ones by old knights-errant against dragons and wizards in enchanted wildernesses and waste howling solitudes; not achievable except by nearly superhuman exercise of all the four cardinal virtues, and unexpected favour of the special blessing of Heaven. His adventure achieved or found unachievable, he has returned with experiences new to him in the affairs of men. What this Colonial Office, inhabiting the head of Downing Street, really *was*, and had to do, or try doing, in God's practical Earth, he could not by any means precisely get to know; believes that it does not itself in the least precisely know. Believes that nobody knows;—that it is a mystery, a kind of Heathen myth;—and stranger than any piece of the old mythological Pantheon; for *it* practically presides over the destinies of many millions of living men.

Such is his report of the Colonial Office: and if we oftener hear such a report of that than we do of the Home Office, Foreign Office or the rest,—the reason probably is, that Colonies excite more attention at present than any of our other interests. The Forty Colonies, it appears, are all pretty like rebelling just now; and are to be pacified with constitutions;—luckier constitutions, let us hope, than some late ones have been. Loyal Canada, for instance, had to quench a rebellion the other year; and this year, in virtue of its constitution, it is called upon to pay the rebels their damages; which surely is a rather surprising result, however constitutional!—Men have rents and moneys dependent in the Colonies; Emigration schemes, Black Emancipations, New-Zealand and other schemes; and feel and publish more emphatically what their Downing-Street woes in these respects have been.

Were the state of poor *sallow* English ploughers and weavers, what we may call the Sallow or Yellow Emancipation interest, as much an object with Exeter-Hall Philanthropists as that of the Black blockheads now all emancipated, and going at large without work, or need of working, in West-India clover (and fattening very much in it, one delights to hear),—then perhaps the Home Office, its huge virtual task better understood, and its small actual performance better seen into, might be found still more deficient, and behind the wants of the age, than the Colonial itself is.

How it stands with the Foreign Office, again, one still less knows. Seizures of Sapienza, and the like sudden appearances of Britain in the character of Hercules-Harlequin, waving, with big bully-voice, her huge sword-of-sharpness over field-mice, and in the air making horrid circles (horrid catharine-wheels and death-disks of metallic terror from said huge sword), to see how they will like it,—do from time to time astonish the world, in a not pleasant manner. Hercules-Harlequin, the Attorney Triumphant, the World's Busybody: none of these are parts this Nation has a turn for; she, if you consulted her, would rather *not* play these parts, but another! Seizures of Sapienza, correspondences with Sotomayor, remonstrances to Otho King of Athens, fleets hanging by their anchor in behalf of the Majesty of Portugal; and in short the whole, or at present very nearly the whole, of that industry of protocolling, diplomatising, remonstrating, admonishing, and 'having the honour to be,'—has sunk justly in public estimation to a very low figure.

For in fact, it is reasonably asked, What vital interest has England in any cause now deciding itself in foreign parts? Once there was a Papistry and Protestantism, important as life eternal and death eternal; more lately there was an interest of Civil Order and Horrors of the French Revolution, important at least as rent-roll and preservation of the game; but now what is there? No cause in which any god or man of this British Nation can be thought to be concerned. Sham-kingship, now recognised and even self-recognised everywhere to be sham, wrestles and struggles with mere ballot-box Anarchy: not a pleasant spectacle to British minds. Both parties in the wrestle professing earnest wishes of peace to us, what have we to do with it except answer earnestly, "Peace, yes certainly," and mind our affairs elsewhere. The British Nation has no concern with that indispensable sorrowful and shameful wrestle now going on everywhere in foreign parts. The British Nation already, by self-experience centuries old, understands all that; was lucky enough to transact the greater part of that, in noble ancient ages, while the wrestle had not yet become a shameful one, but on *both* sides of it there was wisdom, virtue, heroic nobleness fruitful to all time,—thrice-lucky British Nation! The British Nation, I say, has nothing to learn there; has now quite another set of lessons to learn, far ahead of what is going on there. Sad example there, of what the issue is, and how inevitable and how imminent, might admonish the British Nation to be speedy with its new lessons; to bestir itself, as men in peril of conflagration do, with the neighbouring houses all on fire! To obtain, for its own very pressing behoof, if by possibility it could, some real Captaincy instead of an imaginary one: to remove resolutely, and replace by a better sort, its own peculiar species of teaching and guiding histrios of various name, who here too are numerous exceedingly, and much in need of gentle removal, while the play is still good, and the comedy has not yet become *tragic*;—and to be a little swift about it withal; and so to escape the otherwise inevitable evil day! This Britain might learn: but she does not need a protocolling establishment, with much 'having the honour to be,' to teach it her.

No:—she has in fact certain cottons, hardwares and suchlike to sell in foreign parts, and certain wines, Portugal oranges, Baltic tar and other products to buy; and does need, I suppose, some kind of Consul, or accredited agent, accessible to British voyagers, here and there, in the chief cities of the Continent: through which functionary, or through the penny-post, if she had any specific message to foreign courts, it would be easy and proper to transmit the same. Special message-carriers, to be still called Ambassadors, if the name gratified them, could be sent when occasion great enough demanded; not sent when it did not. But for all purposes of a resident ambassador, I hear persons extensively and well acquainted among our foreign embassies at this date declare, That a well-selected *Times* reporter or 'own correspondent' ordered to reside in foreign capitals, and keep his eyes open, and (though sparingly) his pen going, would in reality be much more effective;—and surely we see well, he would come a good deal cheaper! Considerably cheaper in expense of money; and in expense of falsity and grimacing hypocrisy (of which no human arithmetic can count the ultimate *cost*) incalculably cheaper! If this is the fact, why not treat it as such? If this is so in any measure, we had better in that measure admit it to be so! The time, I believe, has come for asking with considerable severity, How far is it so? Nay, there are men now current in political society, men of weight though also of wit, who have been heard to say, "That there was but one reform for the Foreign Office,—to set a live coal under it," and with, of course, a fire-brigade which could prevent the undue spread of the devouring element into neighbouring houses, let that reform it! In such odour is the Foreign Office too, if it were not that the Public, oppressed and nearly stifled with a mere infinitude of bad odours, neglects this one,—in fact, being able nearly always to avoid the street where it is, *escapes* this one, and (except a passing curse, once in the quarter or so) as good as forgets the existence of it.

Such, from sad personal experience and credited prevailing rumour, is the exoteric public conviction about these sublime establishments in Downing Street and the neighbourhood,—the esoteric mysteries of which are indeed still held sacred by the initiated, but believed by the world to be mere Dalai-Lama pills, manufactured let not refined lips hint how, and quite *un*salvatory to mankind. Every one may remark what a hope animates the eyes of any circle, when it is reported or even confidently asserted, that Sir Robert Peel has in his mind privately resolved to go, one day, into that stable of King Augias, which appals human hearts, so rich is it, high-piled with the droppings of two-hundred years; and Hercules-like to load a thousand night-wagons from it, and turn running water into it, and swash and shovel at it, and never leave it till the antique pavement, and real basis of the matter, show itself clean again! In any intelligent circle such a rumour, like the first break of day to men in darkness, enlightens all eyes; and each says devoutly, "*Faxitis*, O ye righteous Powers that have pity on us! All England grateful, with kindling looks, will rise in the rear of him, and from its deepest heart bid him good speed!"

For it is universally felt that some *esoteric* man, well acquainted with the mysteries and properties good and evil of the administrative stable, is the fittest to reform it, nay, can alone reform it otherwise than by sheer violence and destruction, which is a way we would avoid; that in fact Sir Robert Peel is, at present, the one likely or possible man to reform it. And secondly it is felt that 'reform' in that Downing-Street department of affairs is precisely the reform which were worth all others; that those administrative establishments in Downing Street are really the Government of this huge ungoverned Empire; that to clean-out the dead pedantries, unveracities, indolent somnolent impotences, and accumulated dung-mountains there, is the beginning of all practical good whatsoever. Yes, get down once again to the actual *pavement* of that; ascertain what the thing is, and was before dung accumulated in it; and what it should and may, and must, for the life's sake of this Empire, henceforth become: here clearly lies the heart of the whole matter. Political reform, if this be not reformed, is naught and a mere mockery.

What England wants, and will require to have, or sink in nameless anarchies, is not a Reformed Parliament, meaning thereby a Parliament elected according to the six or the four or any other number of 'points' and cunningly-devised improvements in hustings mechanism, but a Reformed Executive or Sovereign Body of Rulers and Administrators,—some improved method, innumerable improvements in our poor blind methods, of getting hold of these. Not a better

Talking-Apparatus, the best conceivable Talking-Apparatus would do very little for us at present;—but an infinitely better Acting-Apparatus, the benefits of which would be invaluable now and henceforth. The practical question puts itself with ever-increasing stringency to all English minds: Can we, by no industry, energy, utmost expenditure of human ingenuity, and passionate invocation of the Heavens and the Earth, get to attain some twelve or ten or six men to manage the affairs of this nation in Downing Street and the chief posts elsewhere, who are abler for the work than those we have been used to, this long while? For it is really a heroic work, and cannot be done by histrios, and dextrous talkers having the honour to be: it is a heavy and appalling work; and, at the starting of it especially, will require Herculean men; such mountains of pedant exuviæ and obscene owl-droppings have accumulated in those regions, long the habitation of doleful creatures; the old *pavements*, the natural facts and real essential functions of those establishments, have not been seen by eyes for these two-hundred years last past! Herculean men acquainted with the virtues of running water, and with the divine necessity of getting down to the clear pavements and old veracities; who tremble before no amount of pedant exuviæ, no loudest shrieking of doleful creatures; who tremble only to live, themselves, like inane phantasms, and to leave their life as a paltry *contribution* to the guano mountains, and not as a divine eternal protest against them!

These are the kind of men we want; these, the nearest possible approximation to these, are the men we must find and have, or go bankrupt altogether; for the concern as it is will evidently not hold long together. How true is this of Crabbe: 'Men sit in Parliament eighty-three hours per week, debating about many things. Men sit in Downing Street, doing protocols, Syrian treaties, Greek questions, Portuguese, Spanish, French, Egyptian and Æthiopian questions; dextrously writing despatches, and having the honour to be. Not a question of them is at all pressing in comparison with the English question. Pacifico the miraculous Gibraltar Jew has been hustled by some populace in Greece: upon him let the British Lion drop, very rapidly indeed, a constitutional tear. Radetzky is said to be advancing upon Milan;—I am sorry to hear it, and perhaps it does deserve a despatch, or friendly letter, once and away: but the Irish Giant, named of Despair, is advancing upon London itself, laying waste all English cities, towns and villages; that is the interesting Government-despatch of the day! I notice him in Piccadilly, blue-visaged, thatched in rags, a blue child on each arm; hunger-driven, wide-mouthed, seeking whom he may devour: he, missioned by the just Heavens, too truly and too sadly their "divine missionary" come at last in *this* authoritative manner, will throw us all into Doubting Castle, I perceive! That is the phenomenon worth protocolling about, and writing despatches upon, and thinking of with all one's faculty day and night, if one wishes to have the honour to be —anything but a Phantasm Governor of England just now! I entreat your Lordship's all-but undivided attention to that Domestic Irish Giant, named of Despair, for a great many years to come. Prophecy of him there has long been; but now by the rot of the potato (blessed be the just gods, who send us either swift death or some beginning of cure at last!), he is here in person, and there is no denying him, or disregarding him any more; and woe to the public watchman that ignores *him*, and sees Pacifico the Gibraltar Jew instead!'

What these strange Entities in Downing Street intrinsically are; who made them, why they were made; how they do their function; and what their function, so huge in appearance, may in net-result amount to,—is probably known to no mortal. The unofficial mind passes by in dark wonder; not pretending to know. The official mind must not blab;—the official mind, restricted to its own square foot of territory in the vast labyrinth, is probably itself dark, and unable to blab. We see the outcome; the mechanism we do not see. How the tailors clip and sew, in that sublime sweating establishment of theirs we know not: that the coat they bring us out is the sorrowfulest fantastic mockery of a coat, a mere intricate artistic net-work of traditions and formalities, an embroiled reticulation made of web-listings and superannuated thrums and tatters, endurable to no grown Nation as a coat, is mournfully clear!—

Two kinds of fundamental error are supposable in such a set of Offices; these two, acting and reacting, are the vice of all inefficient Offices whatever. *First*, that the work, such as it may be, is ill-done in these establishments. That it is delayed, neglected, slurred over, committed to hands that cannot do it well; that, in a word, the questions sent thither are not wisely handled, but unwisely; not decided truly and rapidly, but with delays and wrong at last: which is the principal character, and the infallible result, of an insufficient Intellect being set to decide them. Or *second*, what is still fataler, the work done there may itself be quite the wrong kind of work. Not the kind of supervision and direction which Colonies, and other such interests, Home or Foreign, do by the nature of them require from the Central Government; not that, but a quite other kind! The Sotomayor correspondence, for example, is considered by many persons not to be mismanaged merely, but to be a thing which should never have been managed at all; a quite superfluous concern, which and the like of which the British Government has almost no call to get into, at this new epoch of time. And not Sotomayor only, nor Sapienza only, in regard to that Foreign Office, but innumerable other things, if our witty friend of the 'live coal' have reason in him! Of the Colonial Office, too, it is urged that the questions they decide and operate upon are, in very great part, questions which they never should have meddled with, but almost all of which should have been decided in the Colonies themselves,

—Mother Country or Colonial Office reserving its energy for a quite other class of objects, which are terribly neglected just now.

These are the two vices that beset Government Offices; both of them originating in insufficient Intellect,—that sad insufficiency from which, directly or indirectly, all evil whatsoever springs! And these two vices act and react, so that where the one is, the other is sure to be; and each encouraging the growth of the other, both (if some cleaning of the Augias stable have not intervened for a long while) will be found in frightful development. You cannot have your work well done, if the work be not of the right kind, if it be not work prescribed by the law of Nature as well as by the rules of the office. Laziness, which lies in wait round all human labour-offices, will in that case infallibly leak in, and vitiate the doing of the work. The work is but idle; if the doing of it will but pass, what need of more? The essential problem, as the rules of office prescribe it for you, if Nature and Fact say nothing, is that your work be got to pass; if the work itself is worth nothing, or little or an uncertain quantity, what more can gods or men require of it, or, above all, can I who am the doer of it require, but that it be got to pass?

And now enters another fatal effect, the mother of ever-new mischiefs, which renders well-doing or improvement impossible, and drives bad everywhere continually into worse. The work being what we see, a stupid subaltern will do as well as a gifted one; the essential point is, that he be a quiet one, and do not bother me who have the driving of him. Nay, for this latter object, is not a certain height of intelligence even dangerous? I want no mettled Arab horse, with his flashing glances, arched neck and elastic step, to draw my wretched sand-cart through the streets; a broken, grassfed galloway, Irish garron, or painful ass with nothing in the belly of him but patience and furze, will do it safelier for me, if more slowly. Nay, I myself, am I the worse for being of a feeble order of intelligence; what the irreverent speculative world calls barren, redtapish, limited, and even intrinsically dark and small, and if it must be said, stupid?—To such a climax does it come in all Government and other Offices, where Human Stupidity has once introduced itself (as it will everywhere do), and no Scavenger God intervenes. The work, at first of some worth, is ill done, and becomes of less worth and of ever less, and finally of none: the worthless work can now *afford* to be ill done; and Human Stupidity, at a double geometrical ratio, with frightful expansion grows and accumulates,—towards the unendurable.

The reforming Hercules, Sir Robert Peel or whoever he is to be, that enters Downing Street, will ask himself this question first of all, What work *is* now necessary, not in form and by traditionary use and wont, but in very fact, for the vital interests of the British Nation, to be done here? The second question, How to get it well done, and to keep the best hands doing it well, will be greatly simplified by a good answer to that. O for an eye that could see in those hideous mazes, and a heart that could dare and do! Strenuous faithful scrutiny, not of what is *thought* to be what in the redtape regions, but of what really is what in the realms of Fact and Nature herself; deep-seeing, wise and courageous eyes, that could look through innumerable cobweb veils, and detect what fact or no-fact lies at heart of them,—how invaluable these! For, alas, it is long since such eyes were much in the habit of looking steadfastly at any department of our affairs; and poor commonplace creatures, helping themselves along, in the way of makeshift, from year to year, in such an element, do wonderful works indeed. Such creatures, like moles, are safe only underground, and their engineerings there become very dædalean. In fact, such unfortunate persons have no resource but to become what we call Pedants; to ensconce themselves in a safe world of habitudes, of applicable or inapplicable traditions; not coveting, rather avoiding the general daylight of common-sense, as very extraneous to them and their procedure; by long persistence in which course they become Completed Pedants, hide-bound, impenetrable, able to *defy* the hostile extraneous element: an alarming kind of men. Such men, left to themselves for a century or two, in any Colonial, Foreign, or other Office, will make a terrible affair of it!

For the one enemy we have in this Universe is Stupidity, Darkness of Mind; of which darkness, again, there are many sources, every *sin* a source, and probably self-conceit the chief source. Darkness of mind, in every kind and variety, does to a really tragic extent abound: but of all the kinds of darkness, surely the Pedant darkness, which asserts and believes itself to be *light*, is the most formidable to mankind! For empires or for individuals there is but one class of men to be trembled at; and that is the Stupid Class, the class that cannot see, who, alas, are they mainly that will not see. A class of mortals under which as administrators, kings, priests, diplomatists, etc., the interests of mankind in every European country have sunk overloaded, as under universal nightmare, near to extinction; and indeed are at this moment convulsively writhing, decided either to throw off the unblessed superincumbent nightmare, or roll themselves and it to the Abyss. Vain to reform Parliament, to invent ballot-boxes, to reform this or that; the real Administration, practical Management of the Commonwealth, goes all awry; choked-up with long-accumulated pedantries, so that your appointed workers have been reduced to work as moles; and it is one vast boring and counterboring, on the part of eyeless persons irreverently called stupid; and a dædalean bewilderment, writing 'impossible' on all efforts or proposals, supervenes.

The State itself, not in Downing Street alone but in every department of it, has altered much from what it was in past times; and it will again have to alter very much, to alter, I think, from top to bottom, if it means to continue existing in the times that are now coming and come!

The State, left to shape itself by dim pedantries and traditions, without distinctness of conviction, or purpose beyond that of helping itself over the difficulty of the hour, has become, instead of a luminous vitality permeating with its light all provinces of our affairs, a most monstrous agglomerate of inanities, as little adapted for the actual wants of a modern community as the worst citizen need wish. The thing it is doing is by no means the thing we want to have done. What we want! Let the dullest British man endeavour to raise in his mind this question, and ask himself in sincerity what the British Nation wants at this time. Is it to have, with endless jargoning, debating, motioning and counter-motioning, a settlement effected between the Honourable Mr. This and the Honourable Mr. That, as to their respective pretensions to ride the high horse? Really it is unimportant which of them ride it. Going upon past experience long continued now, I should say with brevity, "Either of them—Neither of them." If our Government is to be a No-Government, what is the matter who administers it? Fling an orange-skin into St. James's Street; let the man it hits be your man. He, if you breed him a little to it, and tie the due official bladders to his ankles, will do as well as another this sublime problem of balancing himself upon the vortexes, with the long loaded-pole in his hands; and will, with straddling painful gestures, float hither and thither, walking the waters in that singular manner for a little while, as well as his foregoers did, till he also capsize, and be left floating feet uppermost; after which you choose another.

What an immense pother, by parliamenting and palavering in all corners of your empire, to decide such a question as that! I say, if that is the function, almost any human creature can learn to discharge it: fling out your orange-skin again; and save an incalculable labour, and an emission of nonsense and falsity, and electioneering beer and bribery and balderdash, which is terrible to think of, in deciding. Your National Parliament, in so far as it has only that question to decide, may be considered as an enormous National Palaver existing mainly for imaginary purposes; and certain, in these days of abbreviated labour, to get itself sent home again to its partridge-shootings, fox-huntings,—and above all, to its rat-catchings, if it could but understand the time of day, and know (as our indignant Crabbe remarks) that 'the *real* Nimrod of this era, who alone does any good to the era, is the rat-catcher!'

The notion that any Government is or can be a No-Government, without the deadliest peril to all noble interests of the Commonwealth, and by degrees slower or swifter to all ignoble ones also, and to the very gullydrains, and thief lodging-houses, and Mosaic sweating establishments, and at last without destruction to such No-Government itself,—was never my notion: and I hope it will soon cease altogether to be the world's or to be anybody's. But if it be the correct notion, as the world seems at present to flatter itself, I point out improvements and abbreviations. Dismiss your National Palaver; make the *Times* Newspaper your National Palaver, which needs no beer-barrels or hustings, and is *cheaper* in expense of money and of falsity a thousand and a million fold; have an economical redtape drilling establishment (it were easier to devise such a thing than a right *Modern University*);—and fling out your orange-skin among the graduates, when you want a new Premier.

A mighty question indeed! Who shall be Premier, and take in hand the 'rudder of government,' otherwise called the 'spigot of taxation'; shall it be the Honourable Felix Parvulus, or the Right Honourable Felicissimus Zero? By our electioneerings and Hansard Debatings, and ever-enduring tempest of jargon that goes on everywhere, we manage to settle that; to have it declared, with no bloodshed except insignificant blood from the nose in hustings-time, but with immense beershed and inkshed and explosion of nonsense, which darkens all the air, that the Right Honourable Zero is to be the man. That we firmly settle; Zero, all shivering with rapture and with terror, mounts into the high saddle; cramps himself on, with knees, heels, hands and feet; and the horse gallops—whither it lists. That the Right Honourable Zero should attempt controlling the horse—Alas, alas, he, sticking on with beak and claws, is too happy if the horse will only gallop anywhither, and not throw him. Measure, polity, plan or scheme of public good or evil, is not in the head of Felicissimus; except, if he could but devise it, some measure that would please his horse for the moment, and encourage him to go with softer paces, godward or devilward as it might be, and save Felicissimus's leather, which is fast wearing. This is what we call a Government in England, for nearly two centuries now.

I wish Felicissimus were saddle-sick forever and a day! He is a dreadful object, however much we are used to him. If the horse had not been bred and broken in, for a thousand years, by real riders and horse-subduers, perhaps the best and bravest the world ever saw, what would have become of Felicissimus and him long since? This horse, by second-nature, religiously respects all fences; gallops, if never so madly, on the highways alone;—seems to me, of late, like a desperate Sleswick thunder-horse who had lost his way, galloping in the labyrinthic lanes of a woody flat country; passionate to reach his goal; unable to reach it, because in the flat leafy lanes there is no outlook whatever, and in the bridle there is no guidance whatever. So he gallops stormfully along, thinking it is forward and forward; and alas, it is only round and round, out of one old lane into the other;—nay, (according to some) 'he mistakes *his own footprints*, which of course grow ever more numerous, for the sign of a more and more frequented road'; and his despair is hourly increasing. My impression is, he is certain soon, such is the growth of his necessity and his despair, to—plunge *across* the fence, into an opener survey of the country; and to sweep Felicissimus off his back, and comb him away very tragically in the process! Poor Sleswicker, I wish you were better ridden. I perceive it lies in the Fates you must now either be better ridden, or else not long at all. This plunging in the heavy labyrinth of over-shaded lanes, with one's stomach getting empty, one's Ireland falling into cannibalism, and no vestige of a goal either visible or possible, cannot last.

Colonial Offices, Foreign, Home and other Offices, got together under these strange circumstances, cannot well be expected to be the best that human ingenuity could devise; the wonder rather is to see them so good as they are. Who made them, ask me not. Made they clearly were; for we see them here in a concrete condition, writing despatches, and drawing salary with a view to buy pudding. But how those Offices in Downing Street were made; who made them, or for what kind of objects they were made, would be hard to say at present. Dim visions and phantasmagories gathered from the Books of Horace Walpole, Memoirs of Bubb Doddington, Memoirs of my Lady Sundon, Lord Fanny Hervey, and innumerable others, rise on us, beckoning fantastically towards, not an answer, but some conceivable intimations of an answer, and proclaiming very legibly the old text, '*Quam parvâ sapientiâ*,' in respect of this hard-working much-subduing British Nation;—giving rise to endless reflections in a thinking Englishman of this day. Alas, it is ever so: each generation has its task, and does it better or worse; greatly neglecting what is not immediately its task. Our poor grandfathers, so busy conquering Indias, founding Colonies, inventing spinning-jennies, kindling Lancashires and Bromwichams, took no thought about the government of all that; left it all to be governed by Lord Fanny and the Hanover Succession, or how the gods pleased. And now we the poor grandchildren find that it will not stick together on these terms any longer; that our sad, dangerous and sore task is to discover some government for this big world which has been conquered to us; that the redtape Offices in Downing Street are near the end of their rope; that if we can get nothing better, in the way of government, it is all over with our world and us. How the Downing-Street Offices originated, and what the meaning of them was or is, let Dryasdust, when in some lucid moment the whim takes him, instruct us. Enough for us to know and see clearly, with urgent practical inference derived from such insight, That they were not made for us or for our objects at all; that the devouring Irish Giant is here, and that he cannot be fed with redtape, and will eat us if we cannot feed him.

On the whole, let us say Felicissimus made them;—or rather it was the predecessors of Felicissimus, who were not so dreadfully hunted, sticking to the wild and ever more desperate Sleswicker in the leafy labyrinth of lanes, as he now is. He, I think, will never make anything; but be combed off by the elm-boughs, and left sprawling in the ditch. But in past time, this and the other heavy-laden redtape soul had withal a glow of patriotism in him; now and then, in his whirling element, a gleam of human ingenuity, some eye towards business that must be done. At all events, for him and every one, Parliament needed to be persuaded that business was done. By the contributions of many such heavy-laden souls, driven on by necessity outward and inward, these singular Establishments are here. Contributions—who knows how far back they go, far beyond the reign of George the Second, or perhaps the reign of William Conqueror. Noble and genuine some of them were, many of them were, I need not doubt: for there is no human edifice that stands long out has got itself planted, here and there, upon the basis of fact; and being built, in many respects, according to the laws of statics: no standing edifice, especially no edifice of State, but has had the wise and brave at work in it, contributing their lives to it; and is 'cemented,' whether it know the fact or not, 'by the blood of heroes!' None; not even the Foreign Office, Home Office, still less the National Palaver itself. William Conqueror, I find, must have had a first-rate Home Office, for his share. The *Domesday Book*, done in four years, and done as it is, with such an admirable brevity, explicitness and completeness, testifies emphatically what kind of under-secretaries and officials William had. Silent officials and secretaries, I suppose; not wasting themselves in parliamentary talk; reserving all their intelligence for silent survey of the huge dumb fact, silent consideration how they might compass the mastery of that. Happy secretaries, happy William!

But indeed nobody knows what inarticulate traditions, remnants of old wisdom, priceless though quite anonymous, survive in many modern things that still have life in them. Ben Brace, with his taciturnities, and rugged stoical ways, with his tarry breeches, stiff as plank-breeches, I perceive is still a kind of *Lod-brog* (Loaded-breeks) in more senses than one; and derives, little conscious of it, many of his excellences from the old Sea-kings and Saxon Pirates themselves; and how many Blakes and Nelsons since have contributed to Ben! "Things are not so false always as they seem," said a certain Professor to me once: "of this you will find instances in every country, and in your England more than any—and I hope will draw lessons from them. An English Seventy-four, if you look merely at the articulate law and methods of it, is one of the impossiblest entities. The captain is appointed not by preëminent merit in sailorship, but by parliamentary connexion; the men" (this was spoken some years ago) "are got by impressment; a press-gang goes out, knocks men down on the streets of sea-towns, and drags them on board,—if the ship were to be stranded, I have heard they would nearly all run ashore and desert. Can anything be more unreasonable than a Seventy-four? Articulately almost nothing. But it has inarticulate traditions, ancient methods and habitudes in it, stoicisms, noblenesses, *true* rules both of sailing and of conduct; enough to keep it afloat on Nature's veridical bosom, after all. See; if you bid it sail to the end of the world, it will lift anchor, go, and arrive. The raging oceans do not beat it back; it too, as well as the raging oceans, has a relationship to Nature, and it does not sink, but under the due conditions is borne along. If it meet with hurricanes, it rides them out; if it meet an Enemy's ship, it shivers it to powder; and in short, it holds on its way, and to a wonderful extent *does* what it means and pretends to do. Assure yourself, my friend, there is an immense fund of truth somewhere or other stowed in that Seventy-four."

More important than the past history of these Offices in Downing Street, is the question of their future history; the question, How they are to be got mended! Truly an immense problem, inclusive of all others whatsoever; which demands to be attacked, and incessantly persisted in, by all good citizens, as the grand problem of Society, and the one thing needful for the Commonwealth! A problem in which all men, with all their wisdoms and all their virtues, faithfully and continually coöperating at it, will never have done *enough*, and will still only be struggling *towards* perfection in it. In which some men can do much;—in which every man can do something. Every man, and thou my present Reader canst do this: *Be* thyself a man abler to be governed; more reverencing the divine faculty of governing, more sacredly detesting the diabolical semblance of said faculty in self and others; so shalt thou, if not govern, yet actually according to thy strength assist in real governing. And know always, and even lay to heart with a quite unusual solemnity, with a seriousness altogether of a religious nature, that as 'Human Stupidity' is verily the accursed parent of all this mischief, so Human Intelligence alone, to which and to which only is victory and blessedness appointed here below, will or can cure it. If we knew this as devoutly as we ought to do, the evil, and all other evils were curable;—alas, if we had from of old known this, as all men made in God's image ought to do, the evil never would have been! Perhaps few Nations have ever known it less than we, for a good while back, have done. Hence these sorrows.

What a people are the poor Thibet idolaters, compared with us and our 'religions,' which issue in the worship of King Hudson as our Dalai-Lama! They, across such hulls of abject ignorance, have seen into the heart of the matter; we, with our torches of knowledge everywhere brandishing themselves, and such a human enlightenment as never was before, have quite missed it. Reverence for Human Worth, earnest devout search for it and encouragement of it, loyal furtherance and obedience to it: this, I say, is the outcome and essence of all true 'religions,' and was and ever will be. We have not known this. No; loud as our tongues sometimes go in that direction, we have no true reverence for Human Intelligence, for Human Worth and Wisdom: none, or too little,—and I pray for a restoration of such reverence, as for the change from Stygian darkness to Heavenly light, as for the return of life to poor sick moribund Society and all its interests. Human Intelligence means little for most of us but Beaver Contrivance, which produces spinning mules, cheap cotton, and large fortunes. Wisdom, unless it give us railway scrip, is not wise.

True nevertheless it forever remains that Intellect is the real object of reverence, and of devout prayer, and zealous wish and pursuit, among the sons of men; and even, well understood, the one object. It is the Inspiration of the Almighty that giveth men understanding. For it must be repeated, and ever again repeated till poor mortals get to discern it, and awake from their baleful paralysis, and degradation under foul enchantments, That a man of Intellect, of real and not sham Intellect, is by the nature of him likewise inevitably a man of nobleness, a man of courage, rectitude, pious strength; who, even *because* he is and has been loyal to the Laws of this Universe, is initiated into *discernment* of the same; to this hour a Missioned of Heaven; whom if men follow, it will be well with them; whom if men do not follow, it will not be well. Human Intellect, if you consider it well, is the exact summary of Human *Worth*; and the essence of all worth-ships and worships is reverence for that same. This much surprises you, friend Peter; but I assure you it is the fact;—and I would advise you to consider it, and to try if you too do not gradually find it so. With me it has long been an article, not of 'faith' only, but of settled insight, of conviction as to what the ordainments of the Maker in this Universe are. Ah, could you and the rest of us but get to know it, and everywhere religiously act upon it,—as our *Fortieth* Article, which includes all the other Thirty-nine, and without which the Thirty-nine are good for almost nothing,—there might then be some hope for us! In this world there is but one appalling creature: the Stupid man *considered* to be the Missioned of Heaven, and followed by men. He is our King, men say, he;—and they follow him, through straight or winding courses, I for one know well whitherward.

Abler men in Downing Street, abler men to govern us: yes, that, sure enough, would gradually remove the dung-mountains, however high they are; that would be the way, nor is there any other way, to remedy whatsoever has gone wrong in Downing Street and in the wide regions, spiritual and temporal, which Downing Street presides over! For the Able Man, meet him where you may, is definable as the born enemy of Falsity and Anarchy, and the born soldier of Truth and Order: into what absurdest element soever you put him, he is there to make it a little less absurd, to fight continually with it till it become a little sane and human again. Peace on other terms he, for his part, cannot make with it; not he, while he continues *able*, or possessed of real intellect and not imaginary. There is but one man fraught with blessings for this world, fated to diminish and successively abolish the curses of the world; and it is he. For him make search, him reverence and follow; know that to find *him* or miss him, means victory or defeat for you, in all Downing Streets, and establishments and enterprises here below.— —I leave your Lordship to judge whether this has been our practice hitherto; and would humbly inquire what your Lordship thinks is likely to be the consequence of continuing to neglect this. It ought to have been our practice; ought, in all places and all times, to be the practice in this world; so says the fixed law of things forevermore:—and it must cease to be *not* the practice, your Lordship; and cannot too speedily do so, I think!—

Much has been done in the way of reforming Parliament in late years; but that of itself seems to avail nothing, or almost less. The men that sit in Downing Street, governing us, are not abler men since the Reform Bill than were those before it. Precisely the same kind of men; obedient formerly to Tory traditions, obedient now to Whig ditto and popular clamours. Respectable men of office: respectably commonplace in faculty,—while the situation is becoming terribly original! Rendering their outlooks, and ours, more ominous every day.

Indisputably enough the meaning of all reform-movement, electing and electioneering, of popular agitation, parliamentary eloquence, and all political effort whatsoever, is that you may get the ten Ablest Men in England put to preside over your ten principal departments of affairs. To sift and riddle the Nation, so that you might extricate and sift-out the true ten gold grains, or ablest men, and of these make your Governors or Public Officers; leaving the dross and common sandy or silty material safely aside, as the thing to be governed, not to govern; certainly all ballot-boxes, caucuses, Kennington-Common meetings, Parliamentary debatings, Red Republics, Russian Despotisms, and constitutional or unconstitutional methods of society among mankind, are intended to achieve this one end; and some of them, it will be owned, achieve it very ill!—If you have got your gold grains, if the men you have got are actually the ablest, then rejoice; with whatever astonishment, accept your Ten, and thank the gods; under this Ten your destruction will at least be milder than under another. But if you have *not* got them, if you are very far from having got them, then do not rejoice at all, then *lament* very much; then admit that your sublime political constitutions and contrivances do not prove themselves sublime, but ridiculous and contemptible; that your world's wonder of a political mill, the envy of surrounding nations, does not yield you real meal; yields you only powder of millstones (called Hansard Debatings), and a detestable brown substance not unlike the grindings of dried horse-dung or prepared street-mud, which though sold under royal patent, and much recommended by the trade, is quite unfit for culinary purposes!—

But the disease at least is not mysterious, whatever the remedy be. Our disease,—alas, is it not clear as the sun, that we suffer under what is the disease of all the miserable in this world, *want of wisdom*; that in the Head there is no vision, and that thereby all the members are dark and in bonds? No vision in the head; heroism, faith, devout insight to discern what is needful, noble courage to do it, greatly defective there: not seeing eyes there, but spectacles constitutionally ground, which, to the unwary, *seem* to see. A quite fatal circumstance, had you never so many Parliaments! How is your ship to be steered by a Pilot with no *eyes* but a pair of glass ones got from the constitutional optician? He must steer by the *ear*, I think, rather than by the eye; by the shoutings he catches from the shore, or from the Parliamentary benches nearer hand:—one of the frightfulest objects to see steering in a difficult sea! Reformed Parliaments in that case, reform-leagues, outer agitations and excitements in never such abundance, cannot profit: all this is but the writhing, and painful blind convulsion of the limbs that are in bonds, that are all in dark misery till the head be delivered, till the pressure on the brain be removed.

Or perhaps there *is* now no heroic wisdom left in England; England, once the land of heroes, is itself sunk now to a dim owlery, and habitation of doleful creatures, intent only on money-making and other forms of catching mice, for whom the proper gospel is the gospel of M'Croudy, and all nobler impulses and insights are forbidden henceforth? Perhaps these present agreeable Occupants of Downing Street, such as the parliamentary mill has yielded them, are the *best* the miserable soil has grown? The most Herculean Ten Men that could be found among the English Twenty-seven Millions, are these? There *are* not, in any place, under any figure, ten diviner men among us? Well; in that case, the riddling and searching of the twenty-seven millions has been *successful.* Here are our ten divinest men; with these, unhappily not divine enough, we must even content ourselves and die in peace; what help is there? No help, no hope, in that case.

But, again, if these are *not* our divinest men, then evidently there always is hope, there always is possibility of help; and ruin never is quite inevitable, till we *have* sifted out our actually divinest ten, and set these to try their hand at governing!—That this has been achieved; that these ten men are the most Herculean souls the English population held within it, is a proposition credible to no mortal. No, thank God; low as we are sunk in many ways, this is not yet credible! Evidently the reverse of this proposition is the fact. Ten much diviner men do certainly exist. By some conceivable, not forever impossible, method and methods, ten very much diviner men could be sifted out!—Courage; let us fix our eyes on that important fact, and strive all thitherward as towards a door of hope!

Parliaments, I think, have proved too well, in late years, that they are not the remedy. It is not Parliaments, reformed or other, that will ever send Herculean men to Downing

Street, to reform Downing Street for us ; to diffuse therefrom a light of Heavenly Order, instead of the murk of Stygian Anarchy, over this sad world of ours. That function does not lie in the capacities of Parliament. That is the function of a *King*,—if we could get such a priceless entity, which we cannot just now! Failing which, Statesmen, or Temporary-Kings, and at the very lowest one real Statesman, to shape the dim tendencies of Parliament, and guide them wisely to the goal: he, I perceive, will be a primary condition, indispensable for any progress whatsoever.

One such, perhaps, might be attained; one such might prove discoverable among our Parliamentary populations? That one, in such an enterprise as this of Downing Street, might be invaluable! One noble man, at once of natural wisdom and practical experience; one Intellect still really human, and not redtapish, owlish, and pedantical, appearing there in that dim chaos, with word of command; to brandish Hercules-like the divine broom and shovel, and turn running water in upon the place, and say as with a fiat, "Here shall be truth, and real work, and talent to do it henceforth; I will seek for able men to work here, as for the elixir of life to this poor place and me":—what might not one such man effect there!

Nay, one such is not to be dispensed with anywhere in the affairs of men. In every ship, I say, there must be a *seeing* pilot, not a mere hearing one! It is evident you can never get your ship steered through the difficult straits by persons standing ashore, on this bank and that, and shouting *their* confused directions to you: "'Ware that Colonial Sandbank! —Starboard now, the Nigger Question!—Larboard, *larboard*, the Suffrage Movement!—Financial Reform, your Clothing-Colonels overboard! The Qualification Movement, 'Ware-re-re!—Helm-a-lee! Bear a hand there, will you! Hr-r-r, lubbers, imbeciles, fitter for a tailor's shop-board than a helm of Government, Hr-r-r!"—And so the ship wriggles and tumbles, and, on the whole, goes as wind and current drive. No ship was ever steered except to destruction in that manner. I deliberately say so: no ship of a State either. If you cannot get a real pilot on board, and put the helm into his hands, your ship is as good as a wreck. One real pilot on board may save you; all the bellowing from the banks that ever was, will not and by the nature of things cannot. Nay, your pilot will have to succeed, if he do succeed, very much in spite of said bellowing; he will hear all that, and regard very little of it,—in a patient mild-spoken wise manner, will regard all of *it* as what it is. And I never doubt but there is in Parliament itself, in spite of its vague palaverings which fill us with despair in these times, a dumb instinct of inarticulate sense and stubborn practical English insight and veracity, that would manfully support a Statesman who could take command with really manful notions of Reform, and as one deserving to be obeyed. O for one such; even one! More precious to us than all the bullion in the Bank, or perhaps that ever was in it, just now!

For it is Wisdom alone that can recognise wisdom: Folly or Imbecility never can; and that is the fatalest ban it labours under, dooming it to perpetual failure in all things. Failure which, in Downing Street and places of *command*, is especially accursed; cursing not one but hundreds of millions! Who is there that can recognise real intellect, and do reverence to it; and discriminate it well from sham intellect, which is so much more abundant, and deserves the reverse of reverence? He that himself has it!—One really human Intellect, invested with command, and charged to reform Downing Street for us, would continually attract real intellect to those regions, and with a divine magnetism search it out from the modest corners where it lies hid. And every new accession of intellect to Downing Street would bring to it benefit only, and would increase such divine attraction in it, the parent of all benefit there and elsewhere!

"What method, then; by what method?" ask many.—

Method, alas! To secure an increased supply of Human Intellect to Downing Street, there will evidently be no quite effectual 'method' but that of increasing the supply of Human Intellect, otherwise definable as Human Worth, in Society generally; increasing the supply of sacred reverence for it, of loyalty to it, and of life-and-death desire and pursuit of it, among all classes,—if we but knew such a 'method'! Alas, that were simply the method of making all classes Servants of Heaven; and except it be devout prayer to Heaven, I have never heard of any method! To increase the reverence for Human Intellect or God's Light, and the detestation of Human Stupidity or the Devil's Darkness, what method is there? No method,—except even this, that we should each of us 'pray' for it, instead of praying for mere scrip and the like; that Heaven would please to vouchsafe us each a little of it, one by one! As perhaps Heaven, in its infinite bounty, by stern methods, gradually will? Perhaps Heaven has mercy too in these sore plagues that are oppressing us; and means to teach us reverence for Heroism and Human Intellect, by such baleful experience of what issue Imbecility and Parliamentary Eloquence lead to? Such reverence, I do hope, and even discover and observe, is silently yet extensively going on among us even in these sad years. In which small salutary fact there burns for us, in this black coil of universal baseness fast becoming universal wretchedness, an inextinguishable hope; far-off but sure, a divine 'pillar of fire by night.' Courage, courage!—

Meanwhile, that our one reforming Statesman may have free command of what Intellect there is among us, and room to try all means for awakening and inviting ever more of it, there has one small Project of Improvement been suggested; which finds a certain degree of favour wherever I hear it talked of, and which seems to merit much more consideration than it has yet received. Practical men themselves approve of it hitherto, so far as it goes; the one objection being that the world is not yet prepared to insist on it,—which of course the world can never be, till once the world consider it, and in the first place hear tell of it! I have, for my own part, a good opinion of this project. The old unreformed Parliament of rotten boroughs *had* one advantage; but that is hereby, in a far more fruitful and effectual manner, secured to the new.

The Proposal is, That Secretaries under and upper, that all manner of changeable or permanent servants in the Government Offices shall be selected *without* reference to their power of getting into Parliament;—that, in short, the Queen shall have power of nominating the half-dozen or half-score Officers of the Administration, whose presence is thought necessary in Parliament, to official seats there, without reference to any constituency but her own only, which of course will mean her Prime Minister's. A very small encroachment on the present constitution of Parliament; offering the minimum of change in present methods, and I almost think a maximum in results to be derived therefrom.—The Queen nominates John Thomas (the fittest man she, much-inquiring, can hear tell of in her three kingdoms) President of the Poor-Law Board, Under Secretary of the Colonies, Under, or perhaps even Upper Secretary of what she and her Premier find suitablest for a working head so eminent, a talent so precious; and grants him, by her direct authority, seat and vote in Parliament so long as he holds that office. Upper Secretaries, having more to do in Parliament, and being so bound to be in favour there, would, I suppose, at least till new times and habits come, be expected to be chosen from among the *People's* Members as at present. But whether the Prime Minister himself is, in all times, bound to be first a People's Member; and which, or how many, of his Secretaries and subordinates he might be allowed to take as *Queen's* Members, my authority does not say,—perhaps has not himself settled; the project being yet in mere outline or foreshadow, the practical embodiment in all details to be fixed by authorities much more competent than he. The soul of his project is, That the Crown also have power to elect a few members to Parliament.

From which project, however wisely it were embodied, there could probably, at first or all at once, no great 'accession of intellect' to the Government Offices ensue; though a little might, even at first, and a little is always precious: but in its ulterior operation, were that faithfully developed, and wisely presided over, I fancy an immense accession of intellect might ensue;—nay, a natural ingress might thereby be opened to all manner of accessions, and the actual flower of whatever intellect the British Nation had might be attracted towards Downing Street, and continue flowing steadily thither! For, let us see a little what effects this simple change carries in it the possibilities of. Here are beneficent germs, which the presence of one truly wise man as Chief Minister, steadily fostering them for even a few years, with the sacred fidelity and vigilance that would beseem him, might ripen into living practices and habitual facts, invaluable to us all.

What it is that Secretaries of State, Managers of Colonial Establishments, of Home and Foreign Government interests, have really and truly to do in Parliament, might admit of various estimate in these times. An apt debater in Parliament is by no means certain to be an able administrator of Colonies, of Home or Foreign Affairs; nay, rather quite the contrary is to be presumed of him; for in order to become a 'brilliant speaker,' if that is his character, considerable portions of his natural internal endowment must have gone to the surface, in order to make a shining figure there, and precisely so much the less (few men in these days know how much less!) must remain available in the internal silent state, or as faculty for thinking, for devising and acting, which latter and which alone is the function essential for him in his Secretaryship. Not to tell a good story for himself 'in Parliament and to the twenty-seven millions, many of them fools'; not that, but to do good administration, to know with sure eye, and decide with just and resolute heart, what is what in the *things* committed to his charge: this and not that, is the service which poor England, whatever it may think and maunder, does require and want of the Official Man in Downing Street. Given a good Official Man or Secretary, he really ought, as far as it is possible, to be left working in the silent state. No mortal can both work and do good talking in Parliament, or out of it: the feat is impossible as that of serving two hostile masters.

Nor would I, if it could be helped, much trouble my good Secretary with addressing Parliament: needful explanations; yes, in a free country, surely;—but not to every frivolous and vexatious person, in or out of Parliament, who chooses to apply for them. There should be demands for explanation too which were reckoned frivolous and vexatious, and censured as such. These, I should say, are the *not* needful explanations: and if my poor Secretary is to be called out from his workshop to answer every one of these,—his workshop will become (what we at present see it, deservedly or not) little other than a pillory; the poor Secretary a kind of talking-machine, exposed to dead-cats and rotten-eggs; and the 'work' got out of him or of it will, as heretofore, be very inconsiderable indeed!—Alas, on this side also, important improvements are conceivable; and will even, I imagine, get them whence we may, be found indispensable one day. The honourable gentleman whom you interrupt here, he, in his official capacity, is not an individual now, but the embodiment of a Nation; he is the 'People of England' engaged in the work of Secretaryship, this one; and cannot forever afford to let the three Tailors of Tooley-street break in upon him at all hours!—

But leaving this, let us remark one thing which is very plain: That whatever be the uses and duties, real or supposed, of a Secretary in Parliament, his faculty to accomplish these is a point entirely unconnected with his ability to get elected into Parliament, and has no relation or proportion to it, and no concern with it whatever. Lord Tommy and the Honourable John are not a whit better qualified for Parliamentary duties, to say nothing of Secretary duties, than plain Tom and Jack; they are merely better qualified, as matters stand, for getting admitted to try them. Which state of matters a reforming Premier, much in want of abler men to help him, now proposes *altering*. Tom and Jack, once admitted by the Queen's writ, there is every reason to suppose will do quite as well there as Lord Tommy and the Honourable John. In Parliament quite *as* well: and elsewhere, in the other infinitely more important duties of a Government Office, which indeed are and remain the essential, vital and intrinsic duties of such a personage, is there the faintest reason to surmise that Tom and Jack, if well chosen, will fall short of Lord Tommy and the Honourable John? No shadow of a reason. Were the intrinsic genius of the men exactly equal, there is no shadow of a reason: but rather there is quite the reverse; for Tom and Jack have been at least workers all their days, not idlers, game-preservers and mere human clothes-horses, at any period of their lives; and have gained a schooling *thereby*, of which Lord Tommy and the Honourable John, unhappily strangers to it for most part, can form no conception! Tom and Jack have already, on this most narrow hypothesis, a decided *superiority* of likelihood over Lord Tommy and the Honourable John.

But the hypothesis is very narrow, and the fact is very wide; the hypothesis counts by units, the fact by millions. Consider how *many* Toms and Jacks there are to choose from, well or ill! The aristocratic class from whom Members of Parliament can be elected extends only to certain thousands; from these you are to choose your Secretary, if a seat in Parliament is the primary condition. But the general population is of Twenty-seven Millions; from all sections of which you can choose, if the seat in Parliament is not to be primary. Make it ultimate instead of primary, a last investiture instead of a first indispensable condition, and the whole British Nation, learned, unlearned, professional, practical, speculative and miscellaneous, is at your disposal! In the lowest broad strata of the population, equally as in the highest and narrowest, are produced men of every kind of genius; man for man, your chance of genius is as good among the millions as among the units;—and class for class, what must it be! From all classes, not from certain hundreds now but from several millions, whatsoever man the gods had gifted with intellect and nobleness, and power to help his country, could be chosen: O Heavens, *could*,—if not by Tenpound Constituencies and the force of beer, then by a Reforming Premier with eyes in his head, who I think might do it quite infinitely better. Infinitely better. For ignobleness cannot, by the nature of it, choose the noble: no, there needs a seeing man who is himself noble, cognisant by internal experience of the symptoms of nobleness. Shall we never think of this; shall we never more remember this, then? It is forever true; and Nature and Fact, however we may rattle our ballot-boxes, do at no time forget it.

From the lowest and broadest stratum of Society, where the births are by the million, there was born, almost in our own memory, a Robert Burns; son of one who 'had not capital for his poor moor-farm of Twenty Pounds a-year.' Robert Burns never had the smallest chance to get into Parliament, much as Robert Burns deserved, for all our sakes, to have been found there. For the man,—it was not known to men purblind, sunk in their poor dim vulgar element, but might have been known to men of insight who had any loyalty or any royalty of their own,—was a born king of men: full of valour, of intelligence and heroic nobleness; fit for far other work than to break his heart among poor mean mortals, gauging beer! Him no Tenpound Constituency chose, nor did any Reforming Premier: in the deep-sunk British Nation, overwhelmed in foggy stupor, with the load-stars all gone out for it, there was no whisper of a notion that it could be desirable to choose him,—except to come and dine with you, and in the interim to gauge. And yet heaven-born Mr. Pitt, at that period, was by no means without need of Heroic Intellect, for other purposes than gauging! But sorrowful strangulation by redtape, much *tighter* then than it now is when so many revolutionary earthquakes have tussled it, quite tied up the meagre Pitt; and he said, on hearing of this Burns and his sad hampered case, "Literature will take care of itself."—"Yes, and of you too, if you don't mind it!" answers one.

And so, like Apollo taken for a Neatherd, and perhaps for none of the best on the Admetus establishment, this new Norse Thor had to put-up with what was going; to gauge ale, and be thankful; pouring *his* celestial sunlight through Scottish Song-writing,—the narrowest chink ever offered to a Thundergod before! And the meagre Pitt, and his Dundasses and redtape Phantasms (growing very ghastly now to think of), did not in the least know or understand, the impious, god-forgetting mortals, that Heroic Intellects, if Heaven were pleased to send such, were the one salvation for the world and for them and all of us. No; they 'had done very well without' such; did not see the use of such; went along 'very well' without such; well presided over by a singular Heroic Intellect called George the Third: and the Thundergod, as was rather fit of him, departed early, still in the noon of life, somewhat weary of gauging ale!—O Peter, what a scandalous torpid element of yellow London fog, favourable to owls only and their mousing operations, has blotted out the stars of Heaven for us these several generations back,—which, I rejoice to see, is now visibly about to take itself away again, or perhaps to be *dispelled* in a very tremendous manner!

For the sake of my Democratic friends, one other observation. Is not this Proposal the very essence of whatever truth there is in 'Democracy'; this, that the able man be chosen, in whatever rank he is found? That he be searched for as hidden treasure is; be trained, supervised, set to the work which he alone is fit for. All Democracy lies in this; this, I think, is worth all the ballot-boxes and suffrage-movements now going. Not that the noble soul, born poor, should be set to spout in Parliament, but that he should be set to assist in governing men: this is our grand Democratic interest. With this we can be saved; without this, were there a Parliament spouting in every parish, and Hansard Debates to stem the Thames, we perish,—die constitutionally drowned, in mere oceans of palaver.

All reformers, constitutional persons, and men capable of reflection, are invited to reflect on these things. Let us brush the cobwebs from our eyes; let us bid the inane traditions be silent for a moment; and ask ourselves, like men dreadfully intent on having it *done*, "By what method or methods can the able men from every rank of life be gathered, as diamond-grains from the general mass of sand: the able men, not the sham-able;—and set to do the work of governing, contriving, administering and guiding for us!" It is the question of questions. All that Democracy ever meant lies there: the attainment of a truer and truer *Aristocracy*, or Government again by the *Best*.

Reformed Parliaments have lamentably failed to attain it for us; and I believe will and must forever fail. One true Reforming Statesman, one noble worshipper and knower of human intellect, with the quality of an experienced Politician too; he, backed by such a Parliament as England, once recognising him, would loyally send, and at liberty to choose his working subalterns from all the Englishmen alive; he surely might do something? Something, by one means or another, is becoming fearfully necessary to be done! He, I think, might accomplish more for us in ten years, than the best conceivable Reformed Parliament, and utmost extension of the suffrage, in twice or ten times ten.

What is extremely important too, you could try this

method with safety; extension of the suffrage you cannot so try. With even an approximately heroic Prime Minister, you could get nothing but good from prescribing to him thus, to choose the fittest man, under penalties; to choose, not the fittest of the four or the three men that were in Parliament, but the fittest from the whole Twenty-seven Millions that he could hear of,—at his peril. Nothing but good from this. From extension of the suffrage, some think, you might get quite other than good. From extension of the suffrage, till it became a universal counting of heads, one sees not in the least what wisdom could be extracted. A Parliament of the Paris pattern, such as we see just now, might be extracted: and from that? Solution into universal slush; drownage of all interests divine and human, in a Noah's-Deluge of Parliamentary eloquence,—such as we hope our sins, heavy and manifold though they are, have *not* yet quite deserved!

Who, then, is to be the Reforming Statesman, and begin the noble work for us? He is the preliminary; one such; with him we may prosecute the enterprise to length after length; without him we cannot stir in it at all. A true *king*, temporary-king, that dare undertake the government of Britain, on condition of beginning in sacred earnest to 'reform' it, not at this or that extremity, but at the heart and centre. That will expurgate Downing Street, and the practical Administration of our Affairs; clear out its accumulated mountains of pedantries and cobwebs; bid the Pedants and the Dullards depart, bid the Gifted and the Seeing enter and inhabit. So that henceforth there be Heavenly light there, instead of Stygian dusk; that God's vivifying light instead of Satan's deadening and killing dusk, may radiate therefrom, and visit with healing all regions of this British Empire, which now writhes through every limb of it, in dire agony as if of death! The enterprise is great, the enterprise may be called formidable and even awful; but there is none nobler among the sublunary affairs of mankind just now. Nay, tacitly it is the enterprise of every man who undertakes to be British Premier in these times;—and I cannot esteem him an enviable Premier who, because the engagement is *tacit*, flatters himself that it does not exist! "Show it me in the bond," he says. Your Lordship, it actually exists: and I think you will see it yet, in another kind of 'bond' than that sheepskin one!

But truly, in any time, what a strange feeling, enough to alarm a very big Lordship, this: that he, of the size he is, has got to the apex of English affairs! Smallest wrens, we know, by training and the aid of machinery, are capable of many things. For this world abounds in miraculous combinations, far transcending anything they do at Drury Lane in the melodramatic way. A world which, as solid as it looks, is made all of aerial and even of spiritual stuff; permeated all by incalculable sleeping forces and electricities; and liable to go off, at any time, into the hugest developments, upon a scratch thoughtfully or thoughtlessly given on the right point:—Nay, for every one of us, could not the sputter of a poor pistol-shot shrivel the Immensities together like a burnt scroll, and make the Heavens and the Earth pass away with a great noise? Smallest wrens, and canary-birds of some dexterity, can be trained to handle lucifer-matches; and have, before now, fired-off whole powder-magazines and parks of artillery. Perhaps *without* much astonishment to the canary-bird. The canary-bird can hold only its own quantity of astonishment; and may possibly enough retain *its* presence of mind, were even Doomsday to come. It is on this principle that I explain to myself the equanimity of some men and Premiers whom we have known.

This and the other Premier seems to take it with perfect coolness. And yet, I say, what a strange feeling, to find himself Chief Governor of England; girding on, upon his moderately-sized new soul, the old battle-harness of an Oliver Cromwell, an Edward Longshanks, a William Conqueror. "I, then, am the Ablest of English attainable Men? This English People, which has spread itself over all lands and seas, and achieved such works in the ages,—which has done America, India, the Lancashire Cotton-trade, Bromwicham Iron-trade, Newton's Principia, Shakspeare's Dramas, and the British Constitution,—the apex of all its intelligences and mighty instincts and dumb longings: it is I? William Conqueror's big gifts, and Edward's and Elizabeth's; Oliver's lightning soul, noble as Sinai and the thunders of the Lord: these are mine, I begin to perceive,—to a certain extent. These heroisms have I,—though rather shy of exhibiting them. These; and something withal of the huge beaver-faculty of our Arkwrights, Brindleys; touches too of the phœnix-melodies and *sunny* heroisms of our Shakspeares, of our Singers, Sages and inspired Thinkers; all this is in me, I will hope,—though rather shy of exhibiting it on common occasions. The Pattern Englishman, raised by solemn acclamation upon the bucklers of the English People, and saluted with universal 'God save THEE!' —has now the honour to announce himself. After fifteen-hundred years of constitutional study as to methods of raising on the bucklers, which is the operation of operations, the English People, surely pretty well skilled in it by this time, has raised—the remarkable individual now addressing you. The best-combined sample of whatsoever divine qualities are in this big People, the consummate flower of all that they have done and been, the ultimate product of the Destinies, and English man of men, arrived at last in the fulness of time, is—who think you? Ye worlds, the Ithuriel javelin by which, with all these heroisms and accumulated energies old and new, the English People means to smite and pierce, is this poor tailor's-bodkin, hardly adequate to bore an eylet-hole, who now has the honour to"— —Good Heavens, if it were not that men generally are very much of the canary-bird, here are reflections sufficient to annihilate any man, almost before starting!

But to us also it ought to be a very strange reflection! This, then, is the length we have brought it to, with our constitutioning, and ballot-boxing, and incessant talk and effort in every kind for so many centuries back; this? The golden flower of our grand alchemical projection, which has set the world in astonishment so long, and been the envy of surrounding nations, is—what we here see. To be governed by his Lordship, and guided through the undiscovered paths of Time by this respectable degree of human faculty. With our utmost soul's travail we could discover, by the sublimest methods eulogised by all the world, no abler Englishman than this?—

Really it should make us pause upon the said sublime methods, and ask ourselves very seriously, whether, notwithstanding the eulogy of all the world, they can be other than extremely astonishing methods, that require revisal and reconsideration very much indeed! For the kind of 'man' we get to govern us, all conclusions whatsoever centre there, and likewise all manner of issues flow infallibly therefrom. 'Ask well, who is your Chief Governor,' says one: 'for around him men like to him will infallibly gather, and by degrees all the world will be made in his image.' 'He who is himself a noble man, has a chance to know the nobleness of men; he who is not, has none. And as for the poor Public,—alas, is not the kind of "man" you set upon it the liveliest symbol of its and your veracity and victory and blessedness, or unveracity and misery and cursedness; the general summation and practical outcome of all else whatsoever in the Public and in you?'

Time was when an incompetent Governor could not be permitted among men. He was, and had to be, by one method or the other, clutched up from his place at the helm of affairs, and hurled down into the hold, perhaps even overboard, if he could not really steer. And we call those ages barbarous, because they shuddered to see a Phantasm at the helm of their affairs; an eyeless Pilot with constitutional spectacles, steering by the *ear* mainly? And we have changed all that: no-government is now the best; and a tailor's foreman, who gives no trouble, is preferable to any other for governing? My friends, such truly is the current idea; but you dreadfully mistake yourselves, and the fact is not such. The fact, now beginning to disclose itself again in distressed Needlewomen, famishing Connaughts, revolting Colonies, and a general rapid advance towards Social Ruin, remains really what it always was, and will so remain!

Men have very much forgotten it at present; and only here a man and there a man begins again to bethink himself of it: but all men will gradually get reminded of it, perhaps terribly to their cost; and the sooner they all lay it to heart again, I think it will be the better. For in spite of our oblivion of it, the thing remains forever true; nor is there any Constitution or body of Constitutions, were they clothed with never such venerabilities and general acceptabilities, that avails to deliver a Nation from the consequences of forgetting it. Nature, I assure you, does forevermore remember it; and a hundred British Constitutions are but as a hundred cobwebs between her and the penalty she levies for forgetting it. Tell me what kind of man governs a People, you tell me, with much exactness, what the net sum-total of social worth in that People has for some time been. Whether *they* have loved the phylacteries or the eternal noblenesses; whether they have been struggling heavenward like eagles, brothers of the radiances, or groping owl-like with horn-eyed diligence, catching mice and balances at their banker's,—poor devils, you will see it all in that one fact. A fact long prepared beforehand; which, if it is a peaceably received one, must have been acquiesced in, judged to be 'best,' by the poor mousing owls, intent only to have a large balance at their banker's and keep a whole skin.

Such sordid populations, which were long blind to Heaven's

light, are getting themselves burnt-up rapidly, in these days, by street-insurrection and Hellfire;—as is indeed inevitable, my esteemed M'Croudy! Light, accept the blessed light, if you will have it when Heaven vouchsafes. You refuse? You prefer Delolme on the British Constitution, the Gospel according to M'Croudy, and a good balance at your banker's? Very well: the 'light' is more and more withdrawn; and for some time you have a general dusk, very favourable for catching mice; and the opulent owlery is very 'happy,' and well-off at its banker's;—and furthermore, by due sequence, infallible as the foundations of the Universe and Nature's oldest law, the light *returns* on you, condensed, this time, into *lightning*, which there is not any skin whatever too thick for taking in!

No. IV

THE NEW DOWNING STREET

[15TH APRIL 1850]

IN looking at this wreck of Governments in all European countries, there is one consideration that suggests itself, sadly elucidative of our modern epoch. These Governments, we may be well assured, have gone to anarchy for this one reason inclusive of every other whatsoever, That they were not wise enough; that the spiritual talent embarked in them, the virtue, heroism, intellect, or by whatever other synonyms we designate it, was not adequate,—probably had long been inadequate, and so in its dim helplessness had suffered, or perhaps invited falsity to introduce itself; had suffered injustices, and solecisms, and contradictions of the Divine Fact, to accumulate in more than tolerable measure; whereupon said Governments were overset, and declared before all creatures to be too false.

This is a reflection sad but important to the modern Governments now fallen anarchic, That they had not spiritual talent enough. And if this is so, then surely the question, How these Governments came to sink for *want* of intellect? is a rather interesting one. Intellect, in some measure, is born into every Century; and the Nineteenth flatters itself that it is rather distinguised that way! What had become of this celebrated Nineteenth Century's intellect? Surely some of it existed, and was 'developed' withal;—nay, in the 'undeveloped,' unconscious, or inarticulate state, it is not dead; but alive and at work, if mutely not less beneficently, some think even more so! And yet Governments, it would appear, could by no means get enough of it; almost none of it came their way; what had become of it? Truly there must be something very questionable, either in the intellect of this celebrated Century, or in the methods Governments now have of supplying their wants from the same. One or other of two grand fundamental shortcomings, in regard to intellect or human enlightenment, are very visible in this enlightened Century of ours; for it has now become the most anarchic of Centuries; that is to say, has fallen practically into such Egyptian darkness that it cannot grope its way at all!

Nay, I rather think both of these shortcomings, fatal deficits both, are chargeable upon us; and it is the joint harvest of both that we are now reaping, with such havoc to our affairs. I rather guess, the intellect of the Nineteenth Century, so full of miracle to Heavyside and others, is itself a mechanical or *beaver* intellect rather than a high or eminently human one. A dim and mean though authentic kind of intellect, this; venerable only in defect of better. This kind will avail but little in the higher enterprises of human intellect, especially in that highest enterprise of guiding men Heavenward, which, after all, is the one real 'governing' of them on this God's Earth:—an enterprise not to be achieved by beaver intellect, but by other higher and highest kinds. This is deficit *first*. And then *secondly*, Governments have, really to a fatal and extraordinary extent, neglected in late ages to supply themselves with what intellect was going; having, as was too natural in the dim time, taken up a notion that human intellect, or even beaver intellect, was not necessary to them at all, but that a little of the *vulpine* sort (if attainable), supported by routine, redtape traditions, and tolerable parliamentary eloquence on occasion, would very well suffice. A most false and impious notion; leading to fatal lethargy on the part of Governments, while Nature and Fact were preparing strange phenomena in contradiction to it.

These are two very fatal deficits;—the remedy of either of which would be the remedy of both, could we but find it!

For indeed they are vitally connected: one of them is sure to produce the other; and both once in action together, the advent of darkness, certain enough to issue in anarchy by and by, goes on with frightful acceleration. If Governments neglect to invite what noble intellect there is, then too surely all intellect, not omnipotent to resist bad influences, will tend to become beaverish ignoble intellect; and quitting high aims, which seem shut-up from it, will help itself forward in the way of making money and suchlike; or will even sink to be sham intellect: helping itself by methods which are not only beaverish but vulpine, and so 'ignoble' as not to have common honesty. The Government, taking no thought to choose intellect for itself, will gradually find that there is less and less of a good quality to choose from: thus, as in all impieties it does, bad grows worse at a frightful *double* rate of progression; and your impiety is twice cursed. If you are impious enough to tolerate darkness, you will get ever more darkness to tolerate; and at that inevitable stage of the account (inevitable in all such accounts) when actual light or else destruction is the alternative, you will call to the Heavens and the Earth for light, and none will come!

Certainly this evil, for one, has *not* 'wrought its own cure'; but has wrought precisely the reverse, and has been hourly eating away what possibilities of cure there were. And so, I fear, in spite of rumours to the contrary, it always is with evils, with solecisms against Nature, and contradictions to the divine fact of things: not an evil of them has ever wrought its own cure in my experience;—but has continually grown worse and wider and uglier, till some *good* (generally a good *man*) not able to endure the abomination longer, rose upon it and cured or else extinguished it. Evil Governments, divested of God's light because they have loved darkness rather, are not likelier than other evils to work their own cure out of that bad plight.

It is urgent upon all Governments to pause in this fatal course; persisted in, the goal is fearfully evident; every hour's persistence in it is making return more difficult. Intellect exists in all countries; and the function appointed it by Heaven,—Governments had better not attempt to contradict that, for they cannot! Intellect *has* to govern in this world; and will do it, if not in alliance with so-called 'Governments' of redtape and routine, then in divine hostility to such, and sometimes alas in diabolic hostility to such; and in the end, as sure as Heaven is higher than Downing Street, and the Laws of Nature are tougher than redtape, with entire victory over them and entire ruin to them. If there is one thinking man among the Politicians of England, I consider these things extremely well worth his attention just now.

Who are available to your Offices in Downing Street? All the gifted souls, of every rank, who are born to you in this generation. These are appointed, by the true eternal 'divine right' which will never become obsolete, to be your governors and administrators; and precisely as you employ them, or neglect to employ them, will your State be favoured of Heaven or disfavoured. This noble young soul, you can have him on either of two conditions; and on one of them, since he is here in the world, you must have him. As your ally and coadjutor; or failing that, as your natural enemy: which shall it be? I consider that every Government convicts itself of infatuation and futility, or absolves and justifies itself before God and man, according as it answers this question. With all sublunary entities, this is the question of questions. What talent is born to you? How do you employ that? The crop of spiritual talent that is born to you, of human nobleness and intellect and heroic faculty, this is infinitely more important than your crops of cotton or corn, or wine or herrings or whale-oil, which the Newspapers record with such anxiety every season. This is not quite counted by seasons, therefore the Newspapers are silent: but by generations and centuries, I assure you it becomes amazingly sensible; and surpasses, as Heaven does Earth, all the corn and wine, and whale-oil and California bullion, or any other crop you grow. If that crop cease, the other crops—please to take them also, if you are anxious about them. That once ceasing, we may shut shop; for no other crop whatever will stay with us, nor is worth having if it would.

To promote men of talent, to search and sift the whole society in every class for men of talent, and joyfully promote them, has not always been found impossible. In many forms of polity they have done it, and still do it, to a certain degree. The degree to which they succeed in doing it marks, as I have said, with very great accuracy the degree of divine and human worth that is in them, the degree of success or real ultimate victory they can expect to have in this world.—Think, for example, of the old Catholic Church, in its merely terrestrial relations to the State; and see if your reflections, and contrasts with what now is, are of an exulting character. Progress of the species has gone on as with seven-league boots, and in various directions has shot ahead amazingly, with three cheers from all the world; but in this direction, the most vital and indispensable, it has lagged terribly, and has even moved backward, till now it is quite gone out of sight in clouds of cotton-fuzz and railway-scrip, and has fallen fairly over the horizon to rearward!

In those most benighted Feudal societies, full of mere tyrannous steel Barons, and totally destitute of Tenpound Franchises and Ballot-boxes, there did nevertheless authentically preach itself everywhere this grandest of gospels, without which no other gospel can avail us much, to all souls of men, "Awake, ye noble souls; here is a noble career for you!" I say, everywhere a road towards promotion, for human nobleness, lay wide open to all men. The pious soul,—which, if you reflect, will mean the ingenuous and ingenious, the gifted, intelligent and nobly-aspiring soul,—such a soul, in whatever rank of life it were born, had one path inviting it; a generous career, whereon, by human worth and valour, all earthly heights and Heaven itself were attainable. In the lowest stratum of social thraldom, nowhere was the noble soul doomed quite to choke, and die ignobly. The Church, poor old benighted creature, had at least taken care of that: the noble aspiring soul, not doomed to choke ignobly in its penuries, could at least run into the neighbouring Convent, and there take refuge. Education awaited it there; strict training not only to whatever useful knowledge could be had from writing and reading, but to obedience, to pious reverence, self-restraint, annihilation of self,—really to human nobleness in many most essential respects. No questions asked about your birth, genealogy, quantity of money-capital or the like; the one question was, "Is there some human nobleness in you, or is there not?" The poor neatherd's son, if he were a Noble of Nature, might rise to Priesthood, to High-priesthood, to the top of this world,—and best of all, he had still high Heaven lying high enough above him, to keep his head steady, on whatever height or in whatever depth his way might lie!

A thrice-glorious arrangement, when I reflect on it; most salutary to all high and low interests; a truly human arrangement. You made the born noble yours, welcoming him as what he was, the Sent of Heaven: you did not force him either to die or become your enemy; idly neglecting or suppressing him as what he was not, a thing of no worth. You accepted the blessed *light*; and in the shape of infernal *lightning* it needed not to visit you. How, like an immense mine-shaft through the dim oppressed strata of society, this Institution of the Priesthood ran; opening, from the lowest depths towards all heights and towards Heaven itself, a free road of egress and emergence towards virtuous nobleness, heroism and well-doing, for every born man. This we may call the living lungs and blood-circulation of those old Feudalisms. When I think of that immeasurable all-pervading lungs; present in every corner of human society, every meanest hut a *cell* of said lungs; inviting whatsoever noble pious soul was born there to the path that was noble for him; and leading thereby sometimes, if he were worthy, to be the Papa of Christendom, and Commander of all Kings, —I perceive how the old Christian society continued healthy, vital, and was strong and heroic. When I contrast this with the noble aims now held out to noble souls born in remote huts, or beyond the verge of Palace-Yard; and think of what your Lordship has done in the way of making priests and papas,—I see a society *without* lungs, fast wheezing itself to death, in horrid convulsions; and deserving to die.

Over Europe generally in these years, I consider that the State has died, has fairly coughed its last in street musketry, and fallen down dead, incapable of any but *galvanic* life henceforth,—owing to this same fatal want of *lungs*, which includes all other wants for a State. And furthermore that it will never come alive again, till it contrive to get such indispensable vital apparatus; the outlook toward which consummation is very distant in most communities of Europe. If you let it come to death or suspended-animation in States, the case is very bad! Vain to call-in universal-suffrage parliaments at that stage: the universal-suffrage parliaments cannot give you any breath of life, cannot find any *wisdom* for you; by long impiety, you have let the supply of noble human wisdom die out; and the wisdom that now courts your universal-suffrages is beggarly human *attorneyism* or sham-wisdom, which is *not* an insight into the Laws of God's Universe, but into the laws of hungry Egoism and the Devil's Chicane, and can in the end profit no community or man.

No; the kind of heroes that come mounted on the shoulders of the universal-suffrage, and instal themselves as Prime Ministers and healing Statesmen by force of able editorship, do not bid very fair to bring Nations back to the ways of God. Eloquent high-lacquered *pinchbeck* specimens these, expert in the arts of Belial mainly;—fitter to be markers at some exceedingly expensive billiard-table than sacred chief-priests of men! 'Greeks of the Lower Empire'; with a varnish of parliamentary rhetoric; and, I suppose, this other great gift, toughness of character,—proof that they have *persevered* in their Master's service. Poor wretches, their industry is mob-worship, place-worship, parliamentary intrigue, and the multiplex art of tongue-fence: flung into that bad element, there they swim for decades long, throttling and wrestling one another according to their strength,—and the toughest or luckiest gets to land, and becomes Premier. A more entirely unbeautiful class of Premiers was never raked out of the ooze, and set on high places, by any ingenuity of man. Dame Dubarry's petticoat was a better seine-net for fishing out Premiers than that. Let all Nations whom necessity is driving towards that method, take warning in time!

Alas, there is, in a manner, but one Nation that can still take warning! In England alone of European Countries the State yet survives; and might help itself by better methods. In England heroic wisdom is not yet dead, and quite replaced by attorneyism: the honest beaver faculty yet abounds with us, the heroic manful faculty shows itself also to the observant eye, not dead but dangerously sleeping. I said there were many *kings* in England: if these can yet be rallied into strenuous activity, and set to govern England in Downing Street and elsewhere, which their function always is,—then England can be saved from anarchies and universal-suffrages; and that Apotheosis of Attorneyism, blackest of terrestrial curses, may be spared us. If these cannot, the other issue, in such forms as may be appropriate to us, is inevitable. What escape is there? England must conform to the eternal laws of life, or England too must die!

England with the largest mass of real living interests ever intrusted to a Nation; and with a mass of extinct imaginary and quite dead interests piled upon it to the very Heavens, and encumbering it from shore to shore,—does reel and stagger ominously in these years; urged by the Divine Silences and the Eternal Laws to take practical hold of its living interests and manage them: and clutching blindly into its venerable extinct and imaginary interests, as if that were still the way to do it. England must contrive to manage its living interests, and quit its dead ones and their methods, or else depart from its place in this world. Surely England is called as no Nation ever was, to summon-out its *kings*, and set them to that high work!—Huge inorganic England, nigh choked under the exuviæ of a thousand years, and blindly sprawling amid chartisms, ballot-boxes, prevenient graces, and bishops' nightmares, must, as the preliminary and commencement of organisation, learn to *breathe* again,—get 'lungs' for herself again, as we defined it. That is imperative upon her: she too will die, otherwise, and cough her last upon the streets some day;—how can she continue living? To enfranchise whatsoever of Wisdom is born in England, and set that to the sacred task of coercing and amending what of Folly is born in England: Heaven's blessing is purchasable by that; by not that, only Heaven's curse is purchasable. The reform contemplated, my liberal friends perceive, is a truly radical one; no ballot-box ever went so deep into the roots: a radical, most painful, slow and difficult, but most indispensable reform of reforms!

How short and feeble an approximation to these high ulterior results, the best Reform of Downing Street, presided over by the fittest Statesman one can imagine to exist at present, would be, is too apparent to me. A long time yet till we get our living interests put under due administration, till we get our dead interests handsomely dismissed. A long time yet till, by extensive change of habit and ways of thinking and acting, *we* get living 'lungs' for ourselves! Nevertheless, by Reform of Downing Street, we do begin to breathe; we do start in the way towards that and all high results. Nor is there visible to me any other way. Blessed enough were the way once entered on; could we, in our evil days, but see the noble enterprise begun, and fairly in progress!

What the '*New* Downing Street' can grow to, and will and must if England is to have a Downing Street beyond a few years longer, it is far from me, in my remote watch-tower, to say with precision. A Downing Street inhabited by the gifted of the intellects of England; directing all its energies upon the real and living interests of England, and silently but incessantly, in the alembics of the place, burning-up the extinct imaginary interests of England, that we may see God's sky a little plainer overhead, and have all of us a great accession of 'heroic wisdom' to dispose of: such a Downing Street—to draw the plan of it, will require architects; many successive architects and builders will be needed there. Let not editors, and remote unprofessional persons, interfere too much!—Change in the present edifice, however, radical change, all men can discern to be inevitable; and even, if there shall not worse swiftly follow, to be imminent. Outlines of the future edifice paint themselves against the sky (to men that still have a *sky*, and are above the miserable London fogs of the hour); noble elements of new State Architecture, foreshadows of a new Downing Street for the New Era that is to come. These with pious hope all men can see; and it is good that all men, with whatever faculty they have, were earnestly looking thitherward;—trying to get above the fogs, that they might look thitherward!

Among practical men the idea prevails that Government can do nothing but 'keep the peace.' They say all higher tasks are unsafe for it, impossible for it,—and in fine not necessary for it or for us. On this footing a very feeble Downing Street might serve the turn!—I am well aware that Government, for a long time past, has taken in hand no other public task, and has professed to have no other, but that of keeping the peace. This public task, and the private one of ascertaining whether Dick or Jack was to do it, have amply filled the capabilities of Government for several generations now. Hard tasks both, it would appear. In accomplishing the first, for example, have not heavenborn Chancellors of the Exchequer had to shear us very bare; and to leave an overplus of Debt, or of fleeces shorn *before* they are grown, justly esteemed among the wonders of the world? Not a first-rate keeping of the peace, this, we begin to surmise! At least it seems strange to us.

For we, and the overwhelming majority of all our acquaintances, in this Parish and Nation and the adjacent Parishes and Nations, are profoundly conscious to ourselves of being by nature peaceable persons; following our necessary industries: without wish, interest or faintest intention to cut the skin of any mortal, to break feloniously into his industrial premises, or do any injustice to him at all. Because indeed, independent of Government, there is a thing called conscience, and we dare not. So that it cannot but appear to us, 'the peace,' under dextrous management, might be very much more easily kept, your Lordship; nay, we almost think, if well let alone, it would in a measure keep *itself* among such a set of persons! And how it happens that when a poor hardworking creature of us has laboriously earned sixpence, the Government comes in, and (as some compute) says, "I will thank you for threepence of that, as per account, for getting you peace to spend the other threepence," our amazement begins to be considerable,—and I think results will follow from it by and by. Not the most dextrous keeping of the peace, your Lordship, unless it be more difficult to do than appears!

Our domestic peace, we cannot but perceive, as good as keeps itself. Here and there a select Equitable person, appointed by the Public for that end, clad in ermine, and backed by certain companies of blue Police, is amply adequate, without immoderate outlay in money or otherwise, to keep-down the few exceptional individuals of the scoundrel kind; who, we observe, by the nature of them, are always weak and inconsiderable. And as to foreign peace, really all Europe, now especially with so many railroads, public journals, printed books, penny-post, bills of exchange, and continual intercourse and mutual dependence, is more and more becoming (so to speak) one Parish; the Parishioners of which being, as we ourselves are, in immense majority peaceable hardworking people, could, if they were moderately well guided, have almost no disposition to quarrel. Their economic interests are one, 'To buy in the cheapest market, and sell in the dearest'; their faith, any *religious* faith they have, is one, 'To annihilate shams—by all methods, street-barricades included.' Why should they quarrel? The Czar of Russia, in the Eastern parts of the Parish, may have other notions; but he knows too well he must keep them to himself. He, if he meddled with the Western parts, and attempted anywhere to crush or disturb that sacred Democratic Faith of theirs, is aware there would rise from a hundred and fifty million human throats such a *Hymn of the Marseillaise* as was never heard before; and England, France, Germany, Poland, Hungary, and the Nine Kingdoms, hurling themselves upon him in never-imagined fire of vengeance, would swiftly reduce his Russia and him to a strange situation! Wherefore he forbears,—and being a person of some sense, will long forbear. In spite of editorial prophecy, the Czar of Russia does not disturb our night's rest. And with the other parts of the Parish our dreams and our thoughts are of anything but of fighting, or of the smallest need to fight.

For keeping of the peace, a thing highly desirable to us, we strive to be grateful to your Lordship. Intelligible to us, also, your Lordship's reluctance to get out of the old routine. But we beg to say farther, that peace by itself has no feet to stand upon, and would not suit us even if it had. Keeping of the peace is the function of a policeman, and but a small fraction of that of any Government, King or Chief of men. Are not all men bound, and the Chief of men in the name of all, to do properly this: To see, so far as human effort under pain of eternal reprobation can, God's Kingdom incessantly advancing here below, and His will done on Earth as it is in Heaven? On Sundays your Lordship knows this well; forget it not on weekdays. I assure you it is for evermore a fact. That is the immense divine and never-ending task which is laid on every man, and with unspeakable increase of emphasis on every Government or Commonwealth of men. Your Lordship, that is the basis upon which peace and all else depends! That basis once well lost, there is no peace capable of being kept,—the only peace that could then be kept is that of the churchyard. Your Lordship may depend on it, whatever thing takes upon it the name of Sovereign or Government in an English Nation such as this will have to get out of that old routine; and set about keeping something very different from the peace, in these days!

Truly it is high time that same beautiful notion of No-Government should take itself away. The world is daily rushing towards wreck, while that lasts. If your Government is to be a Constituted Anarchy, what issue can it have? Our one interest in such Government is, that it would be kind enough to cease and go its ways, *before* the inevitable arrive. The question, Who is to float atop nowhither upon the popular vortexes, and act that sorry character, 'carcass of the drowned ass upon the mud-deluge'? is by no means an important one for almost anybody,—hardly even for the drowned ass himself. Such drowned ass ought to ask himself, If the function is a sublime one? For him too, though he looks sublime to the vulgar and floats atop, a private situation, down out of sight in his natural ooze, would be a luckier one.

Crabbe, speaking of constitutional philosophies, faith in

the ballot-box and suchlike, has this indignant passage: 'If any voice of deliverance or resuscitation reach us, in this our low and all-but lost estate, sunk almost beyond plummet's sounding in the mud of Lethe, and oblivious of all noble objects,—it will be an intimation that we must put away all this abominable nonsense, and understand, once more, that Constituted Anarchy, with however many ballot-boxes, caucuses, and hustings-beerbarrels, is a continual offence to gods and men. That to be governed by small men is not only a misfortune, but it is a curse and a sin; the effect, and alas the cause also, of all manner of curses and sins. That to profess subjection to phantasms, and pretend to accept guidance from fractional parts of tailors, is what Smelfungus in his rude dialect calls it, "a damned *lie*," and nothing other. A lie which, by long use and wont, we have grown accustomed to, and do not the least feel to be a lie, having spoken and done it continually everywhere for such a long time past;—but has Nature grown to accept it as a veracity, think you, my friend? Have the Parcæ fallen asleep, because you wanted to make money in the City? Nature at all moments knows well that it is a lie; and that, like all lies, it is cursed and damned from the beginning.

'Even so, ye indigent millionaires, and miserable bankrupt populations rolling in gold,—whose note-of-hand will go to any length in Threadneedle Street, and to whom in Heaven's Bank the stern answer is, "No effects!" Bankrupt, I say; and Californias and Eldorados will not save us. And every time we speak such lie, or do it or look it, as we have been incessantly doing, and many of us with clear consciousness, for about a hundred and fifty years now, Nature marks down the exact penalty against us. "Debtor to so much lying: forfeiture of existing stock of worth to such extent;—approach to general damnation by so much." Till now, as we look round us over a convulsed anarchic Europe, and at home over an anarchy not yet convulsed, but only heaving towards convulsion, and to judge by the Mosaic sweating-establishments, cannibal Connaughts and other symptoms, not far from convulsion now, we seem to have pretty much *exhausted* our accumulated stock of worth; and, unless money's "worth" and bullion at the Bank will save us, to be rubbing very close upon that ulterior bourne which I do not like to name again!

'On behalf of nearly twenty-seven millions of my fellow-countrymen, sunk deep in Lethean sleep, with mere owl-dreams of Political Economy and mice-catching, in this pacific thrice-infernal slush-element; and also of certain select thousands, and hundreds and units, awakened or beginning to awaken from it, and with horror in their hearts perceiving where they are, I beg to protest, and in the name of God to say, with poor human ink, desirous much that I had divine thunder to say it with, Awake, arise,—before you sink to death eternal! Unnameable destruction, and banishment to Houndsditch and Gehenna, lies in store for all Nations that, in angry perversity or brutal torpor and owlish blindness, neglect the eternal message of the gods, and vote for the Worse while the Better is there. Like owls they say, "Barabbas will do; any orthodox Hebrew of the Hebrews, and peaceable believer in M'Croudy and the Faith of Leave-alone will do: the Right Honourable Minimus is well enough; he shall be our Maximus, under him it will be handy to catch mice, and Owldom shall continue a flourishing empire."'

One thing is undeniable, and must be continually repeated till it get to be understood again: Of all constitutions, forms of government, and political methods among men, the question to be asked is even this, What kind of man do you set over us? All questions are answered in the answer to this. Another thing is worth attending to: No people or populace, with never such ballot-boxes, can select such man for you; only the man of worth can recognise worth in men;—to the commonplace man of no or of little worth, you, unless you wish to be *mis*led, need not apply on such an occasion. Those poor Tenpound Franchisers of yours, they are not even in earnest; the poor sniffing sniggering Honourable Gentlemen they send to Parliament are as little so. Tenpound Franchisers full of mere beer and balderdash; Honourable Gentlemen come to Parliament as to an Almack's series of evening parties, or big cockmain (battle of all the cocks) very amusing to witness and bet upon: what can or could men in that predicament ever do for you? Nay, if they were in life-and-death earnest, what could it avail you in such a case? I tell you, a million blockheads looking authoritatively into one man of what you call genius, or noble sense, will make nothing but nonsense out of him and his qualities, and his virtues and defects, if they look till the end of time. He understands them, sees what they are; but that they should understand him, and see with rounded outline what his limits are,—this, which would mean that they are bigger than he, is forever denied them. Their one good understanding of him is that they at last should loyally say, "We do not quite understand thee; we perceive thee to be nobler and wiser and bigger than we, and will loyally follow thee."

The question therefore arises, Whether, since reform of parliament and suchlike have done so little in that respect, the problem might not be with some hope attacked in the direct manner? Suppose all our Institutions, and Public Methods of Procedure, to continue for the present as they are; and suppose farther a Reform Premier, and the English Nation once awakening under him to a due sense of the infinite importance, nay, the vital necessity there is of getting able and abler men:—might not some heroic wisdom, and actual 'ability' to do what must be done, prove discoverable to said Premier; and so the indispensable Heaven's-blessing descend to us from *above*, since none has yet sprung from below? From above we shall have to try it; the other is exhausted,—a hopeless method that! The utmost passion of the house-inmates, ignorant of masonry and architecture, cannot avail to cure the house of smoke: not if *they* vote and agitate forever, and bestir themselves to the length even of street-barricades, will the *smoke* in the least abate: how can it? Their passion exercised in such ways, till Doomsday, will avail them nothing. Let their passion rage steadily against the existing majordomos to this effect, "*Find* us men skilled in house-building, acquainted with the laws of atmospheric suction, and capable to cure smoke"; something might come of it! In the lucky circumstance of having one man of real intellect and courage to put at the head of the movement, much would come of it;—a New Downing Street, fit for the British Nation and its bitter necessities in this New Era, would come; and from that, in answer to continuous sacred fidelity and valiant toil, all good whatsoever would gradually come.

Of the Continental nuisance called 'Bureaucracy,'—if this should alarm any reader,—I can see no risk or possibility in England. Democracy is hot enough here, fierce enough; it is perennial, universal, clearly invincible among us henceforth. No danger it should let itself be flung in chains by sham-secretaries of the Pedant species, and accept their vile Age of Pinchbeck for its Golden Age! Democracy clamours, with its Newspapers, its Parliaments, and all its Twenty-seven million throats, continually in this Nation forevermore. I remark, too, that the unconscious purport of all its clamours is even this, "Find us men skilled,"—*make* a New Downing Street, fit for the New Era!

Of the Foreign Office, in its reformed state, we have not much to say. Abolition of imaginary work, and replacement of it by real, is on all hands understood to be very urgent there. Large needless expenditures of money, immeasurable ditto of hypocrisy and grimace; embassies, protocols, worlds of extinct traditions, empty pedantries, foul cobwebs:—but we will by no means apply the 'live coal' of our witty friend; the Foreign Office will repent, and not be driven to suicide! A truer time will come for the Continental Nations too: Authorities based on truth, and on the silent or spoken Worship of Human Nobleness, will again get themselves established there; all Sham-Authorities, and consequent Real-Anarchies based on universal-suffrage and the Gospel according to George Sand, being put away; and noble action, heroic new-developments of human faculty and industry, and blessed fruit as of Paradise getting itself conquered from the waste battle-field of the chaotic elements, will once more, there as here, begin to show themselves.

When the Continental Nations have once got to the bottom of *their* Augean Stable, and begun to have real enterprises based on the eternal facts again, our Foreign Office may again have extensive concerns with them. And at all times, and even now, there will remain the question to be sincerely put and wisely answered, What essential concern *has* the British Nation with them and their enterprises? Any concern at all, except that of handsomely keeping apart from them? If so, what are the methods of best managing it?—At present, as was said, while Red Republic but clashes with foul Bureaucracy; and Nations, sunk in blind ignavia, demand a universal-suffrage Parliament to heal their wretchedness; and wild Anarchy and Phallus-Worship struggle with Sham-Kingship and extinct or galvanised Catholicism; and in the Cave of the Winds all manner of rotten waifs and wrecks are hurled against each other,—our English interest in the controversy, however huge said controversy grow, is quite trifling; we have only in a handsome manner to say to it: "Tumble and rage along, ye rotten waifs and wrecks; clash and collide as seems fittest to you; and smite each other into annihilation at your own good pleasure. In that huge conflict, dismal but unavoidable, we, thanks to our heroic ancestors, having got so far ahead of you, have now no interest at all. Our decided notion is, the dead ought to bury their dead in such a case: and so we have the honour to be, with distinguished consideration, your entirely devoted,—FLIMNAP, SEC. FOREIGN DEPARTMENT."—I really think Flimnap, till truer times come, ought to treat much of his work in this way: cautious to give offence to his neighbours; resolute not to concern himself in any of their self-annihilating operations whatsoever.

Foreign wars are sometimes unavoidable. We ourselves, in the course of natural merchandising and laudable business, have now and then got into ambiguous situations; into quarrels which needed to be settled, and without fighting would not settle. Sugar Islands, Spice Islands, Indias, Canadas,—these, by the real decree of Heaven, were ours; and nobody would or could believe it, till it was tried by cannon law, and *so* proved. Such cases happen. In former times especially, owing very much to want of intercourse and to the consequent mutual ignorance, there did occur misunderstandings: and therefrom many foreign wars, some of them by no means unnecessary. With China, or some distant country, too unintelligent of us and too unintelligible to us, there still sometimes rises necessary occasion for a war. Nevertheless wars,—misunderstandings that get to the length of arguing themselves out by sword and cannon,—have, in these late generations of improved intercourse, been palpably becoming less and less necessary; have in a manner become superfluous,—if we had a little wisdom, and our Foreign Office on a good footing.

Of European wars I really hardly remember any, since Oliver Cromwell's last Protestant or Liberation war with Popish antichristian Spain some two hundred years ago, to which I for my own part could have contributed my life with any heartiness, or in fact would have subscribed money itself to any considerable amount. Dutch William, a man of some heroism, did indeed get into troubles with Louis Fourteenth;

and there rested till some shadow of Protestant Interest, and question of National and individual Independence, over those wide controversies; a little money and human enthusiasm was still due to Dutch William. Illustrious Chatham also, not to speak of his Manilla ransoms and the like, did one thing: assisted Fritz of Prussia, a brave man and king (almost the only sovereign *King* I have known since Cromwell's time) like to be borne down by ignoble men and sham-kings; for this let illustrious Chatham too have a little money and human enthusiasm,—a little, by no means much. But what am I to say of heavenborn Pitt the son of Chatham? England sent forth her fleets and armies; her money into every country; money as if the heavenborn Chancellor had got a Fortunatus' purse; as if this Island had become a volcanic fountain of gold, or new terrestrial sun capable of radiating mere guineas. The result of all which, what was it? Elderly men can remember the tar-barrels burnt for success and thrice-immortal victory in the business; and yet what result had we? The French Revolution, a Fact decreed in the Eternal Councils, could not be put down: the result was, that heavenborn Pitt had actually been fighting (as the old Hebrews would have said) against the Lord,—that the Laws of Nature were stronger than Pitt. Of whom therefore there remains chiefly his unaccountable radiation of guineas, for the gratitude of posterity. Thank you for nothing,—for eight hundred millions *less* than nothing!

Our War Offices, Admiralties, and other Fighting Establishments, are forcing themselves on everybody's attention at this time. Bull grumbles audibly: "The money you have cost me these five-and-thirty years, during which you have stood elaborately ready to fight at any moment, without at any moment being called to fight, is surely an astonishing sum. The National Debt itself might have been half paid by that money, which has all gone in pipeclay and blank cartridges!" Yes, Mr. Bull, the money can be counted in hundreds of millions, which certainly is something:—but the 'strenuously organised idleness,' and what mischief that amounts to—have you computed it? A perpetual solecism, and blasphemy (of its sort), set to march openly among us, dressed in scarlet! Bull, with a more and more sulky tone, demands that such solecism be abated; that these Fighting Establishments be as it were disbanded, and set to do some work in the Creation, since fighting there is now none for them. This demand is irrefragably just, is growing urgent too; and yet this demand cannot be complied with,—not yet while the State grounds itself on unrealities, and Downing Street continues what it is.

The old Romans made their soldiers work during intervals of war. The New Downing Street too, we may predict, will have less and less tolerance for idleness on the part of soldiers or others. Nay, the New Downing Street, I foresee, when once it has got its '*Industrial* Regiments' organised, will make these mainly do its fighting, what fighting there is; and so save immense sums. Or indeed, all citizens of the Commonwealth, as is the right and the interest of every free man in this world, will have themselves trained to arms; each citizen ready to defend his country with his own body and soul,—he is not worthy to have a country otherwise. In a State grounded on veracities, that would be the rule. Downing Street, if it cannot bethink itself of returning to the veracities, will have to vanish altogether!

To fight with its neighbours never was, and is now less than ever, the real trade of England. For far other objects was the English People created into this world; sent down from the Eternities, to mark with its history certain spaces in the current of sublunary Time! Essential too that the English People should discover what its real objects are; and resolutely follow these, resolutely refusing to follow other than these. The State will have victory so far as it can do that; so far as it cannot, defeat.

In the New Downing Street, discerning what its real functions are, and with sacred abhorrence putting away from it what its functions are *not*, we can fancy changes enough in Foreign Office, War Office, Colonial Office, Home Office! Our War-soldiers *Industrial*, first of all; doing nobler than Roman works, when fighting is not wanted of them. Seventy-fours not hanging idly by their anchors in the Tagus, or off Sapienza (one of the saddest sights under the sun), but busy, every Seventy-four of them, carrying-over streams of British Industrials to the immeasurable Britain that lies beyond the sea in every zone of the world. A State grounding itself on the veracities, not on the semblances and the injustices: every citizen a soldier for it. Here would be new *real* Secretaryships and Ministries, not for foreign war and diplomacy, but for domestic peace and utility. Minister of Works; Minister of Justice,—clearing his Model-Prisons of their scoundrelism; shipping his scoundrels wholly abroad, under hard and just drill-sergeants (hundreds of such stand wistfully ready for you, these thirty years, in the Rag-and-Famish Club and elsewhere!) into fertile desert countries; to make railways,—one big railway (says the Major[1]) quite across America; fit to employ all the able-bodied Scoundrels and efficient Half-pay Officers in Nature!

Lastly,—or rather *firstly*, and as the preliminary of all,—would there not be a Minister of Education? Minister charged to get this English People taught a little, at his and our peril! Minister of Education; no longer dolefully embayed amid the wreck of moribund 'religions,' but clear ahead of all that; steering, free and piously fearless, towards *his* divine goal under the eternal stars!— —O Heaven, and are these things forever impossible, then? Not a whit. Tomorrow morning they might all begin to be, and go on through blessed centuries realising themselves, if it were not that—alas, if it were not that we are most of us insincere persons, sham talking-machines and hollow windy fools! Which it is *not* 'impossible' that we should cease to be, I hope?

[1] Major Carmichael Smith: see his Pamphlets on this subject.

Constitutions for the Colonies are now on the anvil; the discontented Colonies are all to be cured of their miseries by Constitutions. Whether that will cure their miseries, or only operate as a Godfrey's-cordial to stop their whimpering, and in the end worsen all their miseries, may be a sad doubt to us. One thing strikes a remote spectator in these Colonial questions: the singular placidity with which the British Statesman at this time, backed by M'Croudy and the British moneyed classes, is prepared to surrender whatsoever interest Britain, as foundress of those establishments, might pretend to have in the decision. "If you want to go from us, go; we by no means want you to stay: you cost us money yearly, which is scarce; desperate quantities of trouble too: why not go, if you wish it?" Such is the humour of the British Statesman, at this time.—Men clear for rebellion, 'annexation' as they call it, walk openly abroad in our American Colonies; found newspapers, hold platform palaverings. From Canada there comes duly by each mail a regular statistic of Annexationism: increasing fast in this quarter, diminishing in that;—Majesty's Chief Governor seeming to take it as a perfectly open question; Majesty's Chief Governor in fact seldom appearing on the scene at all, except to receive the impact of a few rotten eggs on occasion, and then duck in again to his private contemplations. And yet one would think the Majesty's Chief Governor ought to have a kind of interest in the thing? Public liberty is carried to a great length in some portions of her Majesty's dominions. But the question, "Are we to continue subjects of her Majesty, or start rebelling against her? So many as are for rebelling, hold up your hands!" Here is a public discussion of a very extraordinary nature to be going on under the nose of a Governor of Canada. How the Governor of Canada, being a British piece of flesh and blood, and not a Canadian lumber-log of mere pine and rosin, can stand it, is not very conceivable at first view. He does it, seemingly, with the stoicism of a Zeno. It is a constitutional sight like few.

And yet an instinct deeper than the Gospel of M'Croudy teaches all men that Colonies are worth something to a country! That if, under the present Colonial Office, they are a vexation to us and themselves, some other Colonial Office can and must be contrived which shall render them a blessing; and that the remedy will be to contrive such a Colonial Office or method of administration, and by no means to cut the Colonies loose. Colonies are not to be picked off the street every day; not a Colony of them but has been bought dear, well purchased by the toil and blood of those we have the honour to be sons of; and we cannot just afford to cut them away because M'Croudy finds the present management of them cost money. The present management will indeed require to be cut away;—but as for the Colonies, we purpose through Heaven's blessing to retain them a while yet! Shame on us for unworthy sons of brave fathers if we do not. Brave fathers, by valiant blood and sweat, purchased for us, from the bounty of Heaven, rich possessions in all zones; and we, wretched imbeciles, cannot do the function of administering them? And because the accounts do not stand well in the ledger, our remedy is, not to take shame to ourselves, and repent in sackcloth and ashes, and amend our beggarly imbecilities and insincerities in that as in other departments of our business, but to fling the business overboard, and declare the business itself to be bad? We are a hopeful set of heirs to a big fortune! It does not suit our Manton gunneries, grouse-shootings, mousings in the City; and like spirited young gentlemen we will give it up, and let the attorneys take it?

Is there no value, then, in human things, but what can write itself down in the cash-ledger? All men know, and even M'Croudy in his inarticulate heart knows, that to men and Nations there are invaluable values which cannot be sold for money at all. George Robins is great; but he is not omnipotent. George Robins cannot quite sell Heaven and Earth by auction, excellent though he be at the business.

Nay, if M'Croudy offered his own life for *sale* in Threadneedle Street, would anybody buy it? Not I, for one. "Nobody bids: pass on to the next lot," answers Robins. And yet to M'Croudy this unsaleable lot is worth all the Universe:—nay, I believe, to us also it is worth something; good monitions, as to several things, do lie in this Professor of the dismal science; and considerable sums even of money, not to speak of other benefit, will yet come out of his life and him, for which nobody bids! Robins has his own field where he reigns triumphant; but to that we will restrict him with iron limits; and neither Colonies nor the lives of Professors, nor other such invaluable objects shall come under his hammer.

Bad state of the ledger will demonstrate that your way of dealing with your Colonies is absurd, and urgently in want of reform; but to demonstrate that the Empire itself must be dismembered to bring the ledger straight? O never. Something else than the ledger must intervene to do that. Why does not England repudiate Ireland, and insist on the 'Repeal,' instead of prohibiting it under death-penalties? Ireland has never been a paying speculation yet, nor is it like soon to be! Why does not Middlesex repudiate Surrey, and Chelsea Kensington, and each county and each parish, and in the end each individual set up for himself and his cashbox, repudiating the other and his, because their mutual interests have got into an irritating course? They must change the course, seek till they discover a soothing one; that is the remedy, when limbs of the same body come to irritate one another. Because the paltry tatter of a garment, reticulated for you out of thrums and listings in Downing Street, ties foot and hand together in an intolerable manner, will you relieve yourself by cutting off the hand or the foot? You will cut off the paltry tatter of a pretended bodycoat, I think, and fling that to the nettles; and imperatively require one that fits your size better.

Miserabler theory than that of money on the ledger being

the primary rule for Empires, or for any higher entity than City owls and their mice-catching, cannot well be propounded. And I would by no means advise Felicissimus, ill at ease on his high-trotting and now justly impatient Sleswicker, to let the poor horse in its desperation go in that direction for a momentary solace. If by lumber-log Governors, by Godfrey's-cordial Constitutions or otherwise, he contrive to cut off the Colonies or any real right the big British Empire has in her Colonies, both he and the British Empire will bitterly repent it one day! The Sleswicker, relieved in ledger for a moment, will find that it is wounded in heart and honour forever; and the turning of its wild forehoofs upon Felicissimus as he lies in the ditch combed off, is not a thing I like to think of! Britain, whether it be known to Felicissimus or not, has other tasks appointed her in God's Universe than the making of money; and woe will betide her if she forget those other withal. Tasks, colonial and domestic, which are of an eternally *divine* nature, and compared with which all money, and all that is procurable by money, are in strict arithmetic an imponderable quantity, have been assigned this Nation; and they also at last are coming upon her again, clamorous, abstruse, inevitable, much to her bewilderment just now!

This poor Nation, painfully dark about said tasks and the way of doing them, means to keep its Colonies nevertheless, as things which somehow or other must have a value, were it better seen into. They are portions of the general Earth, where the children of Britain now dwell; where the gods have so far sanctioned their endeavour, as to say that they have a right to dwell. England will not readily admit that her own children are worth nothing but to be flung out of doors! England looking on her Colonies can say: "Here are lands and seas, spice-lands, corn-lands, timber-lands, overarched by zodiacs and stars, clasped by many-sounding seas; wide spaces of the Maker's building, fit for the cradle yet of mighty Nations and their Sciences and Heroisms. Fertile continents still inhabited by wild beasts are mine, into which all the distressed populations of Europe might pour themselves, and make at once an Old World and a New World human. By the eternal fiat of the gods, this must yet one day be; this, by all the Divine Silences that rule this Universe, silent to fools, eloquent and awful to the hearts of the wise, is incessantly at this moment, and at all moments, commanded to begin to be. Unspeakable deliverance, and new destiny of thousandfold expanded manfulness for all men, dawns out of the Future here. To me has fallen the godlike task of initiating all that: of me and of my Colonies, the abstruse Future asks, Are you wise enough for so sublime a destiny? Are you too foolish?"

That you ask advice of whatever wisdom is to be had in the Colony, and even take note of what *un*wisdom is in it, and record that too as an existing fact, will certainly be very advantageous. But I suspect the kind of Parliament that will suit a Colony is much of a secret just now! Mr. Wakefield, a democratic man in all fibres of him, and acquainted with Colonial Socialities as few are, judges that the franchise for your Colonial Parliament should be decidedly select, and advises a high money-qualification; as there is in all Colonies a fluctuating migratory mass, not destitute of money, but very much so of loyalty, permanency, or civic availability;—whom it is extremely advantageous *not* to consult on what you are about attempting for the Colony or Mother Country. This I can well believe;—and also that a 'high money-qualification,' in the present sad state of human affairs, might be some help to you in selecting; though whether even that would quite certainly bring 'wisdom,' the one thing indispensable, is much a question with me. It might help, it might help! And if by any means you could (which you cannot) exclude the Fourth Estate, and indicate decisively that Wise Advice was the thing wanted here, and Parliamentary Eloquence was not the thing wanted anywhere just now,—there might really some light of experience and human foresight, and a truly valuable benefit, be found for you in such assemblies.

And there is one thing, too apt to be forgotten, which it much behoves us to remember: In the Colonies, as everywhere else in this world, the vital point is not who decides, but what is decided on! That measures tending really to the best advantage temporal and spiritual of the Colony be adopted, and strenuously put in execution; there lies the grand interest of every good citizen British and Colonial. Such measures, whosoever have originated and prescribed them, will gradually be sanctioned by all men and gods; and clamours of every kind in reference to them may safely to a great extent be neglected, as clamorous merely, and sure to be transient. Colonial Governor, Colonial Parliament, whoever or whatever does an injustice, or resolves on an *un*wisdom, he is the pernicious object, however parliamentary he be!

I have known things done, in this or the other Colony, in the most parliamentary way before now, which carried written on the brow of them sad symptoms of eternal reprobation; not to be mistaken, had you painted an inch thick. In Montreal, for example, at this moment, standing amid the ruins of the 'Elgin Marbles' (as they call the burnt walls of the Parliament House there), what rational British soul but is forced to institute the mournfulest constitutional reflections? Some years ago the Canadas, probably not without materials for discontent, and blown upon by skilful artists, blazed up into crackling of musketry, open flame of rebellion; a thing smacking of the gallows in all countries that pretend to have any 'Government.' Which flame of rebellion, had there been no loyal population to fling themselves upon it at peril of their life, might have ended we know not how. It ended speedily, in the good way; Canada got a Godfrey's-cordial Constitution; and for the moment all was varnished into some kind of feasibility again. A most poor feasibility; momentary, not lasting, nor like to be of profit to Canada! For this year, the Canadian most constitutional Parliament, such a congeries of persons as one can imagine, decides that the aforesaid flame of rebellion shall not only be forgotten as per bargain, but that—the loyal population, who flung their lives upon it and quenched it in the nick of time, shall pay the rebels their damages! Of this, I believe, on sadly conclusive evidence, there is no doubt whatever. Such, when you wash off the constitutional pigments, is the Death's-head that discloses itself. I can only say, if all the Parliaments in the world were to vote that such a thing was just, I should feel painfully constrained to answer, at my peril, "No, by the Eternal, never!" And I would recommend any British Governor who might come across that Business, there or here, to overhaul it again. What the meaning of a Governor, if he is not to overhaul and control such things, may be, I cannot conjecture. A Canadian Lumber-log may as well be made Governor. *He* might have some cast-metal hand or shoulder-crank (a thing easily contrivable in Birmingham) for signing his name to Acts of the Colonial Parliament; he would be a 'native of the country' too, with popularity on that score if on no other;—he is your man, if you really want a Log Governor!—

I perceive therefore that, besides choosing Parliaments never so well, the New Colonial Office will have another thing to do: Contrive to send out a new kind of Governors to the Colonies. This will be the mainspring of the business; without this the business will not go at all. An experienced, wise and valiant British man, to represent the Imperial Interest; he, with such a speaking or silent Collective Wisdom as he can gather round him in the Colony, will evidently be the condition of all good between the Mother Country and it. If you can find such a man, your point is gained; if you cannot, lost. By him and his Collective Wisdom all manner of *true* relations, mutual interests and duties such as they do exist in fact between Mother Country and Colony, can be gradually developed into practical methods and results;

and all manner of true and noble successes, and veracities in the way of governing, be won. Choose well your Governor;—not from this or that poor section of the Aristocracy, military, naval, or redtapist; wherever there are born kings of men, you had better seek them out, and breed them to this work. All sections of the British Population will be open to you: and, on the whole, you must succeed in finding a man *fit*. And having found him, I would farther recommend you to keep him some time! It would be a great improvement to end this present *nomadism* of Colonial Governors. Give your Governor due power; and let him know withal that he is wedded to his enterprise, and having once well learned it, shall continue with it; that it is not a Canadian Lumber-Log you want there, to tumble upon the vortexes and sign its name by a Birmingham shoulder-crank, but a Governor of Men; who, you mean, shall fairly gird himself to his enterprise, and fail with it and conquer with it, and as it were live and die with it: he will have much to learn; and having once learned it, will stay, and turn his knowledge to account.

From this kind of Governor, were you once in the way of finding him with moderate certainty, from him and his Collective Wisdom, all good whatsoever might be anticipated. And surely, were the Colonies once enfranchised from redtape, and the poor Mother Country once enfranchised from it; were our idle Seventy-fours all busy carrying-out streams of British Industrials, and those Scoundrel Regiments all working, under divine drill-sergeants at the grand Atlantic and Pacific Junction Railway,—poor Britain and her poor Colonies might find that they *had* true relations to each other: that the Imperial *Mother* and her constitutionally obedient Daughters was not a redtape fiction, provoking bitter mockery as at present, but a blessed God's-Fact destined to fill half the world with its fruits one day!

But undoubtedly our grand primary concern is the Home

Office, and its Irish Giant named of Despair. When the Home Office begins dealing with this Irish Giant, which it is vitally urgent for us the Home Office should straightway do, it will find its duties enlarged to a most unexpected extent, and, as it were, altered from top to bottom. A changed time now when the question is, What to do with three millions of paupers (come upon you for food, since you have no work for them) increasing at a frightful rate per day? Home Office, Parliament, King, Constitution will find that they have now, if they will continue in this world long, got a quite immense new question and continually-recurring set of questions. That huge question of the Irish Giant, with his Scotch and English Giant-Progeny advancing open-mouthed upon us, will, as I calculate, change from top to bottom not the Home Office only but all manner of Offices and Institutions whatsoever, and gradually the structure of Society itself. I perceive, it will make us a new Society, if we are to continue a Society at all. For the alternative is not, Stay where we are, or change? But Change, with new wise effort fit for the new time, to true and wider nobler National Life; or Change, by indolent folding of the arms, as we are now doing, in horrible anarchies and convulsions to Dissolution, to National Death, or Suspended-animation? Suspended-animation itself is a frightful possibility for Britain: this Anarchy whither all Europe has preceded us, where all Europe is now weltering, would suit us as ill as any! The question for the British Nation is: Can we work our course pacifically, on firm land, into the New Era; or must it be, for us too, as for all the others, through black abysses of Anarchy, hardly escaping, if we do with all our struggles escape, the jaws of eternal Death?

For Pauperism, though it now absorbs its high figure of millions annually, is by no means a question of money only, but of infinitely higher and greater than all conceivable money. If our Chancellor of the Exchequer had a Fortunatus' purse, and miraculous sacks of Indian meal that would stand scooping from forever,—I say, even on these terms Pauperism could not be endured; and it would vitally concern all British Citizens to abate Pauperism, and never rest till they had ended it again. Pauperism is the general leakage through every joint of the ship that is rotten. Were all men doing their duty, or even seriously trying to do it, there would be no Pauper. Were the pretended Captains of the world at all in the habit of commanding; were the pretended Teachers of the world at all in the habit of teaching,—of admonishing said Captains among others, and with sacred zeal apprising them to what *place* such neglect was leading, —how could Pauperism exist? Pauperism would lie far over the horizon; we should be lamenting and denouncing quite inferior sins of men, which were only tending afar off towards Pauperism. A true Captaincy; a true Teachership, either making all men and Captains know and devoutly recognise the eternal law of things, or else breaking its own heart, and going about with sackcloth round its loins, in testimony of continual sorrow and protest, and prophecy of God's vengeance upon such a course of things: either of these divine equipments would have saved us; and it is because we have neither of them that we are come to such a pass!

We may depend upon it, where there is a Pauper, there is a sin; to make one Pauper there go many sins. Pauperism is our Social Sin grown manifest; developed from the state of a spiritual ignobleness, a practical impropriety and base oblivion of duty, to an affair of the ledger. Here is not now an unheeded sin against God; here is a concrete ugly hulk of Beggary demanding that you should buy Indian meal for it. Men of reflection have long looked with a horror for which there was no response in the idle public, upon Pauperism; but the quantity of meal it demands has now awakened men of no reflection to consider it. Pauperism is the poisonous dripping from all the sins, and putrid unveracities and god-forgetting greedinesses and devil-serving cants and jesuitisms, that exist among us. Not one idle Sham lounging about

Creation upon false pretences, upon means which he has not earned, upon theories which he does not practise, but yields his share of Pauperism somewhere or other. His sham-work oozes down; finds at last its issue as human Pauperism,—in a human being that by those false pretences cannot live. The Idle Workhouse, now about to burst of overfilling, what is it but the scandalous poison-tank of drainage from the universal Stygian quagmire of our affairs? Workhouse Paupers; immortal sons of Adam rotted into that scandalous condition, subter-slavish, demanding that you would make slaves of them as an unattainable blessing! My friends, I perceive the quagmire must be drained, or we cannot live. And further, I perceive, this of Pauperism is the corner where we must *begin*, —the levels all pointing thitherward, the possibilities lying all clearly there. On that Problem we shall find that innumerable things, that all things whatsoever hang. By courageous steadfast persistence in that, I can foresee Society itself regenerated. In the course of long strenuous centuries, I can see the State become what it is actually bound to be, the keystone of a most real 'Organisation of Labour,'—and on this Earth a world of some veracity, and some heroism, once more worth living in!

The State in all European countries, and in England first of all, as I hope, will discover that its functions are now, and have long been, very wide of what the State in old pedant Downing Streets has aimed at; that the State is, for the present, not a reality but in great part a dramatic speciosity, expending its strength in practices and objects fallen many of them quite obsolete; that it must come a little nearer the true aim again, or it cannot continue in this world. The 'Champion of England' cased in iron or tin, and 'able to mount his horse with little assistance,'—this Champion and the thousandfold cousinry of Phantasms he has, nearly all dead now but still walking as ghosts, must positively take himself away: who can endure him, and his solemn trumpetings and obsolete gesticulations, in a Time that is full of deadly realities, coming open-mouthed upon us? At Drury Lane let him play his part, him and his thousandfold cousinry; and welcome, so long as any public will pay a shilling to see him: but on the solid earth, under the extremely earnest stars, we dare not palter with him, or accept his tomfooleries any more. Ridiculous they seem to some; horrible they seem to me: all lies, if one look whence they come and whither they go, are horrible.

Alas, it will be found, I doubt, that in England more than in any country, our Public Life and our Private, our State and our Religion, and all that we do and speak (and the most even of what we *think*), is a tissue of half-truths and whole-lies; of hypocrisies, conventionalisms, worn-out traditionary rags and cobwebs; such a life-garment of beggarly incredible and uncredited falsities as no honest souls of Adam's Posterity were ever enveloped in before. And we walk about in it with a stately gesture, as if it were some priestly stole or imperial mantle; not the foulest beggar's-gabardine that ever was. 'No Englishman dare believe the truth,' says one: 'he stands, for these two-hundred years, enveloped in lies of every kind; from nadir to zenith an ocean of traditionary cant surrounds him as his life-element. He really thinks the truth dangerous. Poor wretch, you see him everywhere endeavouring to temper the truth by taking the falsity along with it, and welding them together; this he calls "safe course," "moderate course," and other fine names; there, balanced between God and the Devil, he thinks he *can* serve two masters, and that things will go well with him.'

In the cotton-spinning and similar departments our English friend knows well that truth or God will have nothing to do with the Devil or falsehood, but will ravel all the web to pieces if you introduce the Devil or Non-veracity in any form into it: in this department, therefore, our English friend avoids falsehood. But in the religious, political, social, moral, and all other spiritual departments he freely introduces falsehood, nothing doubting; and has long done so, with a profuseness not elsewhere met with in the world. The unhappy creature, does he not know, then, that every lie is accursed, and the parent of mere curses? That he must *think* the truth; much more speak it? That, above all things, by the oldest law of Heaven and Earth which no man violates with impunity, he must not and shall not wag the tongue of him except to utter his thought? That there is not a grin or beautiful acceptable grimace he can execute upon his poor countenance, but is either an express veracity, the image of what passes within him; or else is a bit of Devil-worship which he and the rest of us will have to pay for yet? Alas, the grins he executes upon his poor *mind* (which is all tortured into St. Vitus dances, and ghastly merry-andrewisms, by the practice) are the most extraordinary this sun ever saw.

We have Puseyisms, black-and-white surplice controversies:—do not, officially and otherwise, the select of the longest heads in England sit with intense application and iron gravity, in open forum, judging of 'prevenient grace'? Not a head of them suspects that it can be improper so to sit, or of the nature of treason against the Power who gave an Intellect to man;—that it can be other than the duty of a good citizen to use his godgiven intellect in investigating prevenient grace, supervenient moonshine, or the colour of the Bishop's nightmare, if that happened to turn up. I consider them far ahead of Cicero's Roman Augurs with their chicken-bowels: "Behold these divine chicken-bowels, O Senate and Roman People; the midriff has fallen eastward!" solemnly intimates one Augur. "By Proserpina and the triple Hecate!" exclaims the other, "I say the midriff has fallen to the west!" And they look at one another with the seriousness of men prepared to die in their opinion,—the authentic seriousness of men betting at Tattersall's, or about to receive judgment in Chancery. There is in the Englishman something great, beyond all Roman greatness, in whatever line you meet him; even as a Latter-Day Augur he seeks his fellow!—Poor devil, I believe it is his intense love of peace, and hatred of breeding discussions which lead nowhither, that has led him into this sad practice of amalgamating true and false.

He has been at it these two-hundred years; and has now carried it to a terrible length. He couldn't follow Oliver Cromwell in the Puritan path heavenward, so steep was it, and beset with thorns,—and becoming uncertain withal. He much preferred, at that juncture, to go heavenward with his Charles Second and merry Nell Gwynns, and old decent formularies and good respectable aristocratic company, for escort; sore he tried, by glorious restorations, glorious revolutions and so forth, to perfect this desirable amalgam; hoped always it might be possible;—is only just now, if even now, beginning to give up the hope; and to see with wide-eyed horror that it is not at Heaven he is arriving, but at the Stygian marshes, with their thirty-thousand Needlewomen, cannibal Connaughts, rivers of lamentation, continual wail of infants, and the yellow-burning gleam of a Hell-on-Earth!—Bull, my friend, you must strip that astonishing pontiff-stole, imperial mantle, or whatever you imagine it to be, which I discern to be a garment of curses, and poisoned Nessus'-shirt now at last about to take fire upon you; you must strip that off your poor body, my friend; and, were it only in a soul's suit of Utilitarian buff, and such belief as that a big loaf is better than a small one, come forth into contact with your world, under *true* professions again, and not false. You wretched man, you ought to weep for half a century on discovering what lies you have believed, and what every lie leads to and proceeds from. O my friend, no honest fellow in this Planet was ever so served by his cooks before; or has eaten such quantities and qualities of dirt as you have been made to do, for these two centuries past. Arise, my horribly maltreated yet still beloved Bull; steep yourself in running water for a long while, my friend; and begin forthwith in every conceivable direction, physical and spiritual, the long-expected *Scavenger Age*.

Many doctors have you had, my poor friend; but I perceive it is the Water-Cure alone that will help you: a complete course of *scavengerism* is the thing you need! A new and veritable heart-divorce of England from the Babylonish woman, who is Jesuitism and Unveracity, and dwells not at Rome now, but under your own nose and everywhere; whom, and her foul worship of Phantasms and Devils, poor England *had* once divorced, with a divine heroism not forgotten yet, and well worth remembering now: a clearing-out of Church and State from the unblessed host of Phantasms which have too long nestled thick there, under those astonishing 'Defenders of the Faith,'—Defenders of the Hypocrisies, the spiritual Vampires and obscene Nightmares, under which England lies in syncope;—this is what you need; and if you cannot get it, you must die, my poor friend!

Like people, like priest. Priest, King, Home Office, all manner of establishments and offices among a people bear a striking resemblance to the people itself. It is because Bull has been eating so much dirt that his Home Offices have got into such a shockingly dirty condition,—the old pavements of them quite gone out of sight and out of memory, and nothing but mountains of long-accumulated dung in which the poor cattle are sprawling and tumbling. Had his own life been pure, had his own daily conduct been grounding itself on the clear pavements or actual beliefs and veracities, would he have let his Home Offices come to such a pass? Not in Downing Street only, but in all other thoroughfares and arenas and spiritual or physical departments of his existence, running water and Herculean scavengerism have become indispensable, unless the poor man is to choke in his own exuviæ, and die the sorrowfulest death.

If the State could once get back to the real sight of its

essential function, and with religious resolution begin doing that, and putting away its multifarious imaginary functions, and indignantly casting out these as mere dung and insalubrious horror and abomination (which they are), what a promise of reform were there! The British Home Office, surely this and its kindred Offices exist, if they will think of it, that life and work may continue possible, and may not become impossible, for British men. If honourable existence, or existence on human terms at all, have become impossible for millions of British men, how can the Home Office or any other Office long exist? With Thirty-thousand Needlewomen, a Connaught fallen into potential cannibalism, and the Idle Workhouse everywhere bursting, and declaring itself an *in*humanity and stupid ruinous brutality not much longer to be tolerated among rational human creatures, it is time the State were bethinking itself.

So soon as the State attacks that tremendous cloaca of Pauperism, which will choke the world if it be not attacked, the State will find its real functions very different indeed from what it had long supposed them! The State is a reality, and not a dramaturgy; it exists here to render existence possible, existence desirable and noble, for the State's subjects. The State, as it gets into the track of its real work, will find that same expand into whole continents of new unexpected, most blessed activity; as its dramatic functions, declared superfluous, more and more fall inert, and go rushing like huge torrents of extinct exuviæ, dung and rubbish, down to the Abyss forever. O Heaven, to see a State that knew a little why it was there, and on what ground, in this Year 1850, it could pretend to exist, in so extremely earnest a world as ours is growing! The British State, if it will be the crown and keystone of our British Social Existence, must get to recognise, with a veracity very long unknown to it, what the real objects and indispensable necessities of our Social Existence are. Good Heavens, it is not prevenient grace, or the colour of the Bishop's nightmare, that is pinching us; it is the impossibility to get along any farther for mountains of accumulated dung and falsity and horror; the total closing-up of noble aims from every man,—of any aim at all, from many men, except that of rotting-out in Idle Workhouses an existence below that of beasts!

Suppose the State to have fairly started its 'Industrial Regiments of the New Era,' which alas, are yet only beginning to be talked of,—what continents of new real work opened out, for the Home and all other Public Offices among us! Suppose the Home Office looking out, as for life and salvation, for proper men to command these 'Regiments.' Suppose the announcement were practically made to all British souls that the want of wants, more indispensable than any jewel in the crown, was that of men *able to command men* in ways of industrial and moral welldoing; that the State would give its very life for such men; that such men *were* the State; that the quantity of them to be found in England, lamentably small at present, was the exact measure of England's worth, —what a new dawn of everlasting day for all British souls! Noble British soul, to whom the gods have given faculty and heroism, what men call genius, here at last is a career for thee. It will not be needful now to swear fealty to the Incredible, and traitorously cramp thyself into a cowardly canting play-actor in God's Universe; or, solemnly forswearing that, into a mutinous rebel and waste bandit in thy generation: here is an aim that is clear and credible, a course fit for a man. No need to become a tormenting and self-tormenting mutineer, banded with rebellious souls, if thou wouldst live; no need to rot in suicidal idleness; or take to platform preaching, and writing in Radical Newspapers, to pull asunder the great Falsity in which thou and all of us are choking. The great Falsity, behold it has become, in the very heart of it, a great Truth of Truths; and invites thee and all brave men to coöperate with it in transforming all the body and the joints into the noble likeness of that heart! Thrice-blessed change. The State aims, once more, with a true aim; and has loadstars in the eternal Heaven. Struggle faithfully for it; noble is *this* struggle; thou too, according to thy faculty, shalt reap in due time, if thou faint not. Thou shalt have a wise command of men, thou shalt be wisely commanded by men,—the summary of all blessedness for a social creature here below. The sore struggle, never to be relaxed, and not forgiven to any son of man, is once more a noble one; glory to the Highest, it is now once more a true and noble one, wherein a man can afford to die! Our path is now again Heavenward. Forward, with steady pace, with drawn weapons, and unconquerable hearts, in the name of God that made us all!—

Wise obedience and wise command, I foresee that the regimenting of Pauper Banditti into Soldiers of Industry is but the beginning of this blessed process, which will extend to the topmost heights of our Society; and, in the course of generations, make us all once more a Governed Commonwealth, and *Civitas Dei*, if it please God! Waste-land Industrials succeeding, other kinds of Industry, as cloth-making, shoe-making, plough-making, spade-making, house-building,—in the end, all kinds of Industry whatsoever, will be found capable of regimenting. Mill-operatives, all manner of free operatives, as yet unregimented, nomadic under private masters, they, seeing such example and its blessedness, will say: "Masters, you must regiment us a little; make our interests with you permanent a little, instead of temporary and nomadic; we will enlist with the State otherwise!" This will go on, on the one hand, while the State-operation goes on, on the other: thus will all Masters of Workmen, private Captains of Industry, be forced to incessantly coöperate with the State and its public Captains; they regimenting in their way, the State in its way, with ever-widening field; till their fields *meet* (so to speak) and coalesce, and there be no unregimented worker, or such only as are fit to remain unregimented, any more.—O my friends, I clearly perceive this horrible cloaca of Pauperism, wearing nearly bottomless now, is the point where we must begin. Here, in this plainly unendurable portion of the general quagmire, the lowest point of all, and hateful even to M'Croudy, must our main drain begin: steadily prosecuting that, tearing that along with Herculean labour and divine fidelity, we shall gradually drain the entire Stygian swamp, and make it all once more a fruitful field!

For the State, I perceive, looking out with right sacred earnestness for persons able to command, will straightway also come upon the question: "What kind of schools and seminaries, and teaching and also preaching establishments have I, for the training of young souls to take command and to yield obedience? Wise command, wise obedience: the capability of these two is the net measure of culture, and human virtue, in every man; all good lies in the possession of these two capabilities; all evil, wretchedness and ill-success in the want of these. He is a good man that can command and obey; he that cannot is a bad. If my teachers and my preachers, with their seminaries, high schools and cathedrals, do train men to these gifts, the thing they are teaching and preaching must be true; if they do not, not true!"

The State, once brought to its veracities by the thumbscrew in this manner, what *will* it think of these same seminaries and cathedrals! I foresee that our Etons and Oxfords with their nonsense-verses, college-logics, and broken crumbs of mere *speech*,—which is not even English or Teutonic speech, but old Grecian and Italian speech, dead and buried and much lying out of our way these two thousand years last past,—will be found a most astonishing seminary for the training of young English souls to take command in human Industries, and act a valiant part under the sun! The State does not want vocables, but manly wisdoms and virtues: the State, does it want parliamentary orators, first of all, and men capable of writing books? What a ragfair of extinct monkeries, high-piled here in the very shrine of our existence, fit to smite the generations with atrophy and beggarly paralysis,—as we see it do! The Minister of Education will not want for work, I think, in the New Downing Street!

How it will go with Souls'-Overseers, and what the *new* kind will be, we do not prophesy just now. Clear it is, however, that the last finish of the State's efforts, in this operation of regimenting, will be to get the *true* Souls'-Overseers set over men's souls, to regiment, as the consummate flower of all, and constitute into some Sacred Corporation, bearing authority and dignity in their generation, the Chosen of the Wise, of the Spiritual and Devout-minded, the Reverent who deserve reverence, who are as the Salt of the Earth;—that not till this is done can the State consider its edifice to have reached the first story, to be safe for a moment, to be other than an arch without the keystones, and supported hitherto on mere wood. How will this be done? Ask not; let the second or the third generation after this begin to ask! Alas, wise men do exist, born duly into the world in every current generation; but the getting of *them* regimented is the highest pitch of human Polity, and the feat of all feats in political engineering:—impossible for us, in this poor age, as the building of St. Paul's would be for Canadian Beavers, acquainted only with the architecture of fish-dams, and with no trowel but their tail.

Literature, the strange entity so-called,—that indeed is here. If Literature continue to be the haven of expatriated spiritualisms, and have its Johnsons, Goethes and *true* Archbishops of the World, to show for itself as heretofore, there may be hope in Literature. If Literature dwindle, as is probable, into mere merry-andrewism, windy twaddle, and feats of spiritual legerdemain, analogous to rope-dancing, opera-dancing, and street-fiddling with a hat carried round for halfpence or for guineas, there will be no hope in Literature. What if our next set of Souls'-Overseers were to be *silent* ones very mainly?——Alas, alas, why gaze into the blessed continents and delectable mountains of a Future based on *truth*, while as yet we struggle far down, nigh suffocated in a slough of lies, uncertain whether or how we shall be able to climb at all!—

Who will begin the long steep journey with us; who of living statesmen will snatch the standard, and say, like a hero on the forlorn-hope for his country, Forward! Or is there none; no one that can and dare? And our lot, too, then, is Anarchy by barricade or ballot-box, and Social Death?—We will not think so.

Whether Sir Robert Peel will undertake the Reform of Downing Street for us, or any Ministry or Reform farther, is not known. He, they say, is getting old, does himself recoil from it, and shudder at it; which is possible enough. The clubs and coteries appear to have settled that he surely will not; and this melancholy wriggling seesaw of redtape Trojans and Protectionist Greeks must continue its course till—what *can* happen, my friends, if this go on continuing?

And yet, perhaps, England has by no means so settled it. Quit the clubs and coteries, you do not hear two rational men speak long together upon politics, without pointing their inquiries towards this man. A Minister that will attack the Augias Stable of Downing Street, and begin producing a real Management, no longer an imaginary one, of our affairs; *he*, or else in few years Chartist Parliament and the Deluge come: that seems the alternative. As I read the omens, there was no man in my time more authentically called to a post of difficulty, of danger, and of honour than this man. The enterprise is ready for him, if he is ready for it. He has but to lift his finger in this enterprise, and whatsoever is wise and manful in England will rally round him. If the faculty and heart for it be in him, he, strangely and almost tragically if we look upon his history, is to have leave to try it; he now, at the eleventh hour, has the opportunity for such a feat in reform as has not, in these late generations, been attempted by all our reformers put together.

As for Protectionist jargon, who in these earnest days would occupy many moments of his time with that? 'A Costermonger in this street,' says Crabbe, 'finding lately that his rope of onions, which he hoped would have brought a shilling, was to go for only sevenpence henceforth, burst forth into lamentation, execration and the most pathetic tears. Throwing up the window, I perceived the other costermongers preparing impatiently to pack this one out of their company as a disgrace to it, if he would not hold his peace and take the market rate for his onions. I looked better at this Costermonger. To my astonished imagination, a star-and-garter dawned upon the dim figure of the man; and I perceived that here was no Costermonger to be expelled with ignominy, but a sublime goddess-born Ducal Individual, whom I forbear to name at this moment! What an omen; —nay, to my astonished imagination, there dawned still fataler omens. Surely, of all human trades ever heard of, the trade of Owning Land in England ought *not* to bully us for drink-money just now!'

'Hansard's Debates,' continues Crabbe farther on, 'present many inconsistencies of speech; lamentable unveracities uttered in Parliament, by one and indeed by all; in which sad list Sir Robert Peel stands for his share among others. Unveracities not a few were spoken in Parliament; in fact, to one with a sense of what is called God's truth, it seemed all one unveracity, a talking from the teeth outward, not as the convictions but as the expediencies and inward astucities directed; and, in the sense of God's *truth*, I have heard no true word uttered in Parliament at all. Most lamentable unveracities continually *spoken* in Parliament, by almost every one that had to open his mouth there. But the largest veracity ever *done* in Parliament in our time, as we all know, was of this man's doing;—and that, you will find, is a very considerable item in the calculation!'

Yes, and I believe England in her dumb way remembers that too. And 'the Traitor Peel' can very well afford to let innumerable Ducal Costermongers, parliamentary Adventurers, and lineal representatives of the Impenitent Thief, say all their say about him, and do all their do. With a virtual England at his back, and an actual eternal sky above him, there is not much in the total net-amount of that. When the master of the horse rides abroad, many dogs in the village bark; but he pursues his journey all the same.

No. V.

STUMP-ORATOR

[1st May 1850.]

It lies deep in our habits, confirmed by all manner of educational and other arrangements for several centuries back, to consider human talent as best of all evincing itself by the faculty of eloquent speech. Our earliest schoolmasters teach us, as the one gift of culture they have, the art of spelling and pronouncing, the rules of correct speech; rhetorics, logics follow, sublime mysteries of grammar, whereby we may not only speak but write. And onward to the last of our schoolmasters in the highest university, it is still intrinsically grammar, under various figures grammar. To speak in various languages, on various things, but on all of them to speak, and appropriately deliver ourselves by tongue or pen,—this is the sublime goal towards which all manner of beneficent preceptors and learned professors, from the lowest hornbook upwards, are continually urging and guiding us. Preceptor or professor, looking over his miraculous seedplot, seminary as he well calls it, or crop of young human souls, watches with attentive view one organ of his delightful little seedlings growing to be men,—the tongue. He hopes we shall all get to speak yet, if it please Heaven. "Some of you shall be book-writers, eloquent review-writers, and astonish mankind, my young friends: others in white neckcloths shall do sermons by Blair and Lindley Murray, nay, by Jeremy Taylor and judicious Hooker, and be priests to guide men heavenward by skilfully brandished handkerchief and the torch of rhetoric. For others there is Parliament and the election beerbarrel, and a course that leads men very high indeed;

these shall shake the senate-house, the Morning Newspapers, shake the very spheres, and by dextrous wagging of the tongue disenthral mankind, and lead our afflicted country and us on the way we are to go. The way if not where noble deeds are done, yet where noble words are spoken,—leading us if not to the real Home of the Gods, at least to something which shall more or less deceptively resemble it!"

So fares it with the son of Adam, in these bewildered epochs; so, from the first opening of his eyes in this world, to his last closing of them, and departure hence. Speak, speak, O speak;—if thou have any faculty, speak it, or thou diest and it is no faculty! So in universities, and all manner of dames' and other schools, of the very highest class as of the very lowest; and Society at large, when we enter there, confirms with all its brilliant review-articles, successful publications, intellectual tea-circles, literary gazettes, parliamentary eloquences, the grand lesson we had. Other lesson in fact we have none, in these times. If there be a human talent, let it get into the tongue, and make melody with that organ. The talent that can say nothing for itself, what is it? Nothing; or a thing that can do mere drudgeries, and at best make money by railways.

All this is deep-rooted in our habits, in our social, educational and other arrangements; and all this, when we look at it impartially, is astonishing. Directly in the teeth of all this it may be asserted that speaking is by no means the chief faculty a human being can attain to; that his excellence therein is by no means the best test of his general human excellence, or availability in this world; nay, that, unless we look well, it is liable to become the very worst test ever devised for said availability. The matter extends very far, down to the very roots of the world, whither the British reader cannot conveniently follow me just now; but I will venture to assert the three following things, and invite him to consider well what truth he can gradually find in them:

First, that excellent speech, even speech *really* excellent, is not, and never was, the chief test of human faculty, or the measure of a man's ability, for any true function whatsoever; on the contrary, that excellent *silence* needed always to accompany excellent speech, and was and is a much rarer and more difficult gift.

Secondly, that really excellent speech,—which I, being possessed of the Hebrew Bible or Book, as well as of other books in my own and foreign languages, and having occasionally heard a wise man's word among the crowd of unwise, do almost unspeakably esteem, as a human gift,—is terribly apt to get confounded with its counterfeit, sham-excellent speech! And furthermore, that if really excellent human speech is among the best of human things, then sham-excellent ditto deserves to be ranked with the very worst. False speech,—capable of becoming, as some one has said, the falsest and basest of all human things:—put the case, one were listening to *that* as to the truest and noblest! Which, little as we are conscious of it, I take to be the sad lot of many excellent souls among us just now. So many as admire parliamentary eloquence, divine popular literature, and suchlike, are dreadfully liable to it just now: and whole nations and generations seem as if getting themselves *asphyxiaed*, constitutionally, into their last sleep, by means of it just now!

For alas, much as we worship speech on all hands, here is a *third* assertion which a man may venture to make, and invite considerate men to reflect upon: That in these times, and for several generations back, there has been, strictly considered, no really excellent speech at all, but sham-excellent merely; that is to say, false or quasi-false speech getting itself admired and worshipped, instead of detested and suppressed. A truly alarming predicament; and not the less so if we find it a quite pleasant one for the time being, and welcome the advent of *asphyxia*, as we would that of comfortable natural sleep;—as, in so many senses, we are doing! Surly judges there have been who did not much admire the 'Bible of Modern Literature,' or anything you could distil from it, in contrast with the ancient Bibles; and found that in the matter of speaking, our far best excellence, where that could be obtained, was excellent silence, which means endurance and exertion, and good *work* with lips closed; and that our tolerablest speech was of the nature of honest commonplace introduced where indispensable, which only set-up for being brief and true, and could not be mistaken for excellent.

These are hard sayings for many a British reader, unconscious of any damage, nay, joyfully conscious to himself of much profit, from that side of his possessions. Surely on this side, if on no other, matters stood not ill with him? The ingenuous arts had softened his manners; the parliamentary eloquences supplied him with a succedaneum for government, the popular literatures with the finer sensibilities of the heart: surely on this *wind*ward side of things the British reader was not ill off?—Unhappy British reader!

In fact, the spiritual detriment we unconsciously suffer, in every province of our affairs, from this our prostrate respect to power of speech is incalculable. For indeed it is the natural consummation of an epoch such as ours. Given a general insincerity of mind for several generations, you will certainly find the Talker established in the place of honour; and the Doer, hidden in the obscure crowd, with activity lamed, or working sorrowfully forward on paths unworthy of him. All men are devoutly prostrate, worshipping the eloquent talker; and no man knows what a scandalous idol he is. Out of whom in the mildest manner, like comfortable natural rest, comes mere asphyxia and death everlasting! Probably there is not in Nature a more distracted phantasm than your commonplace eloquent speaker, as he is found on platforms, in parliaments, on Kentucky stumps, at tavern-dinners, in windy, empty, insincere times like ours. The 'excellent Stump-Orator,' as our admiring Yankee friends define him, he who in any occurrent set of circumstances can start forth, mount upon his 'stump,' his rostrum, tribune, place in parliament, or other ready elevation, and pour forth from him his appropriate 'excellent speech,' his interpretation of the said circumstances, in such manner as poor windy mortals round him shall cry bravo to,—he is not an artist I can much admire, as matters go! Alas, he is in general merely the windiest mortal of them all; and is admired for being so, into the bargain. Not a windy blockhead there who kept silent but is better off than this excellent stump-orator. Better off, for a great many reasons; for this reason, were there no other: the silent one is *not* admired; the silent suspects, perhaps partly admits, that he is a kind of blockhead, from which salutary self-knowledge the excellent stump-orator is debarred. A mouthpiece of Chaos to poor benighted mortals that lend ear to him as to a voice from Cosmos, this excellent stump-orator fills me with amazement. Not empty these musical wind-utterances of his; they are big with prophecy; they announce, too audibly to me, that the end of many things is drawing nigh!

Let the British reader consider it a little; he too is not a little interested in it. Nay, he, and the European reader in general, but he chiefly in these days, will require to consider it a great deal,—and to take important steps in consequence by and by, if I mistake not. And in the mean while, sunk as he himself is in that bad element, and like a jaundiced man struggling to discriminate yellow colours,—he will have to meditate long before he in any measure get the immense meanings of the thing brought home to him; and discern, with astonishment, alarm, and almost terror and despair, towards what fatal issues, in our Collective Wisdom and elsewhere, this notion of talent meaning eloquent speech, so obstinately entertained this long while, has been leading us! Whosoever shall look well into origins and issues, will find this of eloquence and the part it now plays in our affairs, to be one of the gravest phenomena; and the excellent stump-orator of these days to be not only a ridiculous but still more a highly tragical personage. While the many listen to him, the few are used to pass rapidly, with some gust of scornful laughter, some growl of impatient malediction; but he deserves from this latter class a much more serious attention.

In the old Ages, when Universities and Schools were first instituted, this function of the schoolmaster, to teach mere speaking, was the natural one. In those healthy times, guided by silent instincts and the monition of Nature, men had from of old been used to teach themselves what it was essential to learn, by the one sure method of learning anything, practical apprenticeship to it. This was the rule for all classes; as it now is the rule, unluckily, for only one class. The Working Man as yet sought only to know his craft; and educated himself sufficiently by ploughing and hammering, under the conditions given, and in fit relation to the persons given: a course of education, then as now and ever, really opulent in manful culture and instruction to him; teaching him many solid virtues, and most indubitably useful knowledges; developing in him valuable faculties not a few both to do and to endure,—among which the faculty of elaborate grammatical utterance, seeing he had so little of extraordinary to utter, or to learn from spoken or written utterances, was not bargained for; the grammar of Nature, which he learned from his mother, being still amply sufficient for him. This was, as it still is, the grand education of the Working Man.

As for the Priest, though his trade was clearly of a reading and speaking nature, he knew also in those veracious times that grammar, if needful, was by no means the one thing needful, or the chief thing. By far the chief thing needful, and indeed the one thing then as now, was, That there should be in him the feeling and the practice of reverence to God and to men; that in his life's core there should dwell, spoken or silent, a ray of pious wisdom fit for illuminating dark human destinies;—not so much that he should possess the art of speech, as that he should have something to speak! And for that latter requisite the Priest also trained himself by apprenticeship, by actual attempt to practise, by manifold long-continued trial, of a devout and painful nature, such as his superiors prescribed to him. This, when once judged satisfactory, procured him ordination; and his grammar-learning, in the good times of priesthood, was very much of a parergon with him, as indeed in all times it is intrinsically quite insignificant in comparison.

The young Noble again, for whom grammar schoolmasters were first hired and high seminaries founded, he too without these, or over and above these, had from immemorial time been used to learn his business by apprenticeship. The young Noble, before the schoolmaster as after him, went apprentice to some elder noble; entered himself as page with some distinguished earl or duke; and here, serving upwards from step to step, under wise monition, learned his chivalries, his practice of arms and of courtesies, his baronial duties and manners, and what it would beseem him to do and to be in the world,—by practical attempt of his own, and example of one whose life was a daily concrete pattern for him. To such a one, already filled with intellectual substance, and possessing what we may call the practical gold-bullion of human culture, it was an obvious improvement that he should be taught to speak it out of him on occasion; that he should carry a spiritual banknote producible on demand for what of 'gold-bullion' he had, not so negotiable otherwise, stored in the cellars of his mind. A man, with wisdom, insight and heroic worth already acquired for him, naturally demanded of the schoolmaster this one new faculty, the faculty of uttering in fit words what he had. A valuable super-addition of faculty:—and yet we are to remember it was scarcely a new faculty; it was but the tangible sign of what other faculties the man had in the silent state: and many a rugged inarticulate chief of men, I can believe, was most enviably 'educated,' who had not a Book on his premises; whose signature, a true sign-*manual*, was the stamp of his iron hand duly inked and clapt upon the parchment; and whose speech in Parliament, like the growl of lions, did indeed convey his meaning, but would have torn Lindley Murray's nerves to pieces! To such a one the schoolmaster adjusted himself very naturally in that manner; as a man wanted for teaching grammatical utterance; the thing to utter being already there. The thing to utter, here was the grand point! And perhaps this is the reason why among earnest nations, as among the Romans for example, the craft of the schoolmaster was held in little regard; for indeed as mere teacher of grammar, of ciphering on the abacus and suchlike, how did he differ much from the dancing-master or fencing-master, or deserve much regard?—Such was the rule in the ancient healthy times.

Can it be doubtful that this is still the rule of human education; that the human creature needs first of all to be educated not that he may speak, but that he may have something weighty and valuable to say! If speech is the banknote for an inward capital of culture, of insight and noble human worth, then speech is precious, and the art of speech shall be honoured. But if there *is* no inward capital; if speech represent no real culture of the mind, but an imaginary culture; no bullion, but the fatal and now almost hopeless deficit of such? Alas, alas, said banknote is then a *forged* one; passing freely current in the market; but bringing damages to the receiver, to the payer, and to all the world, which are in sad truth infallible, and of amount incalculable. Few think of it at present; but the truth remains forever so. In parliaments and other loud assemblages, your eloquent talk, *dis*united from Nature and her facts, is taken as wisdom and the correct image of said facts: but Nature well knows what it is, Nature will not have it as such, and will reject your forged note one day, with huge costs. The foolish traders in the market pass it freely, nothing doubting, and rejoice in the dextrous execution of the piece: and so it circulates from hand to hand, and from class to class; gravitating ever downwards towards the *practical* class; till at last it reaches some poor *working* hand, who can pass it no farther, but must take it to the bank to get bread with it, and there the answer is, "Unhappy caitiff, this note is forged. It does not mean performance and reality, in parliaments and elsewhere, for thy behoof; it means fallacious semblance of performance; and thou, poor dupe, art thrown into the stocks on offering it here!"

Alas, alas, looking abroad over Irish difficulties, Mosaic sweating-establishments, French barricades, and an anarchic Europe, is it not as if all the populations of the world were rising or had risen into incendiary madness; unable longer to endure such an avalanche of forgeries, and of penalties in consequence, as had accumulated upon them? The speaker is 'excellent'; the notes he does are beautiful? Beautifully fit for the market, yes; *he* is an excellent artist in his business;—and the more excellent he is, the more is my desire to lay him by the heels, and fling *him* into the treadmill, that I might save the poor sweating tailors, French Sansculottes, and Irish Sanspotatoes from bearing the smart!

For the smart must be borne; some one must bear it, as sure as God lives. Every word of man is either a note or a forged-note:—have these eternal skies forgotten to be in earnest, think you, because men go grinning like enchanted apes? Foolish souls, this now as of old is the unalterable law of your existence. If you know the truth and do it, the Universe itself seconds you, bears you on to sure victory everywhere:—and, observe, to sure defeat everywhere if you do *not* do the truth. And alas, if you *know* only the eloquent fallacious semblance of the truth, what chance is there of your ever doing it? You will do something very different from *it*, I think!—He who well considers, will find this same 'art of speech,' as we moderns have it, to be a truly astonishing product of the Ages; and the longer he considers it, the more astonishing and alarming. I reckon it the saddest of all the curses that now lie heavy on us. With horror and amazement, one perceives that this much-celebrated 'art,' so diligently practised in all corners of the world just now, is the chief destroyer of whatever good is born to us (softly, swiftly shutting-up all nascent good, as if under exhausted glass-receivers, there to choke and die); and the grand parent-manufactory of evil to us,—as it were, the last finishing and varnishing workshop of all the Devil's ware that circulates under the sun. No Devil's sham is fit for the market till it have been polished and enamelled here; this is the general assaying-house for such, where the artists examine and answer, "Fit for the market; not fit!" Words will not express what mischiefs the misuse of words has done, and is doing, in these heavyladen generations.

Do you want a man *not* to practise what he believes, then encourage him to keep often speaking it in words. Every time he speaks it, the tendency to do it will grow less. His empty speech of what he believes, will be a weariness and an affliction to the wise man. But do you wish his empty speech of what he believes to become farther an insincere speech of what he does not believe? Celebrate to him his gift of speech; assure him that he shall rise in Parliament by means of it, and achieve great things without any performance; that eloquent speech, whether performed or not, is admirable. My friends, eloquent unperformed speech, in Parliament or elsewhere, is horrible! The eloquent man that delivers, in Parliament or elsewhere, a beautiful speech, and will perform nothing of it, but leaves it as if already performed,—what can you make of that man? He has enrolled himself among the *Ignes Fatui* and Children of the Wind; means to serve, as beautifully illuminated Chinese Lantern, in that corps henceforth. I think, the serviceable thing you could do to that man, if permissible, would be a severe one: To *clip-off* a bit of his eloquent tongue by way of penance and warning; another bit, if he again spoke without performing; and so again, till you had clipt the whole tongue away from him,—and were delivered, you and he, from at least one miserable mockery: "There, eloquent friend, see now in silence if there be any redeeming deed in thee; of blasphemous wind-eloquence, at least, we shall have no more!" How many pretty men have gone this road, escorted by the beautifulest marching music from all the 'public organs'; and have found at last that it ended—where? It is the *broad* road, that leads direct to Limbo and the Kingdom of the Inane. Gifted men, and once valiant nations, and as it were the whole world with one accord, are marching thither, in melodious triumph, all the drums and hautboys giving out their cheerfulest *Ça-ira*. It is the universal humour of the world just now. My friends, I am very sure you will *arrive*, unless you halt!—

Considered as the last finish of education, or of human culture, worth and acquirement, the art of speech is noble, and even divine; it is like the kindling of a Heaven's light to *show* us what a glorious world exists, and has perfected itself, in a man. But if no world exist in the man; if nothing but continents of empty vapour, of greedy self-conceits, commonplace hearsays, and indistinct loomings of a sordid *chaos* exist in him, what will be the use of 'light' to show us that? Better a thousand times that such a man do not speak; but keep his empty vapour and his sordid chaos to himself, hidden to the utmost from all beholders. To look on that, can be good for no human beholder; to look away from that, must be good. And if, by delusive semblances of rhetoric, logic, first-class degrees, and the aid of elocution-masters and parliamentary reporters, the poor proprietor of said chaos should be led to persuade himself, and get others persuaded,—which it is the nature of his sad task to do, and which, in certain eras of the world, it is fatally possible to do,—that this is a *cosmos* which he owns; that *he*, being so perfect in tongue-exercise and full of college-honours, is an 'educated' man, and pearl of great price in his generation; that round him, and his parliament emulously listening to him, as round some divine apple of gold set in a picture of silver, all the world should gather to adore: what is likely to become of him and the gathering world? An apple of Sodom set in the clusters of Gomorrah: that, little as he suspects it, is the definition of the poor chaotically eloquent man, with his emulous parliament and miserable adoring world!—Considered as the whole of education, or human culture, which it now is in our modern manners; all apprenticeship except to mere handicraft having fallen obsolete, and the 'educated man' being with us emphatically and exclusively the man that can speak well with tongue or pen, and astonish men by the quantities of speech he has *heard* ('tremendous *reader*,' 'walking encyclopædia,' and suchlike),—the Art of Speech is probably definable in that case as the short summary of all the Black Arts put together.

But the Schoolmaster is secondary, an effect rather than a cause in this matter: what the Schoolmaster with his universities shall manage or attempt to teach will be ruled by what the Society with its practical industries is continually demanding that men should learn. We spoke once of vital *lungs* for Society: and in fact this question always rises as the alpha and omega of social questions, What methods the Society has of summoning aloft into the high places, for its help and governance, the wisdom that is born to it in all places, and of course is born chiefly in the more populous or lower places? For this, if you will consider it, expresses the ultimate available result, and net sum-total, of all the efforts, struggles and confused activities that go on in the Society; and determines whether they are true and wise efforts, certain to be victorious, or false and foolish, certain to be futile, and to fall captive and caitiff. How do men rise in your Society? In all Societies, Turkey included, and I suppose Dahomey included, men do rise; but the question of questions always is, What kind of men? Men of noble gifts, or men of ignoble? It is the one or the other; and a life-and-death inquiry which! For in all places and all times, little as you may heed it, Nature most silently but most inexorably demands that it be the one and *not* the other. And you need not try to palm an ignoble sham upon her, and call it noble; for she is a judge. And her penalties, as quiet as she looks, are terrible; amounting to world-earthquakes, to anarchy and death everlasting; and admit of no appeal!—

Surely England still flatters herself that she has *lungs*; that she can still breathe a little? Or is it that the poor creature, driven into mere blind industrialisms; and as it were, gone pearl-diving this long while many fathoms deep, and tearing-up the oyster-beds so as never creature did before, hardly knows,—so busy in the belly of the oyster-chaos, where is no thought of 'breathing,'—whether she has lungs or not? Nations of a robust habit, and fine deep chest, can sometimes take-in a deal of breath *before* diving; and live long, in the muddy deeps, without new breath: but they too come to need it at last, and will die if they cannot get it!

To the gifted soul that is born in England, what is the career, then, that will carry him, amid noble Olympic dust, up to the immortal gods? For his country's sake, that it may not lose the service he was born capable of doing it; for his own sake, that his life be not choked and perverted, and his light from Heaven be not changed into lightning from the Other Place,—it is essential that there be such a career. The country that can offer no career in that case, is a doomed country; nay, it is already a dead country: it has secured the ban of Heaven upon it; will not have Heaven's light, will have the Other Place's lightning; and may consider itself as appointed to expire, in frightful coughings of street musketry or otherwise, on a set day, and to be in the eye of law dead. In no country is there not some career, inviting to it either the noble Hero, or the tough Greek of the Lower Empire: which of the two do your careers invite? There is no question more important. The kind of careers you offer in countries still living, determines with perfect exactness the kind of the life that is in them,—whether it is natural blessed life, or galvanic accursed ditto, and likewise what degree of strength is in the same.

Our English careers to born genius are twofold. There is the silent or unlearned career of the Industrialisms, which are very many among us; and there is the articulate or learned career of the three professions, Medicine, Law (under which we may include Politics), and the Church. Your born genius, therefore, will first have to ask himself, Whether he can hold his tongue or cannot? True, all human talent, especially all deep talent, is a talent to *do*, and is intrinsically of silent nature; inaudible, like the Sphere Harmonies and Eternal Melodies, of which it is an incarnated fraction. All real talent, I fancy, would much rather, if it listened only to Nature's monitions, express itself in rhythmic facts than in melodious words, which latter at best, where they are good for anything, are only a feeble echo and shadow or foreshadow of the former. But talents differ much in this of power to be silent; and circumstances, of position, opportunity and suchlike, modify them still more;—and Nature's monitions, oftenest quite drowned in foreign hearsays, are by no means the only ones listened to in deciding!—The Industrialisms are all of silent nature; and some of them are heroic and eminently human; others, again, we may call unheroic, not eminently human: *beaverish* rather, but still honest; some are even *vulpine*, altogether inhuman and dishonest. Your born genius must make his choice.

If a soul is born with divine intelligence, and has its lips touched with hallowed fire, in consecration for high enterprises under the sun, this young soul will find the question asked of him by England every hour and moment: "Canst thou turn thy human intelligence into the beaver sort, and make honest contrivance, and accumulation of capital by it? If so, do it; and avoid the vulpine kind, which I don't recommend. Honest triumphs in engineering and machinery await thee;

scrip awaits thee, commercial successes, kingship in the counting-room, on the stock-exchange;—thou shalt be the envy of surrounding flunkies, and collect into a heap more gold than a dray-horse can draw."—"Gold, so much gold?" answers the ingenuous soul, with visions of the envy of surrounding flunkies dawning on him; and in very many cases decides that he will contract himself into beaverism, and with such a horse-draught of gold, emblem of a never-imagined success in beaver heroism, strike the surrounding flunkies yellow.

This is our common course; this is in some sort open to every creature, what we call the beaver career; perhaps more open in England, taking in America too, than it ever was in any country before. And, truly, good consequences follow out of it: who can be blind to them? Half of a most excellent and opulent result is realised to us in this way; baleful only when it sets-up (as too often now) for being the whole result. A half-result which will be blessed and heavenly so soon as the other half is had,—namely, wisdom to guide the first half. Let us honour all honest human power of contrivance in its degree. The beaver intellect, so long as it stedfastly refuses to be vulpine, and answers the tempter pointing out short routes to it with an honest "No, no," is truly respectable to me; and many a highflying speaker and singer whom I have known, has appeared to me much less of a developed man than certain of my mill-owning, agricultural, commercial, mechanical, or otherwise industrial friends, who have held their peace all their days and gone on in the silent state. If a man *can* keep his intellect silent, and make it even into honest beaverism, several very manful moralities, in danger of wreck on other courses, may comport well with that, and give it a genuine and partly human character; and I will tell him, in these days he may do far worse with himself and his intellect than change it into beaverism, and make honest money with it. If indeed he could become a *heroic* industrial, and have a life 'eminently human'! But that is not easy at present. Probably some ninety-nine out of every hundred of our gifted souls, who have to seek a career for themselves, go this beaver road. Whereby the first half-result, national wealth namely, is plentifully realised; and only the second half, or wisdom to guide it, is dreadfully behindhand.

But now if the gifted soul be not of taciturn nature, be of vivid, impatient, rapidly-productive nature, and aspire much to give itself sensible utterance,—I find that, in this case, the field it has in England is narrow to an extreme; is perhaps narrower than ever offered itself, for the like object, in this world before. Parliament, Church, Law: let the young vivid soul turn whither he will for a career, he finds among variable conditions one condition invariable, and extremely surprising, That the proof of excellence is to be done by the tongue. For heroism that will not speak, but only act, there is no account kept:—The English Nation does not need that silent kind, then, but only the talking kind? Most astonishing. Of all the organs a man has, there is none held in account, it would appear, but the tongue he uses for talking. Premiership, woolsack, mitre, and quasi-crown: all is attainable if you can talk with due ability. Everywhere your proof-shot is to be a well-fired volley of talk. Contrive to talk well, you will get to Heaven, the modern Heaven of the English. Do not talk well, only work well, and heroically hold your peace, you have no chance whatever to get thither; with your utmost industry you may get to Threadneedle Street, and accumulate more gold than a drayhorse can draw. Is not this a very wonderful arrangement?

I have heard of races done by mortals tied in sacks; of human competitors, high aspirants, climbing heavenward on the soaped pole; seizing the soaped pig; and clutching with deft fist, at full gallop, the fated goose tied aloft by its foot; —which feats do prove agility, toughness and other useful faculties in man: but this of dextrous talk is probably as strange a competition as any. And the question rises, Whether certain of these other feats, or perhaps an alternation of all of them, relieved now and then by a bout of grinning through the collar, might not be profitably substituted for the solitary proof-feat of talk, now getting rather monotonous by its long continuance? Alas, Mr. Bull, I do find it is all little other than a proof of toughness, which is a quality I respect, with more or less expenditure of falsity and astucity superadded, which I entirely condemn. Toughness *plus* astucity:—perhaps a simple wooden mast set up in Palace-Yard, well soaped and duly presided over, might be the honester method? Such a method as this by trial of talk, for filling your chief offices in Church and State, was perhaps never heard of in the solar system before. You are quite used to it, my poor friend; and nearly dead by the consequences of it: but in the other Planets, as in other epochs of your own Planet it would have done had you proposed it, the thing awakens incredulous amazement, world-wide Olympic laughter, which ends in tempestuous hootings, in tears and horror! My friend, if you can, as heretofore this good while, find nobody to take care of your affairs but the expertest talker, it is all over with your affairs and you. Talk never yet could guide any man's or nation's affairs; nor will it yours, except towards the *Limbus Patrum*, where all talk, except a very select kind of it, lodges at last.

Medicine, guarded too by preliminary impediments, and frightful medusa-heads of quackery, which deter many generous souls from entering, is of the *half*-articulate professions, and does not much invite the ardent kinds of ambition. The intellect required for medicine might be wholly human, and indeed should by all rules be,—the profession of the Human Healer being radically a sacred one and connected with the highest priesthoods, or rather being itself the outcome and acme of all priesthoods, and divinest conquests of intellect here below. As will appear one day, when men take off their old monastic and ecclesiastic spectacles, and look with eyes again! In essence the Physician's task is always heroic, eminently human: but in practice most unluckily at present we find it too become in good part *beaverish*; yielding a money-result alone. And what of it is not beaverish,—does not that too go mainly to ingenious talking, publishing of yourself, ingratiating of yourself; a partly human exercise or waste of intellect, and, alas, a partly vulpine ditto;—making the once sacred Ἰατρὸς, or Human Healer, more impossible for us than ever!

Angry basilisks watch at the gates of Law and Church just now; and strike a sad damp into the nobler of the young aspirants. Hard bonds are offered you to sign; as it were, a solemn engagement to constitute yourself an impostor, before ever entering; to declare your belief in incredibilities, —your determination, in short, to take Chaos for Cosmos, and Satan for the Lord of things, if he come with money in his pockets, and horsehair and bombazeen decently wrapped about him. Fatal preliminaries, which deter many an ingenuous young soul, and send him back from the threshold, and I hope will deter ever more. But if you do enter, the condition is well known: "Talk; who can talk best here? His shall be the mouth of gold, and the purse of gold; and with my μίτρα (once the head-dress of unfortunate-females, I am told) shall his sacred temples be begirt."

Ingenuous souls, unless forced to it, do now much shudder at the threshold of both these careers, and not a few desperately turn back into the wilderness rather, to front a very rude fortune, and be devoured by wild-beasts as is likeliest. But as to Parliament, again, and its eligibility if attainable, there is yet no question anywhere; the ingenuous soul, if possessed of money-capital enough, is predestined by the parental and all manner of monitors to that career of talk; and accepts it with alacrity and clearness of heart, doubtful only whether he shall be *able* to make a speech. Courage, my brave young fellow. If you can climb a soaped pole of any kind, you will certainly be able to make a speech. All mortals have a tongue; and carry on some jumble, if not of thought, yet of stuff which they could talk. The weakest of animals has got a cry in it, and can give voice before dying. If you are tough enough, bent upon it desperately enough, I engage you shall make a speech:—but whether that will be the way to Heaven for you, I do not engage.

These, then, are our two careers for genius: mute Industrialism, which can seldom become very human, but remains beaverish mainly: and the three Professions named learned, —that is to say, able to talk. For the heroic or higher kinds of human intellect, in the silent state, there is not the smallest inquiry anywhere; apparently a thing not wanted in this country at present. What the supply may be, I cannot inform M'Croudy; but the market-demand, he may himself see, is *nil*. These are our three professions that require human intellect in part or whole, not able to do with mere beaverish; and such a part does the gift of talk play in one and all of them. Whatsoever is not beaverish seems to go forth in the shape of talk. To such length is human intellect wasted or suppressed in this world!

If the young aspirant is not rich enough for Parliament, and is deterred by the basilisks or otherwise from entering on Law or Church, and cannot altogether reduce his human intellect to the beaverish condition, or satisfy himself with the prospect of making money,—what becomes of him in such case, which is naturally the case of very many, and ever of more? In such case there remains but one outlet for him, and notably enough that too is a talking one: the outlet of Literature, of trying to write Books. Since, owing to preliminary basilisks, want of cash, or superiority to cash, he cannot mount aloft by eloquent talking, let him try it by dextrous eloquent writing. Here happily, having three fingers, and capital to buy a quire of paper, he can try it to all lengths and in spite of all mortals: in this career there is happily no public impediment that can turn him back; nothing but private starvation,—which is itself a *finis* or kind of goal,—can pretend to hinder a British man from prosecuting Literature to the very utmost, and wringing the final secret from her: "A talent is in thee; No talent is in thee." To the British subject who fancies genius may be lodged in him, this liberty remains; and truly it is, if well computed, almost the only one he has.

A crowded portal this of Literature, accordingly! The haven of expatriated spiritualisms, and, alas, also of expatriated vanities and prurient imbecilities: here do the windy aspirations, foiled activities, foolish ambitions, and frustrate human energies reduced to the vocable condition, fly as to the one refuge left; and the Republic of Letters increases in population at a faster rate than even the Republic of America. The strangest regiment in her Majesty's service, this of the Soldiers of Literature:—would your Lordship much like to march through Coventry with them? The immortal gods are there (quite irrecognisable under these disguises), and also the lowest broken valets;—an extremely miscellaneous regiment. In fact the regiment, superficially viewed, looks like an immeasurable motley flood of discharged playactors, funambulists, false prophets, drunken ballad-singers; and marches not as a regiment, but as a boundless canaille,—without drill, uniform, captaincy or billet; with huge *over*-proportion of drummers; you would say, a regiment gone wholly to the drum, with hardly a good musket to be seen in it,—more a canaille than a regiment. Canaille of all the loud-sounding levities, and general winnowings of Chaos, marching through the world in a most ominous manner; proclaiming, audibly if you have ears: "Twelfth hour of the Night; ancient graves yawning; pale clammy Puseyisms screeching in their winding-sheets; owls busy in the City regions; many goblins abroad! Awake, ye living; dream no more; arise to judgment! Chaos and Gehenna are broken loose; the Devil with his Bedlams must be flung in chains again, and the Last of the Days is about to dawn!" Such is Literature to the reflective soul at this moment.

But what now concerns us most is the circumstance that here too the demand is, Vocables, still vocables. In all appointed courses of activity and paved careers for human genius, and in this unpaved, unappointed, broadest career of Literature, broad way that leadeth to destruction for so many, the one duty laid upon you is still, Talk, talk. Talk well with pen or tongue, and it shall be well with you; do not talk well, it shall be ill with you. To wag the tongue with dextrous acceptability, there is for human worth and faculty, in our England of the Nineteenth Century, that one method of emergence and no other. Silence, you would say, means annihilation for the Englishman of the Nineteenth Century. The worth that has not spoken itself, is not; or is potentially only, and as if it were not. Vox is the God of this Universe. If you have human intellect, it avails nothing unless you either make it into beaverism, or talk with it. Make it into beaverism, and gather money; or else make talk with it, and gather what you can. Such is everywhere the demand for talk among us; to which, of course, the supply is proportionate.

From dinners up to woolsacks and divine mitres, here in England, much may be gathered by talk; without talk, of the human sort nothing. Is Society become wholly a bag of wind, then, ballasted by guineas? Are our interests in it as a sounding brass and a tinkling cymbal?—In Army or Navy, when unhappily we have war on hand, there is, almost against our will, some kind of demand for certain of the silent talents. But in peace, that too passes into mere demand of the ostentations, of the pipeclays and the blank cartridges; and,—except that Naval men are occasionally, on long voyages, forced to hold their tongue, and converse with the dumb elements, and illimitable oceans, that moan and rave there without you and within you, which is a great advantage to the Naval man,—our poor United Services have to make conversational wind-bags and ostentational paper-lanterns of themselves, or do worse, even as the others.

My friends, must I assert, then, what surely all men know, though all men seem to have forgotten it, That in the learned professions as in the unlearned, and in human things throughout, in every place and in every time, the true function of intellect is *not* that of talking, but of understanding and discerning with a view to performing! An intellect may easily talk too much, and perform too little. Gradually, if it get into the noxious habit of talk, there will less and less performance come of it, talk being so delightfully handy in comparison with work; and at last there will no work, or thought of work, be got from it at all. Talk, except as the preparation for work, is worth almost nothing;—sometimes it is worth infinitely less than nothing; and becomes, little conscious of playing such a fatal part, the general summary of pretentious nothingnesses, and the chief of all the curses the Posterity of Adam are liable to in this sublunary world! Would you discover the Atropos of Human Virtue; the sure Destroyer, 'by painless extinction,' of Human Veracities, Performances, and Capabilities to perform or to be veracious, —it is this, you have it here.

Unwise talk is matchless in unwisdom. Unwise work, if it but persist, is everywhere struggling towards correction, and restoration to health; for it is still in contact with Nature, and all Nature incessantly contradicts it, and will heal it or annihilate it: not so with unwise talk, which addresses itself, regardless of veridical Nature, to the universal suffrages; and can, if it be dextrous, find harbour there till all the suffrages are bankrupt and gone to Houndsditch, Nature not interfering with her protest till then. False speech, definable as the acme of unwise speech, is capable, as we already said, of becoming the falsest of all things. Falsest of all things:—and whither will the general deluge of that, in Parliament and Synagogue, in Book and Broadside, carry you and your affairs, my friend, when once they are embarked on it as now?

Parliament, *Parliamentum*, is by express appointment the Talking Apparatus; yet not in Parliament either is the essential function, by any means, talk. Not to speak your opinion well, but to have a good and just opinion worth speaking,—for every Parliament, as for every man, this latter is the point. Contrive to have a true opinion, you will get it told in some way, better or worse; and it will be a blessing to all creatures. Have a false opinion, and tell it with the tongue of Angels, what can that profit? The better you *tell* it, the worse it will be!

In Parliament and out of Parliament, and everywhere in this Universe, your one salvation is, That you can discern with just insight, and follow with noble valour, what the law of the case before you is, what the appointment of the Maker in regard to it has been. Get this out of one man, you are saved; fail to get this out of the most August Parliament wrapt in the sheepskins of a thousand years, you are lost,—your Parliament, and you, and all your sheepskins are lost. Beautiful talk is by no means the most pressing want in Parliament! We have had some reasonable modicum of talk in Parliament! What talk has done for us in Parliament, and is now doing, the dullest of us at length begins to see!

Much has been said of Parliament's breeding men to business; of the training an Official Man gets in this school of argument and talk. He is here inured to patience, tolerance; sees what is what in the Nation and in the Nation's Government; attains official knowledge, official courtesy and manners; —in short, is polished at all points into official articulation, and here better than elsewhere qualifies himself to be a Governor of men. So it is said.—Doubtless, I think, he will see and suffer much in Parliament, and inure himself to several things;—he will, with what eyes he has, gradually *see* Parliament itself, for one thing; what a high-soaring, helplessly floundering, ever babbling yet inarticulate dark dumb Entity it is (certainly one of the strangest under the sun just now): which doubtless, if he have in view to get measures voted there one day, will be an important acquisition for him. But as to breeding himself for a Doer of Work, much more for a King, or Chief of Doers, here in this element of talk; as to that I confess the fatalest doubts, or rather, alas, I have no doubt! Alas, it is our fatalest misery just now, not easily alterable, and yet urgently requiring to be altered, That no British man can attain to be a Statesman, or Chief of *Workers*, till he has first proved himself a Chief of *Talkers*: which mode of trial for a Worker, is it not precisely, of all the trials you could set him upon, the falsest and unfairest?

Nay, I doubt much you are not likely ever to meet the fittest material for a Statesman, or Chief of Workers, in such an element as that. Your Potential Chief of Workers, will he come there at all, to try whether he can talk? Your poor ten-pound franchisers and electoral world generally, in love with eloquent talk, are they the likeliest to discern what man it is that has worlds of silent work in him? No. Or is such a man, even if born in the due rank for it, the likeliest to present himself, and court their most sweet voices? Again, no.

The Age that admires talk so much can have little discernment for inarticulate work, or for anything that is deep and genuine. Nobody, or hardly anybody, having in himself an earnest sense for truth, how can anybody recognise an inarticulate Veracity, or Nature-fact of any kind; a Human *Doer* especially, who is the most complex, profound, and inarticulate of all Nature's Facts? Nobody can recognise him: till once he is patented, get some public stamp of authenticity, and has been articulately proclaimed, and asserted to be a Doer. To the worshipper of talk, such a one is a sealed book. An excellent human soul, direct from Heaven,—how shall any excellence of man become recognisable to this unfortunate? Not except by announcing and placarding itself as excellent,—which, I reckon, it above other things will probably be in no great haste to do.

Wisdom, the divine message which every soul of man brings into this world; the divine prophecy of what the new man has got the new and peculiar capability to do, is intrinsically of silent nature. It cannot at once, or completely at all, be read-off in words; for it is written in abstruse facts, of endowment, position, desire, opportunity, granted to the man; — interprets itself in presentiments, vague struggles, passionate endeavours; and is only legible in whole when his work is *done*. Not by the noble monitions of Nature, but by the ignoble, is a man much tempted to publish the secret of his soul in words. Words, if he have a secret, will be forever inadequate to it. Words do but disturb the real answer of fact which could be given to it; disturb, obstruct, and will in the end abolish, and render impossible, said answer. No grand Doer in this world can be a copious speaker about his doings. William the Silent spoke himself best in a country liberated; Oliver Cromwell did not shine in rhetoric; Goethe, when he had but a book in view, found that he must say nothing even of that, if it was to succeed with him.

Then as to politeness, and breeding to business. An official man must be bred to business; of course he must: and not for essence only, but even for the manners of office he requires breeding. Besides his intrinsic faculty, whatever that may be, he must be cautious, vigilant, discreet,—above all things, he must be reticent, patient, polite. Certain of these qualities are by nature imposed upon men of station; and they are trained from birth to some exercise of them: this constitutes their one intrinsic qualification for office;— this is their one advantage in the New Downing Street projected for this New Era; and it will not go for much in that Institution. One advantage, or temporary advantage; against which there are so many counterbalances. It is the indispensable preliminary for office, but by no means the complete outfit,—a miserable outfit where there is nothing farther.

Will your Lordship give me leave to say that, practically,

the intrinsic qualities will presuppose these preliminaries too, but by no means *vice versâ*. That, on the whole, if you have got the intrinsic qualities, you have got everything, and the preliminaries will prove attainable; but that if you have got only the preliminaries, you have yet got nothing. A man of real dignity will not find it impossible to bear himself in a dignified manner; a man of real understanding and insight will get to know, as the fruit of his very first study, what the laws of his situation are, and will conform to these. Rough old Samuel Johnson, blustering Boreas and rugged Arctic Bear as he often was, defined himself, justly withal, as a polite man: a noble manful attitude of soul is his; a clear, true and loyal sense of what others are, and what he himself is, shines through the rugged coating of him; comes out as grave deep rhythmus when his King honours him, and he will not 'bandy compliments with his King';—is traceable too in his indignant trampling-down of the Chesterfield patronages, tailor-made insolences, and contradictions of sinners; which may be called his *revolutionary* movements, hard and peremptory by the law of them; these could not be soft like his *constitutional* ones, when men and kings took him for somewhat like the thing he was. Given a noble man, I think your Lordship may expect by and by a polite man. No 'politer' man was to be found in Britain than the rustic Robert Burns: high duchesses were captivated with the chivalrous ways of the man; recognised that here was the true chivalry, and divine nobleness of bearing,—as indeed they well might, now when the Peasant God and Norse Thor had come down among them again! Chivalry this, if not as they do chivalry in Drury Lane or West-End drawing-rooms, yet as they do it in Valhalla and the General Assembly of the Gods.

For indeed, who *invented* chivalry, politeness, or anything that is noble and melodious and beautiful among us, except precisely the like of Johnson and of Burns? The select few who in the generations of this world were wise and valiant, they, in spite of all the tremendous majority of blockheads and slothful belly-worshippers, and noisy ugly persons, have devised whatsoever is noble in the manners of man to man. I expect they will learn to be polite, your Lordship, when you give them a chance!—Nor is it as a school of human culture, for this or for any other grace or gift, that Parliament will be found first-rate or indispensable. As experience in the river is indispensable to the ferryman, so is knowledge of his Parliament to the British Peel or Chatham;—so was knowledge of the Œil-de-Bœuf to the French Choiseul. Where and how said river, whether Parliament with Wilkeses, or Œil-de-Bœuf with Pompadours, can be waded, boated, swum; how the miscellaneous cargoes, 'measures' so-called, can be got across it, according to their kinds, and landed alive on the hither side as facts:—we have all of us our *ferries* in this world; and must know the river and its ways, or get drowned some day! In that sense, practice in Parliament is indispensable to the British Statesman; but not in any other sense.

A school, too, of manners and of several other things, the Parliament will doubtless be to the aspirant Statesman; a school better or worse;—as the Œil-de-Bœuf likewise was, and as all scenes where men work or live are sure to be. Especially where many men work together, the very rubbing against one another will grind and polish off their angularities into roundness, into 'politeness' after a sort; and the official man, place him how you may, will never want for schooling, of extremely various kinds. A first-rate school one cannot call this Parliament for him;—I fear to say what rate at present! In so far as it teaches him vigilance, patience, courage, toughness of lungs or of soul, and skill in any kind of swimming, it is a good school. In so far as it forces him to speak where Nature orders silence; and even, lest all the world should learn his secret (which often enough would kill his secret, and little profit the world), forces him to speak falsities, vague ambiguities, and the froth-dialect usual in Parliaments in these times, it may be considered one of the worst schools ever devised by man; and, I think, may almost challenge the Œil-de-Bœuf to match it in badness.

Parliament will train your men to the manners required of a statesman; but in a much less degree to the intrinsic functions of one. To these latter, it is capable of *mis*training as nothing else can. Parliament will train you to talk; and above all things to hear, with patience, unlimited quantities of foolish talk. To tell a good story for yourself, and to make it *appear* that you have done your work: this, especially in constitutional countries, is something;—and yet in all countries, constitutional ones too, it is intrinsically nothing, probably even less. For it is not the function of any mortal, in Downing Street or elsewhere here below, to wag the tongue of him, and make it appear that he has done work; but to wag some quite other organs of him, and to do work; there is no danger of his work's appearing by and by. Such an accomplishment, even in constitutional countries, I grieve to say, may become much *less* than nothing. Have you at all computed how much less? The human creature who has once given way to satisfying himself with 'appearances,' to seeking his salvation in 'appearances,' the moral life of such human creature is rapidly bleeding out of him. Depend upon it, Beelzebub, Satan, or however you may name the too authentic Genius of Eternal Death, has got that human creature in his claws. By and by you will have a dead parliamentary bagpipe, and your living man fled away without return!

Such parliamentary bagpipes I myself have heard play tunes, much to the satisfaction of the people. Every tune lies within their compass; and their mind (for they still call it *mind*) is ready as a hurdygurdy on turning of the handle: "My Lords, this question now before the House"— —Ye Heavens, O ye divine Silences, was there in the womb of Chaos, then, such a product, liable to be evoked by human art, as that same? While the galleries were all applausive of heart, and the Fourth Estate looked with eyes enlightened, as if you had touched its lips with a staff dipped in honey,—I have sat with reflections too ghastly to be uttered. A poor human creature and learned friend, once possessed of many fine gifts, possessed of intellect, veracity, and manful conviction on a variety of objects, has he now lost all that;—converted all that into a glistering phosphorescence which can show itself on the outside; while within, all is dead, chaotic, dark; a painted sepulchre full of dead-men's bones! Discernment, knowledge, intellect, in the human sense of the words, this man has now none. His opinion you do not ask on any matter: on the *matter* he has no opinion, judgment, or insight; only on what may be said about the matter, how it may be argued of, what tune may be played upon it to enlighten the eyes of the Fourth Estate.

Such a soul, though to the eye he still keeps tumbling about in the Parliamentary element, and makes 'motions,' and passes bills, for aught I know,—are we to define him as a *living* one, or as a dead? Partridge the Almanac-maker, whose 'publications' still regularly appear, is known to be dead! The dog that was drowned last summer, and that floats up and down the Thames with ebb and flood ever since,—is it not dead? Alas, in the hot months, you meet here and there such a floating dog; and at length, if you often use the river steamers, get to know him by sight. "There he is again, still astir there in his quasi-stygian element!" you dejectedly exclaim (perhaps reading your Morning Newspaper at the moment); and reflect, with a painful oppression of nose and imagination, on certain completed professors of parliamentary eloquence in modern times. Dead long since, but *not* resting; daily doing motions in that Westminster region still,—daily from Vauxhall to Blackfriars, and back again; and cannot get away at all! Daily (from Newspaper or river steamer) you may see him at some point of his fated course, hovering in the eddies, stranded in the ooze, or rapidly progressing with flood or ebb; and daily the odour of him is getting more intolerable; daily the condition of him appeals more tragically to gods and men.

Nature admits no lie; most men profess to be aware of this, but few in any measure lay it to heart. Except in the departments of mere material manipulation, it seems to be taken practically as if this grand truth were merely a polite flourish of rhetoric. What is a lie? The question is worth asking, once and away, by the practical English mind.

A voluntary spoken divergence from the fact as it stands, as it has occurred and will proceed to develop itself: this clearly, if adopted by any man, will so far forth *mis*lead him in all practical dealing with the fact; till he cast that statement out of him, and reject it as an unclean poisonous thing, he can have no success in dealing with the fact. If such spoken divergence from the truth be involuntary, we lament it as a misfortune; and are entitled, at least the speaker of it is, to lament it extremely as the most palpable of all misfortunes, as the indubitablest losing of his way, and turning aside from the goal instead of pressing towards it, in the race set before him. If the divergence is voluntary,—there superadds itself to our sorrow a just indignation: we call the voluntary spoken divergence a lie, and justly abhor it as the essence of human treason and baseness, the desertion of a man to the Enemy of men against himself and his brethren. A lost deserter; who has gone over to the Enemy, called Satan; and cannot *but* be lost in the adventure! Such is every liar with the tongue; and such in all nations is he, at all epochs, considered. Men pull his nose, and kick him out of doors; and by peremptory expressive methods signify that they can and will have no trade with him. Such is spoken divergence from the fact: so fares it with the practiser of that sad art.

But have we well considered a divergence *in thought* from what is the fact? Have we considered the man whose very thought is a lie to him and to us! He too is a frightful man; repeating about this Universe on every hand what is not, and driven to repeat it; the sure herald of ruin to all that follow him, that know with *his* knowledge! And would you learn how to get a mendacious thought, there is no surer recipe than carrying a loose tongue. The lying thought, you already either have it, or will soon get it by that method. He who lies with his very tongue, *he* clearly enough has long ceased to think truly in his mind. Does he, in any sense, 'think'? All his thoughts and imaginations, if they extend beyond mere beaverisms, astucities and sensualisms, are false, incomplete, perverse, untrue even to himself. He has become a false mirror of this Universe; not a small mirror only, but a crooked, bedimmed and utterly deranged one. But all loose tongues too are akin to lying ones; are insincere at the best, and go rattling with little meaning; the thought lying languid at a great distance behind them, if thought there be behind them at all. Gradually there will be none or little! How can the thought of such a man, what he calls thought, be other than false?

Alas, the palpable liar with his tongue does at least know that he is lying, and has or might have some faint vestige of remorse and chance of amendment; but the impalpable liar, whose tongue articulates mere accepted commonplaces, cants and babblement, which means only, "Admire me, call me an excellent stump-orator!"—of him what hope is there? His thought, what thought he had, lies dormant, inspired only to invent vocables and plausibilities; while the tongues goes so glib, the thought is absent, gone a-woolgathering; getting itself drugged with the applausive 'Hear, hear!'—what will become of such a man? His idle thought has run all to seed, and grown false and the giver of falsities; the inner light of his mind has gone out; all his light is mere putridity and phosphorescence henceforth. Whosoever is in quest of ruin, let him with assurance follow that man; he or no one is on the right road to it.

Good Heavens, from the wisest Thought of a man to the actual truth of a Thing as it lies in Nature, there is, one would suppose, a sufficient interval! Consider it,—and what other intervals we introduce! The faithfulest, most glowing word of a man is but an imperfect image of the thought, such as it is, that dwells within him; his best word will never but with error convey his thought to other minds: and then between *his* poor thought and Nature's Fact, which is the Thought of the Eternal, there may be supposed to lie some discrepancies, some shortcomings! Speak your sincerest, think your wisest, there is still a great gulf between you and the fact. And now, do *not* speak your sincerest, and, what will inevitably follow out of that, do not think your wisest, but think only your plausiblest, your showiest for parliamentary purposes, where will you land with that guidance?—I invite the British Parliament, and all the Parliamentary and other Electors of Great Britain, to reflect on this till they have well understood it; and then to ask, each of himself, What probably the horoscopes of the British Parliament, at this epoch of World-History, may be?—

Fail, by any sin or any misfortune, to discover what the truth of the fact is, you are lost so far as that fact goes! If your thought do not image truly but do image falsely the fact, you will vainly try to work upon the fact. The fact will not obey you, the fact will silently resist you; and ever, with silent invincibility, will go on resisting you, till you do get to image it truly instead of falsely. No help for you whatever, except in attaining to a true image of the fact. Needless to vote a false image true; vote it, revote it by overwhelming majorities, by jubilant unanimities and universalities; read it thrice or three hundred times, pass acts of parliament upon it till the Statute-book can hold no more,—it helps not a whit: the thing is not so, the thing is otherwise than so; and Adam's whole Posterity, voting daily on it till the world finish, will not alter it a jot. Can the sublimest sanhedrim, constitutional parliament, or other Collective Wisdom of the world, persuade fire not to burn, sulphuric acid to be sweet milk, or the Moon to become green cheese? The fact is much the reverse:—and even the Constitutional British Parliament abstains from such arduous attempts as these latter in the voting line; and leaves the multiplication-table, the chemical, mechanical, and other qualities of material substances to take their own course; being aware that voting and perorating, and reporting in Hansard, will not in the least alter any of these. Which is indisputably wise of the British Parliament.

Unfortunately the British Parliament does not, at present, quite know that *all* manner of things and relations of things, spiritual equally with material, all manner of qualities, entities, existences whatsoever, in this strange visible and invisible Universe, are equally inflexible of nature; that they will, one and all, with precisely the same obstinacy, continue to obey their own law, not our law; deaf as the adder to all charm of parliamentary eloquence, and of voting never so often repeated; silently, but inflexibly and forevermore, declining to change themselves, even as sulphuric acid declines to become sweet milk, though you vote so to the end of the world. This, it sometimes seems to me, is not quite sufficiently laid hold of by the British and other Parliaments just at present. Which surely is a great misfortune to said Parliaments! For, it would appear, the grand point, after all constitutional improvements, and such wagging of wigs in Westminster as there has been, is precisely what it was before any constitution was yet heard of, or the first official wig had budded out of nothing: namely, to ascertain what the truth of your question, in Nature, really is! Verily so. In this time and place, as in all past and in all future times and places. Today in St. Stephen's, where constitutional, philanthropical, and other great things lie in the mortarkit; even as on the Plain of Shinar long ago, where a certain Tower, likewise of a very philanthropic nature, indeed one of the desirablest towers I ever heard of, was to be built,—but couldn't! My friends, I do not laugh; truly I am more inclined to weep.

Get, by six-hundred and fifty-eight votes, or by no vote at all, by the silent intimation of your own eyesight and understanding given you direct out of Heaven, and more sacred to you than anything earthly, and than all things earthly,—a correct image of the fact in question, as God and Nature have made it: that is the one thing needful; with that it shall be well with you in whatsoever you have to do with said fact. Get, by the sublimest constitutional methods, belauded by all the world, an *in*correct image of the fact: so shall it be other than well with you; so shall you have laud from able-editors and vociferous masses of mistaken human creatures; and from the Nature's Fact, continuing quite silently the same as it was, contradiction, and that only. What else? Will Nature change, or sulphuric acid become sweet milk, for the noise of vociferous blockheads? Surely not. Nature, I assure you, has not the smallest intention of doing so.

On the contrary, Nature keeps silently a most exact Savings-bank, and official register, correct to the most evanescent item, Debtor and Creditor, in respect to one and all of us; silently marks down, Creditor by such and such an unseen act of veracity and heroism; Debtor to such a loud blustery blunder, twenty-seven million strong or one unit strong, and to all acts and words and thoughts executed in consequence of that, —Debtor, Debtor, Debtor, day after day, rigorously as Fate (for this *is* Fate that is writing); and at the end of the account you will have it all to pay, my friend; there is the rub! Not the infinitesimalist fraction of a farthing but will be found marked there, for you and against you; and with the due rate of interest you will have to pay it, neatly, completely, as sure as you are alive. You will have to pay it even in money if you live:—and, poor slave, do you think there is no payment but in money? There is a payment which Nature rigorously exacts of men, and also of Nations, and this I think when her wrath is sternest, in the shape of dooming you to possess money. To possess it; to have your bloated vanities fostered into monstrosity by it, your foul passions blown into explosion by it, your heart and perhaps your very stomach ruined with intoxication by it; your poor life and all its manifold activities stunned into frenzy and comatose sleep by it,—in one word, as the old Prophets said, your soul forever lost by it. Your soul; so that, through the Eternities, *you* shall have no soul, or manful trace of ever having had a soul; but only, for certain fleeting moments, shall have had a moneybag, and have given soul and heart and (frightfuler still) stomach itself in fateful exchange for the same. You wretched mortal, stumbling about in a God's Temple, and thinking it a brutal Cookery-shop! Nature, when her scorn of a slave is divinest, and blazes like the blinding lightning against his slavehood, often enough flings him a bag of money, silently saying: "That! Away; thy doom is that!"—

For no man, and for no body or biggest multitude of men, has Nature favour, if they part company with her facts and her. Excellent stump-orator; eloquent parliamentary dead-dog, making motions, passing bills; reported in the Morning Newspapers, and reputed the 'best speaker going'? From the Universe of Fact he has turned himself away; he is gone into partnership with the Universe of Phantasm; finds it profitablest to deal in forged-notes, while the foolish shop-keepers will accept them. Nature for such a man, and for Nations that follow such, has her patibulary forks, and prisons of death everlasting:—dost thou doubt it? Unhappy mortal, Nature otherwise were herself a Chaos and no Cosmos. Nature was not made by an Impostor; not she, I think, rife as they are!—In fact, by money or otherwise, to the uttermost fraction of a calculable and incalculable value, we have, each one of us, to settle the exact balance in the abovesaid Savings-bank, or official register kept by Nature: Creditor by the quantity of veracities we have done, Debtor by the quantity of falsities and errors; there is not, by any conceivable device, the faintest hope of escape from that issue for one of us, nor for all of us.

This used to be a well-known fact; and daily still, in certain edifices, steeple-houses, joss-houses, temples sacred or other, everywhere spread over the world, we hear some dim mumblement of an assertion that such is still, what it was always and will forever be, the fact: but meseems it has terribly fallen out of memory nevertheless; and, from Dan to Beersheba, one in vain looks out for a man that really in his heart believes it. In his heart he believes, as we perceive, that scrip will yield dividends: but that Heaven too has an office of account, and unerringly marks down, against us or for us, whatsoever thing we do or say or think, and treasures up the same in regard to every creature,—this I do not so well perceive that he believes. Poor blockhead, no: he reckons that all payment is in money, or approximately representable by money; finds money go a strange course; disbelieves the parson and his Day of Judgment; discerns not that there is any judgment except in the small or big debt court: and lives (for the present) on that strange footing in this Universe. The unhappy mortal, what is the use of his 'civilisations' and his 'useful knowledges,' if he have forgotten that beginning of human knowledge; the earliest perception of the awakened human soul in this world; the first dictate of Heaven's inspiration to all men? I cannot account him a man any more; but only a kind of human beaver, who has acquired the art of ciphering. He lives without rushing hourly towards suicide, because his soul, with all its noble aspirations and imaginations, is sunk at the bottom of his stomach, and lies torpid there, unaspiring, unimagining, unconsidering, as if it were the vital principle of a mere *four*-footed beaver. A soul of a man, appointed for spinning cotton and making money, or, alas, for merely shooting grouse and gathering rent; to whom Eternity and Immortality, and all human Noblenesses and divine Facts that did not tell upon the stock-exchange, were meaningless fables, empty as the inarticulate wind. He will recover out of that persuasion one day, or be ground to powder, I believe!—

To such a pass, by our beaverisms and our mammonisms; by canting of 'prevenient grace' everywhere, and so boarding and lodging our poor souls upon supervenient moonshine everywhere, for centuries long; by our sordid stupidities and our idle babblings; through faith in the divine Stump-Orator, and Constitutional Palaver, or august Sanhedrim of Orators, —have men and Nations been reduced, in this sad epoch! I cannot call them happy Nations; I must call them Nations like to perish; Nations that will either begin to recover, or else soon die. Recovery is to be hoped;—yes, since there is in Nature an Almighty Beneficence, and His voice, divinely terrible, can be heard in the world-whirlwind now, even as from of old and forevermore. Recovery, or else destruction and annihilation, is very certain; and the crisis, too, comes rapidly on: but by Stump-Orator and Constitutional Palaver, however perfected, my hopes of *recovery* have long vanished. Not by them, I should imagine, but by something far the reverse of them, shall we return to truth and God!—

I tell you, the ignoble intellect cannot think the *truth*, even within its own limits, and when it seriously tries! And of the ignoble intellect that does not seriously try, and has even reached the 'ignobleness' of seriously trying the reverse, and of lying with its very tongue, what are we to expect? It is frightful to consider. Sincere wise speech is but an imperfect corollary, and insignificant outer manifestation, of sincere wise thought. He whose very tongue utters falsities, what has his heart long been doing? The thought of his heart is not its wisest, not even *its* wisest; it is its foolishest; —and even of that we have a false and foolish copy. And it is Nature's Fact, or the Thought of the Eternal, which we want to arrive at in regard to the matter,—which if we do *not* arrive at, we shall not save the matter, we shall drive the matter into shipwreck!

The practice of modern Parliaments, with reporters sitting

among them, and twenty-seven millions mostly fools listening to them, fills me with amazement. In regard to no *thing*, or fact as God and Nature have made it, can you get so much as the real thought of any honourable head,—even so far as *it*, the said honourable head, still has capacity of thought. What the honourable gentleman's wisest thought is or would have been, had he led from birth a life of piety and earnest veracity and heroic virtue, you, and he himself poor deep-sunk creature, vainly conjecture as from immense dim distances far in the rear of what he is led to *say*. And again, far in the rear of what his thought is,—surely long infinitudes beyond all *he* could ever think,—lies the Thought of God Almighty, the Image itself of the Fact, the thing you are in quest of, and must find or do worse! Even his, the honourable gentleman's, actual bewildered, falsified, vague surmise or quasi-thought, even this is not given you; but only some falsified copy of this, such as he fancies may suit the reporters and twenty-seven millions mostly fools. And upon that latter you are to act;— —with what success, do you expect? That is the thought you are to take for the Thought of the Eternal Mind,—that double-distilled falsity of a blockheadism from one who is false even as a blockhead!

Do I make myself plain to Mr. Peter's understanding? Perhaps it will surprise him less that parliamentary eloquence excites more wonder than admiration in me; that the fate of countries governed by that sublime alchemy does not appear the hopefulest just now. Not by that method, I should apprehend, will the Heavens be scaled and the Earth vanquished; not by that, but by another.

A benevolent man once proposed to me, but without pointing out the methods how, this plan of reform for our benighted world: To cut from one generation, whether the current one or the next, all the tongues away, prohibiting Literature too; and appoint at least one generation to pass its life in silence. "There, thou one blessed generation, from the vain jargon of babble thou art beneficently freed. Whatsoever of truth, traditionary or original, thy own god-given intellect shall point-out to thee as true, that thou wilt go and *do.* In doing of it there will be a verdict for thee; if a verdict of True, thou wilt hold by it, and ever again do it; if of Untrue, thou wilt never try it more, but be eternally delivered from it. To do aught because the vain hearsays order thee, and the big clamours of the sanhedrim of fools, is not thy lot,—what worlds of misery are spared thee! Nature's voice heard in thy own inner being, and the sacred Commandment of thy Maker: these shall be thy guidances, thou happy tongueless generation. What is good and beautiful thou shalt know; not merely what is said to be so. Not to talk of thy doings, and become the envy of surrounding flunkies, but to taste of the fruit of thy doings themselves, is thine. What the Eternal Laws will sanction for thee, do; what the Froth Gospels and multitudinous long-eared Hearsays never so loudly bid, all this is already chaff for thee,—drifting rapidly along, thou knowest whitherward, on the eternal winds."

Good Heavens, if such a plan were practicable, how the chaff might be winnowed out of every man, and out of all human things; and ninety-nine hundredths of our whole big Universe, spiritual and practical, might blow itself away, as mere torrents of chaff;—whole trade-winds of chaff, many miles deep, rushing continually with the voice of whirlwinds towards a certain Fire, which knows how to deal with it! Ninety-nine hundredths blown away; all the lies blown away, and some skeleton of a spiritual and practical Universe left standing for us which were *true*: O Heavens, is it forever impossible, then? By a generation that had no *tongue* it really might be done; but not so easily by one that had. Tongues, platforms, parliaments, and fourth-estates; unfettered presses, periodical and stationary literatures: we are nearly all gone to tongue, I think; and our fate is very questionable!

Truly, it is little known at present, and ought forthwith to become better known, what ruin to all nobleness and fruitfulness and blessedness in the genius of a poor mortal you generally bring about, by ordering him to speak, to do all things with a view to their being seen! Few good and fruitful things ever were done, or could be done, on those terms. Silence, silence; and be distant ye profane, with your jargonings and superficial babblements, when a man has anything to *do*! Eye-service,—dost thou know what that is, poor England?—eye-service is all the man can do in these sad circumstances; grows to be all he has the idea of doing, of his or any other man's ever doing, or ever having done, in any circumstances. Sad enough. Alas, it is our saddest woe of all;—too sad for being spoken of at present, while all or nearly all men consider it an imaginary sorrow on my part!

Let the young English soul, in whatever logic-shop and nonsense-verse establishment of an Eton, Oxford, Edinburgh, Halle, Salamanca, or other High Finishing-School, he may be getting his young idea taught how to speak and spout, and print sermons and review-articles, and thereby show himself and fond patrons that it *is* an idea,—lay this solemnly to heart; this is my deepest counsel to him! The idea you have once spoken, if it even were an idea, is no longer yours; it is gone from you, so much life and virtue is gone, and the vital circulations of your self and your destiny and activity are henceforth deprived of it. If you could not get it spoken, if you could still constrain it into silence, so much the richer are you. Better keep your idea while you can: let it still circulate in your blood, and there fructify; inarticulately inciting you to good activities; giving to your whole spiritual life a ruddier health. When the time does come for speaking it, you will speak it all the more concisely, the more expressively, appropriately; and if such a time should never come, have you not already acted it, and uttered it as no words can? Think of this, my young friend; for there is nothing truer, nothing more forgotten in these shabby gold-laced days. Incontinence is half of all the sins of man. And among the many kinds of that base vice, I know none baser, or at present half so fell and fatal, as that same Incontinence of Tongue. 'Public speaking,' 'parliamentary eloquence': it is a Moloch, before whom young souls are made to pass through the fire. They enter, weeping or rejoicing, fond parents consecrating them to the redhot Idol, as to the Highest God: and they come out spiritually *dead.* Dead enough; to live thenceforth a galvanic life of mere Stump-Oratory; screeching and gibbering, words without wisdom, without veracity, without conviction more than skin-deep. A divine gift, that? It is a thing admired by the vulgar, and rewarded with seats in the Cabinet and other preciosities; but to the wise, it is a thing not admirable, not adorable; unmelodious rather, and ghastly and bodeful, as the speech of sheeted spectres in the streets at midnight!

Be not a Public Orator, thou brave young British man, thou that art now growing to be something: not a Stump-Orator, if thou canst help it. Appeal not to the vulgar, with its long ears and its seats in the Cabinet; not by spoken words to the vulgar; *hate* the profane vulgar, and bid it begone. Appeal by silent work, by silent suffering if there be no work, to the gods, who have nobler than seats in the Cabinet for thee! Talent for Literature, thou hast such a talent? Believe it not, be slow to believe it! To speak, or to write, Nature did not peremptorily order thee; but to work she did. And know this: there never was a talent even for real Literature, not to speak of talents lost and damned in doing sham Literature, but was primarily a talent for something infinitely better of the silent kind. Of Literature, in all ways, be shy rather than otherwise, at present! There where thou art, work, work; whatsoever thy hand findeth to do, do it,—with the hand of a man, not of a phantasm; be that thy unnoticed blessedness and exceeding great reward. Thy words, let them be few, and well-ordered. Love silence rather than speech in these tragic days, when, for very speaking, the voice of man has fallen inarticulate to man; and hearts, in this loud babbling, sit dark and dumb toward one another. Witty,—above all, O be not witty: none of us is bound to be witty, under penalties; to be wise and true we all are, under the terriblest penalties!

Brave young friend, dear to me, and *known* too in a sense, though never seen, nor to be seen by me,—you are, what I am not, in the happy case to learn to *be* something and to *do* something, instead of eloquently talking about what has been and was done and may be! The old are what they are, and will not alter; our hope is in you. England's hope, and the world's, is that there may once more be millions such, instead of units as now. *Mactè; i fausto pede.* And may future generations, acquainted again with the silences, and once more cognisant of what is noble and faithful and divine, look back on *us* with pity and incredulous astonishment!

No. VI

PARLIAMENTS

[1st June 1850]

By this time it is sufficiently apparent the present Editor is not one of those who expect to see the Country saved by farther 'reforming' the reformed Parliament we have got. On the contrary, he has the sad conviction that from such Parliament never so ingeniously reformed, there can no salvation come, but only a speedy finale far different from salvation. It is his effort and desire to teach this and the other thinking British man that said finale, the advent namely of actual open Anarchy, cannot be distant, now when virtual disguised Anarchy, long-continued and waxing daily, has got to such a height; and that the one method of staving-off that fatal consummation, and steering towards the Continents of the Future, lies not in the direction of reforming Parliament, but of what he calls reforming Downing Street; a thing infinitely urgent to be begun, and to be strenuously carried on. To find a Parliament more and more the express image of the People, could, unless the People chanced to be wise as well as miserable, give him no satisfaction. Not this at all; but to find some sort of *King*, made in the image of God, who could a little achieve for the People, if not their spoken wishes, yet their dumb wants, and what they would at last find to have been their instinctive *will*,—which is a far different matter usually, in this babbling world of ours.

Qualification movement, universal-suffrage movement, Reform Association, and suchlike, this Editor does not enjoin upon his readers;—his readers whom (as every crow is known to think her own eggs whitest) he considers to be a select class, the true Aristocracy of England, capable of far better things than these. Which better things, and not the worse, it is his heart's wish to urge them upon doing. And yet, alas, how can he forbid any reader of his, or of other people's, to join such suffrage movement, or still more distracted Chartism of Six Points, if it seem hopeful? Where we are, is no continuing. Men say: "The finale must come, ought to come; perhaps the sooner it comes, it will be the lighter to bear. If the foul universal boil is to go on ripening, under mere Leave-alone and Premiers of the Phantasm order, perhaps the sooner it bursts, and declares itself as universal gangrene and social death, the better!" Good Heavens, have men computed what the bursting-out of virtual disguised Anarchy into open undeniable Anarchy, such as they have in the Continental countries just now, amounts to in human affairs; what a game that of trying for cure in the Medea's-caldron of Revolution is! Must we also front the Apotheosis of Attorneyism; and know what the blackest of terrestrial curses means?

But if the captains of the ship are of that scandalous class who refuse to be warned *except* by iceberg counsellors nudging them, what are the miserable crew to do? Yes, the crew had better consider of that; they have greatly too little considered it of late. They will find that in Nature there is no such alarming creature as a Chief Governor of that humour, in getting round a Cape Horn like this of ours; that, if pity did not check our rage, there is no such traitor in the ship as this unconscious one! Who, placidly assured, nothing doubting but he is the friend of gods and men, can stand with imperturbable attitude, quietly steering, by his old Whig and other charts of the British Channel (as if we were still *there* or thereabouts), into the yawning mouth of Chaos, on the other side of the world; and call it passing the Forelands in rough weather, or getting into Cowes, by constitutional methods, and 'remedial measures suited to the occasion.' Our heart's prayer in those circumstances is: From such Chief Governors, good Lord deliver us! And if masses of the desperate common men before the mast do invoke Chartism rather, and *invite* the iceberg counsellors to nudge him,—cannot we too well understand it? I hope, in other quarters of the ship there are men who know wiser courses, and instead of inviting the iceberg counsellors and Six Points, will direct all their strength to fling the Phantasm Captain under hatches. It is with the view of aiding and encouraging these latter that we now institute a few considerations upon Parliaments generally.

Dryasdust in his lumber-masses, which he calls treatises and histories, has not been explicit about Parliaments: but we need not doubt, the English Parliament, as windy a palavering and imaginary entity as it has now grown to be, was at one time a quite solid serious actuality, met for earnest despatch of work which, on the King's part and the Commonwealth's, needed absolutely to be done. Reading in *Eadmerus* and the dim old Books, one finds gradually that the Parliament was at first a most simple Assemblage, quite cognate to the situation; that Red William, or whoever had taken on him the terrible task of being King in England, was wont to invite, oftenest about Christmas time, his subordinate Kinglets, Barons as he called them, to give him the pleasure of their company for a week or two: there, in earnest conference all morning, in freer talk over Christmas cheer all evening, in some big royal Hall of Westminster, Winchester, or whereever it might be, with log-fires, huge rounds of roast and boiled, not lacking malmsey and other generous liquor, they took counsel concerning the arduous matters of the kingdom. "You Taillebois, what have you to propose in this arduous matter?—Frontdebœuf has another view; thinks, in his southern counties, they will go with the Protectionist movement, and repeal the malt-tax, the African Squadron, and the window-duty itself.—Potdevin, what is your opinion of the measure; will it hold in your parts? So, Fitzurse disagrees, then!—Tête-d'étoupes, speak out. And first, the pleasure of a glass of wine, my infant?"—Thus, for a fortnight's space, they carried on, after a human manner, their grand National Consult or *Parliamentum*; intermingling Dinner with it (as is still the modern method); debating everything, as Tacitus describes the Ancient Germans to have done, two times: once sober, and once what he calls 'drunk,'—not dead-drunk, but jolly round their big table;—that so both sides of the matter might be seen; and, midway between rash hope and unreasonable apprehension, the true decision of it might be hit. To this hour no public matter, with whatever serious argument, can be settled in England till it have been dined upon, perhaps repeatedly dined upon.

To King Rufus there could no more natural method present itself, of getting his affairs of sovereignty transacted, than this same. To assemble all his working Sub-kings about him; and gather in a human manner, by the aid of sad speech and of cheerful, what their real notions, opinions, and determinations were. No way of making a law, or of getting one executed when made, except by even such a General Consult in one form or another.—Naturally too, as in all places where men meet, there established themselves modes of proceeding in this Christmas *Parliamentum*: secretaries from the first were needed there, strict record of the results arrived-at being indispensable: and the methods of arriving, marginally noted or otherwise, would not be forgotten: such methods, with trials of ever new methods, accumulating, and in the course of continual practice getting sifted, rejected, adopted, and committed to record,—the vast elaboration, now called Law of Parliament, Privilege, Practice of Parliament, and that huge sheepskin quarry, in which Dryasdust bores and grovels as if the world's or England's secret lay there, grew to be what we see.

So likewise in the time of the Edwards, when Parliament gradually split itself into Two Houses; and Borough Members and Knights of the Shire were summoned up to answer, Whether they could stand such and such an impost? and took upon them to answer, "Yes, your Majesty; but we have such and such grievances greatly in need of redress first,"—nothing could be more natural and human than such a Parliament still was. And so, granting subsidies, stating grievances, and notably widening its field in that latter direction, accumulating new modes, and practices of Parliament greatly important in world-history, the old Parliament continued an eminently human, veracious, and indispensable entity, achieving real work in the Centuries. Down, we may say, to the Century of Charles First, when being constrained by unforeseen necessity to do so, it took suddenly, like water at the boiling point, a quite immense development of function; and performed that new function too, to the world's and its own amazement, in an eminently human, authentic and effectual manner,—the 'supply' it granted his Majesty, this time (in front of Whitehall, as it ultimately proved), being of a very unexpected yet by no means unessential nature; and the 'grievance' it now stated for redress being the transcendent one of Compulsion towards Spiritual Nightmare, towards Canting Idolatry, and Death Eternal,—which I do not wonder that they couldn't endure, and wouldn't! Which transcendent grievance, it is well known, they did get redressed, in a most conspicuous manner, they, for the time being;—and so have since set all the world upon similar but far less hopeful attempts, by methods which *appear* the same, and are not the same but different.

This Long Parliament which conquered its King, and even extinguished him, since he would in no way be quiet when conquered; and which thus, the first of such Assemblages, declared that it was Sovereign in the Nation, and more royal than any King who could be there,—has set a flaming pattern to all the world, which now after centuries all the world is fruitlessly bent to emulate. This ever-memorable Long Parliament is definable, both in regard to its destinies in History, and to its intrinsic collective and individual worth among Deliberative Assemblies, as the Acme of Parliaments;

the highest that it lay in them to be, or to do, in human affairs. The consummation, this, and slow cactus-flowerage of the parliamentary tree among mankind, which blossoms only in thousands of years, and is seen only once by men: the Father, this, of all Congresses, National Conventions and sublunary Parliaments that have since been.

But what I had to remark of this Long Parliament, and of its English predecessors generally from the times of Rufus downwards, is their perfect veracity of purpose, their exact adaptation to getting the business done that was in hand. Supplies did, in some way, need to be granted; grievances, such as never fail, did in some way need to be stated and redressed. The silent Peoples had their *Parliamentum*; and spake by it to their Kings who governed them. In all human Government, wherever a man will attempt to govern men, this is a function necessary as the breath of life: and it must be said the old European Populations and the fortunate English best of all, did this function *well*. The old Parliaments were authentic entities; came upon indispensable work; and were in earnest to their very finger-ends about getting it done. No conclave of railway directors, met with closed doors upon the sacred cause of scrip and dividends, could be more intent upon the business necessary, or be more appropriate for it, than those old Parliaments were.

In modern Parliaments, again, indeed ever down from the Long Parliament, I note a sad gradual falling-off in this matter of 'veracity,'—which, alas, means a falling-off in all real use, or possible advantage, there can be to mankind in such Institutions. The Parliament, if we examine well, has irrevocably lost certain of its old functions, which it still pretends to do; and has got certain new functions, which it never can do, and yet pretends to be doing: a doubly fatal predicament for the Parliament. Its functions growing ever more confused in this twofold way, the position of the Parliament has become a false, and has gradually been becoming an impossible one, in modern affairs. While on the other hand, the poor Parliament, little conscious of all that, and long dimly struggling to remedy all that, and exist amidst it; or in later years, still more fatally admitting all that, and quietly consenting to exist beside it *without* remedy,—has had to distort and pervert its poor activity in all manner of ways; and at length has diffused itself into oceans of windy talk reported in *Hansard*; has grown, in short, a National Palaver; and is, as I said lately, one of the strangest entities this sun ever looked down upon. For, I think, a National Palaver recognised as Sovereign, a solemn Convocation of all the Stump-Orators in the Nation to come and govern us, was not seen in the earth till recently. I consider it has been reserved for these our Latter Generations; a product long ripening for us from afar;—and would fain hope that, like the Long Parliament, or acme and consummate flower in any kind, it can only be a transient phenomenon!

Some functions that are and continue real the Parliament still has;—and these it becomes infinitely necessary to dissever, and extricate alive, from the ocean of unreality in which they swim. Unreality is death, to Parliaments and to all things. The real functions whatsoever they are, these, most certainly, are all the good we shall ever get of Parliament; and the question now is, Shall said good be drowned, or not be drowned, in the immeasurable accompaniment of imaginary functions which are evil and falsity, and that only?

In the way of changed times I note two grand modern facts, omitting many minor, which have, one of them irrevocably, and the other hopelessly for the present, altered from top to bottom the function and position of all Parliaments; and which do now fatally vitiate their procedure everywhere, rendering much of what they do a superfluity, a mere hypocrisy, or noxious grimace; and thus infecting even what is real in their function with a windy falsity, lamentable to behold and greatly requiring to be altered: Fact *first*, the existence of an Unfettered Press, with its perennial ever-increasing torrent of morning newspapers, pamphlets, books: fact *second*, that there is now no King present in Parliament; no King now there, the *King* having vanished,—in front of Whitehall, long since! Fact first I take to be unalterable. Complete alteration of fact second I discern to be distant, but likewise to be indispensable and inevitable; and to require urgently here and now (by *New Downing Streets* or otherwise) a strenuous beginning, from all good citizens who would do any reform in their generation. Both facts together have dislocated every joint of the old arrangement, and made the modern Parliament a new creature; and whosoever means to work reform there, will either open his eyes, and keep them open, to both these facts, or work only mischief and ruin.

In countries that can stand a Free Press,—which many cannot, but which England, thanks to her long good training, still can,—it is evident the National Consult or *real* Parliamentary Debate goes on of itself, everywhere, continually. Is not the *Times* newspaper an open Forum, open as never Forum was before, where all mortals vent their opinion, state their grievance,—all manner of grievances, from loss of your umbrella in a railway, to loss of your honour and fortune by unjust sovereign persons? One grand branch of the Parliament's trade is evidently dead forever! And the beautiful Elective Parliament itself is nothing like so living as it used to be. If we will consider it, the essential truth of the matter is, every British man can now elect *himself* to Parliament without consulting the hustings at all. If there be any vote, idea or notion in him, on any earthly or heavenly thing, cannot he take a pen, and therewith autocratically pour forth the same into the ears and hearts of all people, so far as it will go? Precisely so far; and, what is a great advantage too, no farther. The discussion of questions goes on, not in St. Stephen's now, but from Dan to Beersheba by able-editors and articulate-speaking creatures that *can* get others to listen to them. This is the fact; and it demands to be attended to as such,—and will produce changes, I think, by and by.

What is the good of men collected, with effort, to debate on the benches of St. Stephen's, now when there is a *Times* Newspaper? Not the discussion of questions; only the ultimate voting of them (a very brief process, I should think!) requires to go on, or can veritably go on, in St. Stephen's now. The honourable gentleman is oftenest very wearisome in St. Stephen's now: his and his Constituency's *Aye* or *No*, is all we want of the honourable gentleman there; all we are ever like to get of him there,—could it but be had without admixtures! If your Lordship will reflect on it, you will find it an obsolete function, this debating one of his; useless in these new times, as a set of riding postboys would be, along the line of the Great Western Railway. Loving my life, and time which is the stuff of life, I read no Parliamentary Debates, rarely any Parliamentary Speech; but I am told there is not, once in the seven years, the smallest gleam of new intelligence thrown on any matter, earthly or divine, by an honourable gentleman on his legs in Parliament. Nothing offered you but wearisome, dreary, thrice-boiled colewort;—a bad article at first, and served and again served in Newspapers and Periodical and other Literatures, till even the inferior animals would recoil from it. Honourable gentlemen have complained to myself that under the sky there was not such a bore. What is or can be the use of this, your Lordship?

Let an honourable gentleman who has colewort, or stump-oratory of that kind, send it direct to the *Times*; perhaps they will print it for him, and then all persons can read it there who hope instruction from it. If the *Times* refuse to print it, let the honourable gentleman, if still so minded, print it at his own expense; let him advertise it at a penny the gross, distribute it gratis as handbill, or even offer a small reward per head to any citizen that will read it: but if, after all, no body of citizens will read it even for a reward, then let the honourable gentleman retire into himself, and consider what such omens mean! So much I take to be fair, or at least unavoidable in a free country: Let every creature try to get his opinion listened to; and let honourable gentlemen who can print their own stump-oratory, and offer the public a reward for using it, by all means do so. But that, when no human being will incline or even consent to have their said oratory, they can get upon their legs in Parliament and pour it out still, to the burdening of many Newspapers, to the boring of their fellow-creatures, and generally to the despair of all thinking citizens in the community: this is and remains, I must crave to say, an infatuation, and, whatever respectable old coat you put upon it, is fast growing a nuisance which must be abated.

Still more important for a Parliament is the question: King present there, or no King? Certain it always is, and if forgotten, it much requires to be brought to mind, that a Parliament acting in the character of a body to be consulted by the sovereign ruler, or executive King of a Nation, differs immensely from a Parliament which is itself to enact the sovereign ruler, and to be supreme over all things; not merely giving its advice, its remonstrance, dissent or assent, and leaving the ruler still to decide with that new illumination; but deciding of itself, and by its Yes or its No peremptorily ordering all things to be or not to be. These, I say, are two extremely different characters for a Parliament to enact; and they necessitate all manner of distinctions, of the most vital nature, in our idea of a Parliament; so that what applies with full force to a Parliament acting the former character, will not apply at all to one enacting the latter: nay, what is of the highest benefit in the former kind of Parliament, may not only in the latter kind be of no benefit, but be even of the fatalest detriment, and bring destruction to the poor Parliament itself and to all that depends thereon.

It is first of all, therefore, to be inquired, Whether your Parliament is actually in practice the Adviser of the Sovereign; or is the Sovereign itself? For the distinction is profound; goes down to the very roots of Parliament and of the Body Politic: and if you confound the two kinds of Parliaments, and apply to the one the psalmodyings and celebratings of constitutional doctors (very rife through the eighteenth century), which were meant for the other, and were partly true of the other, but are altogether false of this,—you will set forth in a radically wrong course, and will advance incessantly, with whatever psalmodyings of your own or of the world's, to a goal you are like to be much surprised at! —Under which of these two descriptions the British Parliament of our time falls, no one can need to be informed. Apart from certain thin fictions, and constitutional cobwebs which it is not expected any one should not see through, our Parliament is the sovereign ruler and real executive King of this Empire; and constitutional men, who for a century past have been singing praises to that sublime Institution in its old character, are requested to look at it in this new one, and see what praises it has earned for itself there. Hitherto, in these last fifteen years since it has worked without shackle in that new character, one does not find its praises mount very high! The exercise of English Sovereignty, if that mean governance of the Twenty-seven million British souls and guidance of their temporal and eternal interests towards a good issue, does not seem to stand on the very best footing just at present! Not as a Sovereign Ruler of the Twenty-seven million British men, or heroic guide of their temporal or their eternal interests, has the reformed Parliament distinguished itself as yet, but otherwise only if at all.

In fact, there rises universally the complaint, and expression of surprise, That our reformed Parliament cannot get on with any kind of work, except that of talking, which does not serve much; and the Chief Minister has been heard lamenting, in a pathetic manner, that the Business of the Nation (meaning thereby the voting of the supplies) was dreadfully obstructed; and that it would be difficult for him to accomplish the Business of the Nation (meaning thereby the voting of the supplies), if honourable gentlemen would not please to hold their tongues a little. It is really pathetic, after a sort; and unless parliamentary eloquence will suffice the British Nation, and its businesses and wants, one sees not what is to become of us in that direction. For, in fine, the tragic experience is dimly but irrepressibly forcing itself on all the world, that our British Parliament does not shine as Sovereign Ruler of the British Nation; that it was excellent only as Adviser of the Sovereign Ruler; and has not, somehow or other, the art of getting work done; but produces talk merely, not of the most instructive sort for most part, and in vortexes of talk is not unlike to submerge itself and the whole of us, if help come not!

My own private notion, which I invite all reformed British citizens to reflect on, is and has for a long time been, That this dim universal experience, which points towards very tragic facts, will more and more rapidly become a clear universal experience, and disclose a tragic law of Nature little dreamt of by constitutional men of these times. That a Parliament, especially a Parliament with Newspaper Reporters firmly established in it, is an entity which by its very nature cannot do work, but can do talk only,—which at times may be needed, and at other times again may be very needless. Consider, in fact, a body of Six-hundred and fifty-eight miscellaneous persons set to consult about 'business' with Twenty-seven millions mostly fools assiduously listening to them, and checking and criticising them:—was there ever since the world began, will there ever be till the world end, any 'business' accomplished in these circumstances? The beginning of all business everywhere, as all practical persons testify, is decidedly this, That every man *shut* his mouth, and do not open it again till his thinking and contriving faculty have elaborated something worth articulating. Which rule will much abridge the flow of speech in such assemblies! This, however, is the preliminary fundamental rule for business; and this, alas, is precisely the rule which cannot be attended to in constitutional Parliaments.

Add now another most unfortunate condition, That your Parliamentary Assembly is *not* very much in earnest, not at all 'dreadfully in earnest,' to do even the best it can; that in general the Nation it represents is no longer an earnest Nation, but a light, sceptical, epicurean one, which for a century has gone along smirking, grimacing, cutting jokes about all things, and has not been bent with dreadful earnestness on anything at all, except on making money each member of it for himself: here, certainly enough, is a Parliament that will do no business except such as can be done in sport; and unfortunately, it is well known, almost none can be done in that way. To which Parliament, in the centre of such a Nation, introduce now assiduous Newspaper Reporters, and six yards of small type laid on all breakfast-tables every morning; alas, are not the Six-hundred and fifty-eight miscellaneous gentlemen, who sit to do sovereign business in such circumstances, verily a self-contradiction, a solecism in Nature, —Nature having appointed that business shall *not* be done in that way? Incapable they of doing business; capable of speech only, and this none of the best. Speech which, as we can too well see, whether it be speech to the question and to the wise men near, or 'speech to Buncombe' (as the Americans call it), to the distant constituencies and the twenty-seven millions mostly fools, will yearly grow more worthless as speech, and threaten to finish by becoming burdensome to gods and men!

So that the sad conclusion, which all experience, wherever it has been tried, is fatally making good, appears to be, That Parliaments, admirable as Advising Bodies, and likely to be in future universally useful in that capacity, are, as Ruling and Sovereign Bodies, not useful, but useless or worse. That a Sovereign with nine-hundred or with six-hundred and fifty-eight heads, all set to talk against each other in the presence of thirty-four or twenty-seven or eighteen millions, cannot do the work of sovereignty at all; but is smitten with eternal incompetence for that function by the law of Nature itself. Such, alas, is the sad conclusion; and in England, and wherever else it is tried, a sad experience will rapidly make it good.

Only perhaps in the United States, which alone of countries can do *without* governing,—every man being at least able to live, and move-off into the wilderness, let Congress jargon as it will,—can such a form of so-called 'Government' continue, for any length of time, to torment men with the semblance, when the indispensable substance is not there. For America, as the citizens well know, is an 'unparalleled country,'—with mud soil enough and fierce sun enough in the Mississippi Valley alone to grow Indian corn for all the extant Posterity of Adam at this time;—what other country ever stood in such a case? 'Speeches to Buncombe,' and a constitutional battle of the Kilkenny cats, which in other countries are becoming tragical and unendurable, may there still fall under the comical category. If indeed America should ever experience a higher call, as is likely, and begin to feel diviner wants than that of Indian corn with abundant bacon and molasses, and unlimited scope for all citizens to hunt dollars,—America too will find that caucuses, division-lists, stump-oratory and speeches to Buncombe will *not* carry men to the immortal gods; that the Washington Congress, and constitutional battle of Kilkenny cats is, there as here, naught for such objects; quite incompetent for such; and, in fine, that said sublime constitutional arrangement will require to be (with terrible throes, and travail such as few expect yet) remodelled, abridged, extended, suppressed; torn asunder, put together again;—not without heroic labour, and effort quite other than that of the Stump-Orator and the Revival Preacher, one day!

Thus if the first grand branch of parliamentary business, that of stating grievances, has fallen to the Unfettered Presses, and become quite dead for Parliaments, infecting them with mere hypocrisy when they now try it,—the second or new grand branch of business intrusted to them, and passionately expected and demanded of them, is one which they cannot do; the attempt and pretence to do which can only still farther involve them in hypocrisy, in fatal cecity, stump-oratory, futility, and the faster accelerate their doom, and ours if we depend on them.

We may take it as a fact, and should lay it to heart everywhere, That no Sovereign Ruler with six-hundred and fifty-eight heads, set to rule twenty-seven millions, by continually talking in the hearing of them all, can for the life of it make a good figure in that vocation; but must by nature make a bad figure, and ever a worse and worse, till, some good day, by soft recession or by rude propulsion, as the Omnipotent Beneficence may direct, it—get relieved from said vocation.

In the whole course of History I have heard of only two Parliaments of the sovereign sort, that did the work of sovereignty with some effect: the National Convention, in Paris, during the French Revolution; and the Long Parliament, here at London, during our own. Not that the work, in either case, was perfect; far enough from that; but with all imperfections it was got done; and neither of these two workers proved to be quite futile, or a solecism in its place in the world. These two Parliaments succeeded, and did not fail. The conditions, however, were peculiar; not likely to be soon seen again.

In the first place, of both these Parliaments it can be said that they *were* 'dreadfully in earnest'; in earnest as no Parliaments before or since ever were. Nay, indeed, in the end, it had become a matter of life or death with them. But apart from that latter consideration, in the Long Parliament especially, nothing so astonishes a modern man as the serious, solemn, nay, devout, religiously earnest spirit in which almost every member had come up to his task. For the English was yet a serious devout Nation,—as in fact it intrinsically still is, and ever tends and strives to be; this its poor modern levity, sceptical knowingness, and sniffing grinning humour, being forced on it, and sitting it very ill: —ever a devout Nation, I say; and the Divine Presence yet irradiated this poor Earth and its business to most men; and to all Englishmen the Parliament, we can observe, was still what their Temple was to the ancient Hebrews; the most august of terrestrial objects, into which when a man entered, he felt that he was standing on holy ground. Literally so; and much is the modern man surprised at it; and only after much reluctance can he admit it to be credible, to be certain and visible among our old fathers there.—In which temper alone, is there not sure promise of work being done, under any circumstances whatsoever? Given any lamest Talking Parliament, with its Chartisms or its starving Irish, and a starving world getting all into pike-points round it; given the saddest natural solecism discoverable in the Earth or under the Earth;—inform it with this noble spirit, it will from the first hour become a *less* sad solecism; it will, if such divine spirit hold in it, and nerve its continual efforts, cease at last to be a solecism, and by self-sacrifice or otherwise become a veracity, and get itself *adopted* by Nature.

But secondly, what likewise is of immense significance, the Long Parliament had no Reporters. Very far from that; no Member himself durst so much as whisper to any extraneous mortal, without leave given, what went on within those sacred walls. Solemn reprimand from the Speaker, austere lodgment in the Tower, if he did. If a patriot stranger, coming up on express pilgrimage from the country, chance to gaze in from the Lobby too curiously on the august Assemblage (as once or twice happens), he is instantly seized by the fit usher; led, pale as his shirt, into the floor of the honourable House, Speaker Lenthall's and four hundred other pairs of Olympian eyes transfixing him, that it be there ascertained, Whether the Tower, the Tarpeian rock, or what in Nature or out of it, shall be the doom of such a man! A silent place withal, though a talking one; hermetically sealed; no whisper to be published of it, except what the honourable House itself directs. Let a modern honourable member, with his reporters' gallery, his strangers' gallery, his female ventilator, and twenty-seven millions mostly fools listening to him at Buncombe, while all at hand are asleep, consider what a fact is that old one!

But thirdly, what also is a most important fact in this question, the Long Parliament, after not many months of private debating, split itself fairly into two parties; and the Opposition party fairly rode away, designing to *debate* in another manner thenceforth. What an abatement of parliamentary eloquence in that one fact by itself, is evident enough! The Long Parliament, for all manner of reasons, for these three and for others that could be given, was an unexampled Parliament—properly indeed, as I sometimes define it, the Father of all Parliaments which have sat since in this world!

The French Convention did its work, too; and this under circumstances intrinsically similar, much as they differed outwardly. No Parliament more 'in earnest' ever sat in any country or time; and indeed it was the Parliament of a Nation all in deadly earnest; gambling against the world for life or for death. The Convention had indeed Reporters; and encountered much parliamentary eloquence at its starting, and underwent strange handlings and destinies in consequence; but we know how *it* managed with its parliamentary eloquence, and got that reduced to limits, when once business did behove to be done! The Convention, its Girondins and opposition parties once thrown out, had its Committee of *Salut Publique*, consisting of Twelve, of Nine, or even properly of Three; in whose hands lay all sovereign business, and the whole terrible task of ascertaining what was to be done. Of which latter, the latter being itself so immense, so swift and imperatively needful, all parliamentary eloquence was to be the enforcement and publisher and recorder merely. And whatever eloquent heads chose to obstruct this sovereign Committee, the Convention had its guillotine, and swiftly rid itself of these and of their eloquence. Whereby business went on, without let on that side; and actually got itself done!

These are the only instances I know, of Parliaments that succeeded in the business of Government; and these I think are *not* inviting instances to the British reformer of this day. Rather what we may call paroxysms of parliamentary life, than instances of what could be continuously expected of any Parliament,—or perhaps even transiently wished of any. They were the appropriate, and as it proved, the effectual organism for Periods of a quite transcendent character in National Life; such as it is not either likely or desirable that we should see, except at very long intervals, in human affairs.

The fact is, Parliaments have had two great blows, in modern times: and are now in a manner quite shorn of their real strength, and what is still worse, invested with an imaginary. Faust of Mentz, when he invented 'movable types,' inflicted a terrible blow on Parliaments; suddenly, though yet afar off, reducing them to a mere scantling of their former self, and taking all the best business out of their hands. Then again John Bradshaw, when he ordered the hereditary *King* to vanish, in front of Whitehall, and proclaimed that Parliament itself was King,—John, little conscious of it, inflicted a still more terrible blow on Parliaments; appointing them to do (especially with *Faust* too, or the Morning Newspaper, gradually getting in) what Nature and Fact had decided they could never do. In which doubly fatal state, with Faust busier than ever among them, they continue at this moment,—working towards strange issues, I do believe!

Or, speaking in less figurative language, our conclusion is, *first*, That Parliaments, while they continued, as our English ones long did, mere Advisers of the Sovereign Ruler, were invaluable institutions; and did, especially in periods when there was no *Times* Newspaper, or other general Forum free to every citizen who had three fingers and a smattering of grammar,—deserve well of mankind, and achieve services for which we should be always grateful. This is conclusion first. But then, alas, equally irrefragable comes conclusion *second*, That Parliaments when they get to try, as our poor British one now does, the art of governing by themselves as the Supreme Body in the Nation, make no figure in that capacity, and can make none, but by the very nature of the case are unable to do it. Only two instances are on record of Parliaments having, in any circumstances, succeeded as Governing Bodies; and it is even *hoped*, or ought to be, by men generally, that there may not for another thousand years be a third!

As not only our poor British Parliament of those years and decades, but all the sudden European Parliaments at Paris, Frankfort, Erfurt and elsewhere, are Parliaments which undertake that second or impossible function of governing as Parliaments, and must either do it, or sink in black anarchy one knows not whitherward,—the horoscope of Parliaments is by no means cheering at present; and good citizens may justly shudder, if their anticipations point that way, at the prospect of a Chartist Parliament here. For your Chartist Parliament is properly the consummation of that fatal tendency, towards the above-mentioned impossible function, on the part of Parliaments. A tendency not yet consummated with us; for we still have other fragments of old Authority lodged elsewhere than in the Parliament, which still struggles here and there to accomplish a little governing though under strange conditions: and to instal a Parliament of the Six Points would be precisely to extinguish with the utmost rapidity all such fragments, and solemnly by National Charter and Six Points, to bid the Parliament, "Be supreme King over us, thou, in all respects; and rule us, thou,—since it is impossible for thee!"

These are serious considerations, sufficient to create alarm and astonishment in any constitutional man. But really it grows late in the day with constitutional men; and it is time for them to look up from their Delolme. If the constitutional man will take the old Delolme-Bentham spectacles off his nose, and look abroad into the Fact itself with such eyes as he may have, I consider he will find that reform in matters social does *not* now mean, as he has long sleepily fancied, reform in Parliament alone or chiefly or perhaps at all. My alarming message to him is, that the thing we vitally need is not a more and more perfectly elected Parliament, but some reality of a Ruling Sovereign to preside over Parliament; that we have already got the former entity in some measure, but that we are farther than ever from the road towards the latter; and that if the latter be missed and not got, there is no life possible for us. A New Downing Street, an infinitely reformed Governing Apparatus; there some hope might lie. A Parliament, any conceivable Parliament, continuing to attempt the function of Governor, can lead us only into No-Government which is called Anarchy; and the more 'reformed' or Democratic you make it, the swifter will such consummation be.

Men's hopes from a Democratic or otherwise reformed Parliament are various, and rather vague at present; but surely this, as the ultimate essence, lies and has always lain in the heart of them all: That hereby we shall succeed better in doing the commandment of Heaven, instead of everywhere violating or ignoring Heaven's commandment, and incurring Heaven's curse, as now. To ascertain better and better what the will of the Eternal was and is with us, what the Laws of the Eternal are, all Parliaments, Ecumenic Councils, Congresses, and other Collective Wisdoms, have had this for their object. This or else nothing easily conceivable,—except to merit damnation for themselves, and to get it too! Nevertheless, in the inexplicable universal votings and debatings of these Ages, an idea or rather a dumb presumption to the contrary has gone idly abroad; and at this day, over extensive tracts of the world, poor human beings are to be found, whose practical belief it is that if we 'vote' this or that, so this or that will thenceforth *be*. "Who 's to decide it?" they all ask, as if the whole or chief question lay there. "Who 's to decide it?" asks the irritated British citizen, with a sneer in his tone. "Who 's to decide it?" asks he, oftener than any other question of me. Decide it, O irritated British citizen? Why, thou, and I, and each man into whose living soul the Almighty has breathed a gleam of understanding; we are all, and each of us for his own self, to decide it: and woe will befall us, each and all, if we don't decide it *aright*; according as the Almighty has already 'decided' it, as it has been appointed to be and to continue, before all human decidings and after them all!—

Practically men have come to imagine that the Laws of this Universe, like the laws of constitutional countries, are decided by voting; that it is all a study of division-lists, and for the Universe too, depends a little on the activity of the whipper-in. It is an idle fancy. The Laws of this Universe, of which if the Laws of England are not an exact transcript, they should passionately study to become such, are fixed by the everlasting congruity of things, and are not fixable or changeable by voting! Neither properly, we say, are the Laws of England, or those of any other land never so republican or red-republican, fixable or changeable by that poor foolish process; not at all, O constitutional Peter, much as it may astonish you! Voting is a method we have agreed upon for settling temporary discrepancies of opinion as to what is law or not law, in this small section of the Universe called England: a good temporary method, possessing some advantages; which does settle the discrepancy for the moment. Nay, if the votings were sincere and loyal, we might have some chance withal of being *right* as to the question, and of settling it blessedly forever;—though again, if the votings are insincere, selfish, almost professedly *dis*loyal, and given under the influence of beer and balderdash, we have the proportionate sad chance of being *wrong*, and so settling it under curses, to be fearfully unsettled again!

For I must remark to you, and reiterate to you, that a continued series of votings transacted incessantly for sessions long, with three-times-three readings, and royal assents as many as you like, cannot make a law the thing which *is* no law. No, that lies beyond them. They can make it a sheepskin Act of Parliament; and even hang men (though now with difficulty) for not obeying it:—and this they reckon enough; the idle fools! I tell you and them, it is a miserable blunder, this self-styled 'law' of theirs; and I for one will study either to have no concern with it, or else by all judicious methods to *dis*obey said blundering impious pretended 'law.' In which sad course of conduct, very unpleasant to my feelings, but needful at such times, the gods and all good men, and virtually these idle fools themselves, will be on my side; and so I shall succeed at length, in spite of obstacles; and the pretended 'law' will take down its gibbet-ropes, and abrogate itself, and march, with the town-drum beating in the rear of it, and beadles scourging the back of it, and ignominious idle clamour escorting it, to Chaos, one day; and the Prince of Darkness, Father of Delusions, Devil, or whatever his name be, who is and was always *its* true proprietor, will again hold possession of it,—much good may it do him!

My friend, do you think had the united Posterity of Adam voted, and since the Creation done nothing but vote, that three and three were seven,—would this have altered the laws of arithmetic; or put to the blush the solitary Cocker who continued to assert privately that three and three were six? I consider, not. And is arithmetic, think you, a thing more fixed by the Eternal, than the laws of justice are, and what the right is of man towards man? The builder of this world was Wisdom and Divine Foresight, not Folly and Chaotic Accident. Eternal Law is silently present, everywhere and everywhen. By Law the Planets gyrate in their orbits;—by some approach to Law the Street-Cabs ply in their thoroughfares. No pin's point can you mark within the wide circle of the All where God's Laws are not. Unknown to you, or known (you had better try to know them a little!)—inflexible, righteous, eternal; not to be questioned by the sons of men. Wretched being, do you hope to prosper by assembling six-hundred and fifty-eight poor creatures in a certain apartment, and getting them, after debate, and "Divide,—'vide,—'vide," and report in the *Times*, to vote what is *not* is? You will carry it, you, by your voting and your eloquencing and babbling; and the adamantine basis of the Universe shall bend to your third reading, and paltry bit of engrossed sheepskin and dog-latin? What will become of you?

Unless perhaps the Almighty Maker has forgotten this miserable anthill of a Westminster, of an England; and has no Laws in force here which are of moment to Him? Not here and now; only in Judea, and distant countries at remote periods of time? Confess it, Peter, you have some cowardly notion to that effect, though ashamed to say so! Miserable soul! Don't you notice gravitation here, the law of birth and of death, and other laws? Peter, do you know why the Age of Miracles is past? Because you are become an enchanted human ass (I grieve to say it); and merely bray parliamentary eloquence; rejoice in chewed gorse, scrip coupons, or the like; and have no discernible 'Religion,' except a degraded species of Phallus-Worship, whose liturgy is in the Circulating Libraries!

In Parliaments, Constitutional Conclaves and Collective Wisdoms, it is too fatally certain there have been many things approved of, which it was found on trial Nature did not approve but disapprove. Nature told the individual trying to lead his life by such rule, No; the Nation of individuals, No. "Not this way, my children, though the wigs that prescribed it were of great size, and the bowowing they enforced it with was loud; not by this way is victory and blessedness attainable; by other ways than this. Only stagnation, degradation, choked sewers, want of potatoes, uncultivated heaths, overturned mud-cabins, and at length Chartism, street-barricades, Red Republic, and Chaos come again, will prove attainable by this!"

Here below there is but one thing needful; one thing;—and that one will in nowise consent to be dispensed with! He that can ascertain, in England or elsewhere, what the laws of the Eternal are and walk by them voted for or unvoted, with him it will be well; with him that misses said laws, and only gets himself voted for, not well. Voting, in fact, O Peter, is a thing I value but little in any time, and almost at zero in this. Not a divine thing at all, my poor friend, but a human; and in the beer-and-balderdash case, whatever constitutional doctors may say, almost a brutal. Voting, never a divine Apollo, was once a human Bottom the Weaver; and, so long as he continued in the sane and sincere state, was worth consulting about several things. But alas, enveloped now in mere stump-oratory, cecity, mutinous imbecility, and sin and misery, he is now an enchanted Weaver,—wooed by the fatuous Queen of constitutional Faëry,—and feels his cheek hairy to the scratch. Beer rules him, and the Infinite of Balderdash; and except as a horse might vote for tares or hard beans, he had better, till he grow wise again, hardly vote at all. I will thank thee to take him away, into his own place, which is very low down indeed; and to put in the upper place something infinitely worthier. You ask what thing; in a triumphant manner, with erect ear and curved tail, O hapless quadruped? How can I tell *you* what thing? I myself know it, and every soul still human knows it, or may know; but to the soul that has fallen asinine, and thinks the Laws of God are to be voted for, it is unknowable.

'If of ten men nine are recognisable as fools, which is a common calculation,' says our *Intermittent* Friend, 'how, in the name of wonder, will you ever get a ballot-box to grind you out a wisdom from the votes of these ten men? Never by any conceivable ballot-box, nor by all the machinery in Bromwicham or out of it, will you attain such a result. Not by any method under Heaven, except by suppressing, and in some good way reducing to zero, nine of those votes, can wisdom ever issue from your ten.

'Why men have got so universally into such a fond expectation? The reason might lead us far. The reason, alas, is, men have, to a degree never before exampled, forgotten that there is fixed eternal law in this Universe; that except by coming upon the dictates of that, no success is possible for any nation or creature. That we should have forgotten this,—alas, here is an abyss of vacuity in our much-admired opulence, which the more it is looked at saddens the thinking heart the more.

'And yet,' continues he elsewhere, 'it is unavoidable and indispensable at present. With voting and ballot-boxing who can quarrel, as the matter stands? I pass it without quarrel; nay, say respectfully, "Good speed to you, poor friends: Heaven send you not only a good voting-box, but something worth voting for! Sad function yours, giving plumpers or split-votes for or against such a pair of human beings, and such a set of human causes. Adieu!"'

And yet surely, not in England only, where the Institution is like a second nature to us, but in all countries where men have attained any civilisation, it is good that there be a Parliament. Morning Newspapers, and other temporary or permanent changes of circumstances, may much change and almost infinitely abridge its function, but they never can abolish it. Under whatever reformed Downing Street, or indispensable new King, of these New Eras, England be governed, its Parliament too will continue indispensable. And it is much to be desired that all men saw clearly what the Parliament's real function, in these changed times of newspaper reporters and imaginary kings, had grown to be. We must set it to its real function; and, at our peril and its, restrict it to that! Its real function is the maximum of all we shall be able to get out of it. Wrap it in never so many sheepskins, and venerabilities of use-and-wont, you will not get it persuaded to do what its real function is *not*. Endless derangement, spreading into futility on every side, and ultimate ruin even to its real function, will result to you from setting it to work against what Nature and Fact have appointed for it. Your Dray-wagon, excellent for carting beer along the streets,—start not with it from the chimney-tops, as Chariot of the Sun; for it will not act in that capacity!—

As a 'Collective *Wisdom*' of Nations the talking Parliament, I discern too well, can never more serve. Wisdom dwells not with stump-oratory; to the stump-orator Wisdom has waved her sad and peremptory farewell. A Parliament, speaking through reporters to Buncombe and the Twenty-seven millions mostly fools, has properly given up that function; that is not now the function it attempts. But even as the Condensed Folly of Nations; Folly bound up into articulate masses, and able to say Yes and No for itself, it will much avail the Governing Man! To know at what pitch the widespread Folly of the Nation now stands, what may safely be attempted with said Folly, and what not safely: this too is very indispensable for the Governing Man. Below *this* function, in the maddest times and with Faust of

Mentz reverberating every madness *ad infinitum*, no Parliament can fall.

Votes of men are worth collecting, if convenient. True, their opinions are generally of little wisdom, and can on occasion reach to all conceivable and inconceivable degrees of folly; but their instincts, where these can be deciphered, are wise and human; these, hidden under the noisy utterance of what they call their opinions, are the unspoken sense of man's heart, and well deserve attending to. Know well what the people inarticulately feel, for the Law of Heaven itself is dimly written there; nay, do not neglect, if you have opportunity, to ascertain what they vote and say. One thing the stupidest multitude at a hustings can do, provided only it be sincere: Inform you how *it* likes this man or that, this proposed law or that. "I do not like thee, Dr. Fell; the reason why I cannot tell,"—and perhaps indeed there is no reason; nevertheless let the Governor too be thankful to know the fact, 'full well'; for it may be useful to him. Nay, the multitude, even when its nonsense is not sincere, but produced in great part by beer and stump-oratory, will yet by the very act of voting feel itself bound in honour; and so even in that case it apprises you, "Such a man, such a law, will I accept, being persuaded thereto by beer and stump-oratory, and having polled at hustings for the same."

Beyond doubt it will be useful, will be indispensable, for the King or Governor to know what the mass of men think upon public questions legislative and administrative; what they will assent to willingly, what unwillingly; what they will resist with superficial discontents and remonstrances, what with obstinate determination, with riot, perhaps with armed rebellion. No Governor otherwise can go along with clear illumination on his path, however plain the loadstar and ulterior goal be to him; but at every step he must be liable to fall into the ditch; to awaken he knows not what nests of hornets, what sleeping dogkennels, better to be avoided. By all manner of means let the Governor inform himself of all this. To which end, Parliaments, Free Presses, and suchlike are excellent; they keep the Governor fully aware of what the People, wisely or foolishly, think. Without in some way knowing it with moderate exactitude, he has not a possibility to govern at all. For example, the Chief Governor of Constantinople, having no Parliament to tell it him, knows it only by the frequency of incendiary fires in his capital, the frequency of bakers hanged at their shop-lintels; a most inferior *ex-postfacto* method!—Profitable indisputably, essential in all cases where practicable, to know clearly what and where the obstacles are. Marching with noble aim, with the heavenly loadstars ever in your eye, you will thus choose your path with the prudence which is also noble, and reach your aim surely, if more slowly.

With the real or seeming slowness we do not quarrel. The winding route, on uneven surfaces, may often be the swiftest; that is a point for your own prudences, practical sagacities, and qualities as a King: the indispensable point, for both you and us, is that you do always advance, unresting if unhasting, and know in every fibre of you that arrive you must. Rigidly straight routes find some admiration with the vulgar, and are rather apt to please at hustings; but we know well enough they are no clear sign of strength of purpose. The Leming-rat, I have been told, travelling in myriads seaward from the hills of Norway, turns not to the right or the left: if these rats meet a haystack, they eat their way through it; if a stone house, they try the same feat, and not being equal to eating the house, climb the walls of it, pour over the roof of it, and push forward on the old line, swimming or ferrying rivers, scaling or rounding precipices; most consistent Leming-rats. And what is strange, too, their errand seaward is properly none. They all perish, before reaching the sea, or of hunger on the sand-beach; their consistent rigidly straight journey was a journey nowhither! I do not ask your Lordship to imitate the Leming-rat.

But as to universal suffrage, again,—can it be proved that, since the beginning of the world, there was ever given a universal vote in favour of the worthiest man or thing? I have always understood that true worth, in any department, was difficult to recognise; that the worthiest, if he appealed to universal suffrage, would have but a poor chance. John Milton, inquiring of universal England what the worth of *Paradise Lost* was, received for answer, Five Pounds Sterling. George Hudson, inquiring in like manner what his services on the railways might be worth, received for answer (prompt temporary answer), Fifteen Hundred Thousand ditto. Alas, Jesus Christ asking the Jews what *he* deserved, was not the answer, Death on the gallows!—Will your Lordship believe me, I feel it almost a shame to insist on such truisms. Surely the doctrine of judgment by vote of hustings has sunk now, or should be fast sinking, to the condition of obsolete with all but the commonest of human intelligences. With me, I must own, it has never had any existence. The mass of men consulted at hustings, upon any high matter whatsoever, is as ugly an exhibition of human stupidity as this world sees.

Universal suffrage assembled at hustings,—I will consult it about the quality of New-Orleans pork, or the coarser kinds of Irish butter; but as to the character of men, I will if possible ask it no question: or if the question be asked and the answer given, I will generally consider, in cases of any importance, that the said answer is likely to be wrong,—that I have to listen to the said answer and receive it as authentic, and for my own share to go, and with whatever strength may lie in me, do the reverse of the same. Even so, your Lordship; for how should I follow a multitude to do evil? There are such things as multitudes all full of beer and nonsense, even of insincere factitious nonsense, who by hypothesis cannot but be wrong. Or what safety will there be in a thousand or ten thousand brawling potwallopers, or blockheads of any rank whatever, if the Fact, namely the whole

Universe and the Eternal Destinies, be against me? These latter I for my share will try to follow, even if alone in doing so. It will be better for me.

Your Lordship, there are fools, cowards, knaves, and gluttonous traitors true only to their own appetite, in immense majority, in every rank of life; and there is nothing frightfuler than to see these voting and deciding! "Not your way, my unhappy brothers, shall it be decided; no, not while I, and 'a company of poor men' you may have heard of, live in this world. Vote it as you please," my friend Oliver was wont to say or intimate; "vote it so, if you like; there is a company of poor men that will spend all their blood before they see it settled so!"—Who, in such sad moments, but has to *hate* the profane vulgar, and feel that he must and will debar it from him! And alas, the vulgarest vulgar, I often find, are not those in ragged coats at this day; but those in fine, superfine, and superfinest;—the more is the pity! Superfine coat symbolically indicates, like official stamp and signature, *Bank-of-England Thousand-Pound Note*; and blinkard owls, in city and country, accept it cheerfully as such: but look closer, you may find it mere *Bank of Elegance*; a flash-note travelling towards the eternal Fire;—and will have nothing to do with it, you, I hope!

Clearly enough, the King in constitutional countries would wish to ascertain all men's votes, their opinions, volitions on all manner of matters; that so his whole scene of operations, to the last cranny of it, might be illuminated for him, and he, wherever he were working, might work with perfect knowledge of the circumstances and materials. But the King, New Downing Street, or whatever the Sovereign's name is, will be a very poor King indeed if he *admit* all these votes into his system of procedure, and transform them into acts;—indeed I think, in that case, he will not be long for this world as a King! No: though immense acclamation attend him at the first outset in that course, every volition and opinion finding itself admitted into the poor King's procedure,—yet unless the volitions and opinions are wise and not foolish, not the smallest ultimate prosperity can attend him; and all the acclamations of the world will not save him from the ignominious lot which Nature herself has appointed for all creatures that do *not* follow the Law which Nature has laid down.

You ask this and the other man what is his opinion, his notion, about varieties of things: and having ascertained what his notion is, and carried it off as a piece of information,—surely you are bound, many times, most times if you are a wise man, to go directly in the teeth of it, and for his sake and for yours to do directly the contrary of it. Any man's opinion one would accept; all men's opinion, could it be had absolutely without trouble, might be worth accepting. Nay, on certain points I even ask my horse's opinion:—as to whether beans will suit him at this juncture, or a truss of tares; on this and the like points I carefully consult my horse; gather, by such language as he has, what my horse's candid opinion as to beans or the truss of tares is, and unhesitatingly follow the same. As what prudent rider would not? There is no foolishest man but knows one and the other thing more clearly than any the wisest man does; no glimmer of human or equine intelligence but can disclose something which even the intelligence of a Newton, *not* present in that exact juncture of circumstances, would not otherwise have ascertained. To such length you would gladly consult all equine, and much more all human intelligences:—to such length; and, strictly speaking, not any farther.

Of what use towards the general result of finding out what it is wise to do,—which is the one thing needful to all men and nations,—can the fool's vote be? It is either coincident with the wise man's vote, throwing no new light on the matter, and therefore superfluous; or else it is contradictory, and therefore still more superfluous, throwing mere darkness on the matter, and imperatively demanding to be annihilated, and returned to the giver with protest. Woe to you if you leave that valid! There are expressions of volition too, as well as of opinion, which you collect from foolish men, and even from inferior creatures: these can do you no harm, these it may be very beneficial for you to have and know;—but these also, surely it is often imperative on you to contradict, and would be ruinous and baleful for you to *follow*. You have to apprise the unwise man, even as you do the unwiser horse: "On the truss of tares I took your vote, and have cheerfully fulfilled it; but in regard to choice of roads and the like, I regret to say you have no competency whatever. No, my unwise friend, we are for Hammersmith and the West, not for Highgate and the Northern parts, on this occasion: not by that left turn, by this turn to the right runs our road; thither, for reasons too intricate to explain at this moment, it will behove thee and me to go: Along, therefore!"—

"But how?" your Lordship asks, and all the world with you: "Are not two men stronger than one; must not two votes carry it over one?" I answer; No, nor two thousand nor two million. Many men vote; but in the end, you will infallibly find, none counts except the few who were *in the right*. Unit of that class, against as many zeros as you like! If the King's thought *is* according to the will of God, or to the law appointed for this Universe, I can assure your Lordship the King will ultimately carry that, were he but one in it against the whole world.

It is not by rude force, either of muscle or of will, that one man can govern twenty men, much more twenty millions of men. For the moment, if all the twenty are stark against his resolution never so wise, the twenty for the moment must have their foolish way; the wise resolution, for the moment, cannot be carried. Let their votes be taken, or known (as is often possible) without taking; and once well taken, let them be weighed,—which latter operation, also an essential one for the King or Governor, is very difficult. If the weight be in favour of the Governor, let him in general proceed; cheerfully accepting adverse account of heads, and dealing wisely with that according to his means;—often enough, in pressing cases, flatly disregarding that, and walking through the heart of it; for in general it is but frothy folly and loud-blustering rant and wind.

I have known minorities, and even small ones by the account of heads, do grand national feats long memorable to all the world, in these circumstances. Witness Cromwell and his Puritans; a minority at all times, by account of heads; yet the authors or saviours, as it ultimately proved, of whatsoever is divinest in the things we can still reckon ours in England. Minority by tale of heads; but weighed in Heaven's balances, a most clear majority: this 'company of poor men that will spend their blood rather,' on occasion shown,—it has now become a noble army of heroes, whose conquests were appointed to endure forever. Indeed it is on such terms that grand national and other feats, by the sons of Adam, are generally done. Not without risk and labour to the doers of them; no surely, for it never was an easy matter to do the real will of a Nation, much more the real will of this Universe in respect to a Nation. No, that is difficult and heroic; easy as it is to count the voting heads of a Nation at any time, and do the behests of their beer and balderdash; empty behests, very different from even their 'will,' poor blockheads, to say nothing of the Nation's will and the Universe's will! Which two, especially which latter, are alone worth doing.

But if not only the number but the weight of votes preponderate against your Governor, he, never so much in the right, will find it wise to hold his hand; to delay, for a time, this his beneficent execution, which is ultimately inevitable and indispensable, of Heaven's Decrees; the Nation being still unprepared. He will leave the bedarkened Nation yet a while alone. What can he do for it, if not even a small minority will stand by him? Let him strive to enlighten the Nation; let him pray, and in all ways endeavour, that the Nation be enlightened,—that a small minority may open their eyes and hearts to the message of Heaven, which he, heavy-laden man and governor, *has* been commissioned to see done in this transitory earth, at his peril! Heaven's message, sure enough, if it be true; and Hell's if it be not, though voted for by innumerable two-legged animals without feathers or with!

On the whole, honour to small minorities, when they are genuine ones. Severe is their battle sometimes, but it is victorious always like that of gods. Tancred of Hauteville's sons, some eight centuries ago, conquered all Italy; bound it up into organic masses, of vital order after a sort; founded thrones and principalities upon the same, which have not yet entirely vanished,—which, the last dying wrecks of which, still wait for some worthier successor, it would appear. The Tancred Normans were some Four Thousand strong; the Italy they conquered in open fight, and bound up into masses at their ordering will, might count Eight Millions, all as large of bone, as eupeptic and black-whiskered as they. How came the small minority of Normans to prevail in this so hopeless-looking debate? Intrinsically, doubt it not, because they were in the right; because, in a dim, instinctive, but most genuine manner, they were doing the commandment of Heaven, and so Heaven had decided that they were to prevail. But extrinsically also, I can see, it was because the Normans were *not* afraid to have their skin scratched; and were prepared to die in their quarrel where needful. One man of that humour among a thousand of the other, consider it! Let the small minority, backed by the whole Universe, and looked on by such a cloud of invisible witnesses, fall into no despair.

What is to become of Parliament in the New Era, is less

a question with me than what is to become of Downing Street. With a reformed Downing Street strenuously bent on real and not imaginary management of our affairs, I could foresee all manner of reform to England and its Parliament; and at length in the gradual course of years, that highest acme of reform to Parliament and to England, a New Governing Authority, a real and not imaginary King set to preside there. With that, to my view, comes all blessedness whatsoever; without that comes, and can come, nothing but, with ever-accelerated pace, ANARCHY; or the *declaration* of the fact that we have no Governor, and have long had none.

For the rest, Anarchy advances as with seven-league boots, in these years. Either some New Downing Street and Incipiency of a real Hero-Kingship again, or else Chartist Parliament, with Apotheosis of Attorneyism, and Anarchy very undeniable to all the world: one or else the other, it seems to me, we shall soon have. Under a real Kingship the Parliament, we may rest satisfied, would gradually, with whatever difficulty, get itself inducted to its real function, and restricted to that, and moulded to the form fittest for that. If there can be no reform of Downing Street, I care not much for the reform of Parliament. Our doom, I perceive, is the Apotheosis of Attorneyism; into that blackest of terrestrial curses we must plunge, and take our fate there like the others.

For the sake both of the New Downing Street and of whatever its New Parliament may be, let us add here, what will vitally concern both these Institutions, a few facts, much forgotten at present, on the general question of Enfranchisement;—and therewith end. Who is slave, and eternally appointed to be governed; who free, and eternally appointed to govern? It would much avail us all to settle this question.

Slave or free is settled in Heaven for a man; acts of parliament attempting to settle it on earth for him, sometimes make sad work of it. Now and then they correctly copy Heaven's settlement in regard to it; proclaim audibly what is the silent fact, "Here is a free man, let him be honoured!" —and so are of the nature of a God's Gospel to other men concerned. Far oftenest they quite miscopy Heaven's settlement, and copy merely the account of the Ledger, or some quite other settlement in regard to it; proclaiming with an air of discovery, "Here is a Ten-pounder; here is a Thousand-pounder; Heavens, here is a Three-million pounder, —is not he free?" Nay, they are wont, here in England for some time back, to proclaim in the gross, as if it had become credible lately, all two-legged animals without feathers to be 'free.' "Here is a distressed Nigger," they proclaim, "who much prefers idleness to work,—should not he be free to choose which? Is not he a man and brother? Clearly here are two legs and no feathers: let us vote him Twenty millions for enfranchisement, and so secure the blessing of the gods!"—

My friends, I grieve to remind you, but it is eternally the fact: Whom Heaven has made a slave, no parliament of men nor power that exists on Earth can render free. No; he is chained by fetters which parliaments with their millions cannot reach. You can label him free; yes, and it is but labelling him a solecism,—bidding him be the parent of solecisms wheresoever he goes. You can give him pumpkins, houses of tenpound rent, houses of ten-thousand pound: the bigger candle you light within the slave-image of him, it will but show his slave-features on the larger and more hideous scale. Heroism, manful wisdom is not his: many things you can give him, but that thing never. Him the Supreme Powers marked in the making of him, *slave*; appointed him, at his and our peril, not to command but to obey, in this world. Him you cannot enfranchise, not him; to proclaim this man free is not a God's Gospel to other men; it is an alarming Devil's Gospel to himself and to us all. Devil's Gospel little feared in these days; but brewing for the whole of us its big oceans of destruction all the same. States are to be called happy and noble in so far as they settle rightly who is slave and who free; unhappy, ignoble, and doomed to destruction, as they settle it wrong.

We may depend on it, Heaven in the most constitutional countries knows well who is slave, who is not. And with regard to voting, I lay it down as a rule, No real *slave's* vote is other than a nuisance, whensoever or wheresoever or in what manner soever it be given. That is a truth, No slave's vote;—and, alas, here is another not quite so plain, though equally certain, That as Nature and severe Destiny, not mere act of Parliament and possession of money-capital, determine a man's slavehood,—so, by these latter, it has been, in innumerable instances, determined *wrong* just at present! Instances evident to everybody, and instances suspected by nobody but the more discerning:—the fact is, slaves are in a tremendous majority everywhere; and the voting of them (not to be got rid of just yet) is a nuisance in proportion. Nuisance of proportionally tremendous magnitude, properly indeed the grand fountain of all other nuisances whatsoever.

For it is evident, could you entirely exclude the slave's vote, and admit only the heroic free man's vote,—folly, knavery, falsity, gluttonous imbecility, lowmindedness and cowardice had, if not disappeared from the earth, reduced themselves to a rigorous minimum in human affairs; the ultimate New Era, and best possible condition of human affairs, had actually come. This is what I always pray for; rejoicing in everything that furthers it, sorrowing for everything that furthers the reverse of it. And though I know it is yet a great way off, I know also either that it is inevitably coming, or that human society, and the possibility of man's living on this earth, has ended. And so for England too, nay, I think for England most and soonest of all, it will be behooveful that we attain some rectification, innumerable rectifications, in regard to this essential matter; and contrive to bid our Heaven's free men vote, and our Heaven's slaves be silent, with infinitely more correctness than at present. Either on the hither brink of that black sea of Anarchy, wherein other Nations at present lie drowning and plunging, or after weltering through the same, if we can welter,—it will have to be attained. In some measure, in some manner, attained: life depends on that, death on the missing of that.

New definitions of slavery are pressingly wanted just now. The definition of a free man is difficult to find, so that all men could distinguish slave from free; found, it would be invaluable! The free man once universally recognised, we should know him who had the privilege to vote and assist in commanding, at least to go himself uncommanded. Men do not know his definition well at present; never knew it worse; —hence these innumerable sorrows.

The free man is he who is *loyal* to the Laws of this Universe; who in his heart sees and knows, across all contradictions, that injustice *cannot* befall him here; that except by sloth and cowardly falsity evil is not possible here. The first symptom of such a man is not that he resists and rebels, but that he obeys. As poor Henry Marten wrote in Chepstow Castle long ago,

> "Reader, if thou an oft-told tale wilt trust,
> Thou'lt gladly do and suffer what thou must."

Gladly; he that will go gladly to his labour and his suffering, it is to him alone that the Upper Powers are favourable and the Field of Time will yield fruit. 'An oft-told tale,' friend Harry; all the noble of this world have known it, and in various dialects have striven to let us know it! The essence of all 'religion' that was and that will be, is to make men *free*. Who is he that, in this Life-pilgrimage, will consecrate himself at all hazards to obey God and God's servants, and to disobey the Devil and his? With pious valour this free man walks through the roaring tumults, invincibly the way whither he is bound. To him in the waste Saharas, through the grim solitudes peopled by galvanised corpses and doleful creatures, there is a loadstar; and his path, whatever those of others be, is towards the Eternal. A man well worth consulting, and taking the vote of, about matters temporal; and properly the only kind of man. Though always an exceptional, this was once a well-known man. He has become one of the rarest now;—but is not yet entirely extinct; and will become more plentiful, if the Gods intend to keep this Planet habitable long.

Him it were vain to try to find always without mistake; alas, if he were in the majority, this world would be all 'a school of virtue,' which it is far from being. Nevertheless to him, and in all times to him alone, belongs the rule of this world: that he be got to rule, that he be forbidden to rule and not got, means salvation or destruction to the world. Friend Peter, I am perfectly deliberate in calling this the truest doctrine of the constitution you have ever heard. And I recommend you to learn it gradually, and to lay it well to heart; for without it there is no salvation, and all other doctrines of the constitution are leather and prunella. Will any mass of Chancery parchments, think you, of respectablest traditions and Delolme philosophies, save a man or People that forgets this, from the eternal fire? There does burn such a *fire* everywhere under this green earth-rind of ours, and London pavements themselves (as Paris pavements have done) can start up into sea-ridges, with a horrible 'trough of the sea,' if the fire-flood urge!

To this man, I say, belongs eternally the government of the world. Where he reigns, all is blessed; and the gods rejoice, and only the wicked make wail. Where the contrary of him reigns, all is accursed; and the gods lament,—and will, by terrible methods, rectify the matter by and by! Have you forbidden this man to rule? Obey he cannot where the Devil and his servants rule; how can he? He must die thrice ruined, damned by the gods, if he do. He will retire rather, into deserts and rocky inaccessibilities, companion to wild-beasts, to the dumb granites and the eternal stars, far from you and your affairs. You and your affairs, once well quit of him, go by a swift and ever swifter road!

I would recommend your Lordship to attack straightway, by the *Industrial Regiments* or better otherwise, that huge Irish and British Pauper Question, which is evidently the father of questions for us, the *lowest* level in our 'universal stygian quagmire'; and to try whether (without ballot-box) there are no 'kings' discoverable in England who would rally round you, in practical attempt towards draining said quagmire from that point. And to be swift about it; for the time presses,—and if your Lordship is not ready, I think the ballot-boxes and the six points are fast getting ready!

No. VII

HUDSON'S STATUE

[1st July 1850]

At St. Ives in Huntingdonshire, where Oliver Cromwell farmed and resided for some years, the people have determined to attempt some kind of memorial to that memorable character. Other persons in other quarters seem to be, more or less languidly, taking up the question; in Country Papers I have read emphatic leading-articles, recommending and urging that there should be a 'People's Statue' of this great Oliver,—Statue furnished by universal contribution from the English People; and set up, if possible, in London, in Huntingdon, or failing both these places, in St. Ives, or Naseby Field. Indeed a considerable notion seems to exist in the English mind, that some brass or stone acknowledgment is due to Cromwell, and ought to be paid him. So that the vexed question, 'Shall Cromwell have a Statue?' appears to be resuscitating itself; and the weary Public must prepare to agitate it again.

Poor English Public, they really are exceedingly bewildered with Statues at present. They would fain do honour to somebody, if they did but know whom or how. Unfortunately they know neither whom nor how; they are, at present, the farthest in the world from knowing! They have raised a set of the ugliest Statues, and to the most extraordinary persons, ever seen under the sun before. Being myself questioned, in reference to the New Houses of Parliament some years ago, "Shall Cromwell have a Statue?" I had to answer, with sorrowful dubiety: "Cromwell? Side by side with a sacred Charles the Second, sacred George the Fourth, and the other sacred Charleses, Jameses, Georges, and Defenders of the Faith,—I am afraid he wouldn't like it! Let us decide provisionally, No." And now again as to St. Ives and the People's Statue, is it not to be asked in like manner: "Who are the 'People'? Are they a People worthy to build Statues to Cromwell; or worthy only of doing it to Hudson?"——This latter is a consideration that will lead us into far deeper and more momentous than sculptural inquiries; and I will request the reader's excellent company into these for a little.

The truth is, dear Reader, nowhere, to an impartial observant person, does the deep-sunk condition of the English mind, in these sad epochs; and how, in all spiritual or moral provinces, it has long quitted company with fact, and ceased to have veracity of heart, and clearness or sincerity of purpose, in regard to such matters,—more signally manifest itself, than in this affair of Public Statues. Whom doth the king delight to honour? that is the question of questions concerning the king's own honour. Show me the man you honour; I know by that symptom, better than by any other, what kind of man you yourself are. For you show me there what your ideal of manhood is; what kind of man you long inexpressibly to be, and would thank the gods, with your whole soul, for being if you could.

In this point of view, it was always matter of regret with me that Hudson's Statue, among the other wonders of the present age, was not completed. The 25,000*l.* subscribed, or offered as oblation, by the Hero-worshippers of England to their Ideal of a Man, awoke many questions as to what outward figure it could most profitably take, under the eternal canopy; questions never finally settled; nor ever now to be settled, now when the universal Hudson *ragnarök*, or 'twilight of the gods,' has arrived, and it is too clear no statue or cast-metal image of that Incarnation of the English Vishnu will ever be molten now! Why was it not set up; that the whole world might see it; that our 'Religion' might be seen, mounted on some figure of a Locomotive, garnished with Scrip-rolls proper; and raised aloft in some conspicuous place,—for example, on the *other* arch at Hyde-Park Corner? By all opportunities, especially to all subscribers and pious sacrificers to the Hudson Testimonial, I have earnestly urged: Complete your Sin-Offering; buy, with the Five-and-twenty Thousand Pounds, what utmost amount of brazen metal and reasonable sculptural supervision it will cover,—say ten tons of brass, with a tolerable sculptor: model that, with what exactness Art can, into the enduring Brass Portrait and Express Image of King Hudson, as he receives the grandees of this country at his levées or soirées and couchées; mount him on the highest place you can discover in the most crowded thoroughfare, on what you can consider the pinnacle of the English world: I assure you he will have beneficial effects there. To all men who are struggling for your approbation, and fretting their poor souls to fiddlestrings because you will not sufficiently give it, I will say, leading them to the foot of the Hudson mount of vision: "See, my worthy Mr. Rigmarole; consider this surprising Copper Pyramid, in partly human form: did the celestial value of men's approbation ever strike you so forcibly before? The *new* Apollo Belvidere this, or Ideal of the Scrip Ages. What do you think of it? *Allah Ilallah*; there is still one God, you see, in England; and this is his Prophet. Let it be a source of healing to you, my unhappy Mr. Rigmarole; draw from it 'uses of terror,' as the old divines said; uses of amazement, of new wisdom, of unutterable reflection upon the present epoch of the world!"

For, in fact, there was more of real worship in the affair of Hudson than is usual in such. The practical English mind has its own notions as to the Supreme Excellence; knows the real from the spurious Avatar of Vishnu; and does not worship without its reasons. The practical English mind, contemplating its divine Hudson, says with what remainder of reverence is in it: "Yes, you are something like the Ideal of a Man; you are he I would give my right arm and leg, and accept a potbelly, with gout, and an appetite for strong-waters, to be like! You out of nothing can make a world, or huge fortune of gold. A divine intellect is in you, which Earth and Heaven, and Capel Court itself acknowledge; at the word of which are done miracles. You find a dying railway; you say to it, Live, blossom anew with scrip;—and it lives, and blossoms into umbrageous flowery scrip, to enrich with golden apples, surpassing those of the Hesperides, the hungry souls of men. Diviner miracle what god ever did? Hudson,—though I mumble about my thirty-nine articles, and the service of *other* divinities,—Hudson is my god, and to him I will sacrifice this twenty-pound note: if perhaps he will be propitious to me?"

Object not that there was a mixed motive in this worship of Hudson; that perhaps it was not worship at all. Undoubtedly there were two motives mixed, but both of them sincere,—as often happens in worship. 'Transcendent admiration' is defined as the origin of sacrifice; but also the hope of profit joins itself. If by sacrificing a goat, or the like trifle, to Supreme Jove, you can get Supreme Jove's favour, will not that, for one, be a good investment? Jove is sacrificed to, and worshipped, from transcendent admiration: but also, in part, men of practical nature worship him as pumps are primed,—give him a little water, that you may get from him a river. O god-like Hudson, O god-recognising England, why was not the partly anthropomorphous Pyramid of Copper cast, then, and set upon the pinnacle of England, that all men might have seen it, and the sooner got to understand these things! The twenty-five-thousand-pound oblation lay upon the altar at the Bank; this monstrous Copper Vishnu of the Scrip Ages might have been revealed to men, and was not. Unexpected obstacles occurred. In fact, there rose from the general English soul,—lying dumb and infinitely bewildered, but not yet altogether dead, poor wretch,—such a growl of inarticulate amazement, at this unexpected Hudson

Apotheosis, as alarmed the pious worshippers; and their Copper Pyramid remains unrealised; not to be realised to all eternity now, or at least not till Chaos come again, and the ancient mud-gods have dominion! The *Ne-plus-ultra* of Statue-building was within sight; but it was not attained, it was to be forever unattainable.

If the world were not properly *anarchic*, this question 'Who shall have a Statue?' would be one of the greatest and most solemn for it. Who is to have a Statue? means, Whom shall we consecrate and set apart as one of our sacred men? Sacred; that all men may see him, be reminded of him, and, by new example added to old perpetual precept, be taught what is real worth in man. Whom do you wish us to resemble? Him you set on a high column, that all men, looking on it, may be continually apprised of the duty you expect from them. What man to set there, and what man to refuse forevermore the leave to be set there: this, if a country were not anarchic as we say,—ruleless, given up to the rule of Chaos, in the primordial fibres of its being,—would be a great question for a country!

And to the parties themselves, lightly as they set about it, the question is rather great. Whom shall I honour, whom shall I refuse to honour? If a man have any precious thing in him at all, certainly the most precious of all the gifts he can offer is his approbation, his reverence to another man. This is his very soul, this fealty which he swears to another: his personality itself, with whatever it has of eternal and divine, he bends here in reverence before another. Not lightly will a man give this,—if he is still a man. If he is no longer a man, but a greedy blind two-footed animal, 'without soul, except what saves him the expense of salt and keeps his body with its appetites from putrefying'; alas, if he is nothing now but a human money-bag and meat-trough, it is different! In that case his 'reverence' is worth so many pounds sterling; and these, like a gentleman, he will give willingly. Hence the British Statues, such a populace of them as we see. British Statues, and some other more important things! Alas, of how many unveracities, of what a world of *ir*reverence, of sordid debasement, and death in 'trespasses and sins,' is this light unveracious bestowal of one's approbation the fatal outcome! Fatal in its origin; in its developments and thousandfold results so fatal. It is the poison of the universal Upas-tree, under which all human interests, in these bad ages, lie writhing as if in the last struggle of death. Street-barricades rise for that reason, and counterfeit kings have to shave-off their whiskers, and fly like coiners; and it is a world gone mad in misery, by bestowing its approbation wrong!

Give every man the meed of honour he has merited, you have the ideal world of poets; a hierarchy of beneficences, your noblest man at the summit of affairs, and in every place the due gradation of the fittest for that place: a maximum of wisdom works and administers, followed, as is inevitable, by a maximum of success. It is a world such as the idle poets dream of,—such as the active poets, the heroic and the true of men, are incessantly toiling to achieve, and more and more realise. Achieved, realised, it never can be; striven after and approximated to, it must forever be,—woe to us if at any time it be not! Other aim in this Earth we have none. Renounce such aim as vain and hopeless, reject it altogether, what more have you to reject? You have renounced fealty to Nature and its Almighty Maker; you have said practically, "We can flourish very well without minding Nature and her ordinances; perhaps Nature and the Almighty—what are they? A Phantasm of the brain of Priests, and of some chimerical persons that write Books?"—"Hold!" shriek others wildly: "You incendiary infidels;—you should be quiet infidels, and believe! Haven't we a Church? Don't we keep a Church, this long while; best-behaved of Churches, which meddles with nobody, assiduously grinding its organs, reading its liturgies, homiletics, and excellent old moral horn-books, so patiently as Church never did? Can't we doff our hat to it: even look in upon it occasionally, on a wet Sunday; and so, at the trifling charge of a few millions annually, serve *both* God and the Devil? Fools, you should be quiet infidels, and believe!"

To give our approval aright,—alas, to do every one of us what lies in him, that the honourable man everywhere, and he only have honour, that the able man everywhere be put into the place which is fit for him, which is his by eternal right: is not this the sum of all social morality for every citizen of this world? This one duty perfectly done, what more *could* the world have done for it? The world in all departments and aspects of it were a perfect world; everywhere administered by the best wisdom discernible in it, everywhere enjoying the exact maximum of success and felicity possible for it. Imperfectly, and not perfectly done, we know this duty must always be. Not done at all; no longer remembered as a thing which God and Nature and the Eternal Voices do require to be done, —alas, we see too well what kind of a world that ultimately makes for us! A world no longer habitable for quiet persons: a world which in these sad days is bursting into street-barricades, and pretty rapidly turning-out its 'Honoured Men,' as intrusive dogs are turned out, with a kettle tied to their tail. To Kings, Kaisers, Spiritual Papas and Holy Fathers, there is universal "*Apage!* Depart thou; go thou to the—Father of thee!" in a huge world-voice of mob-musketry and sooty execration, uglier than any ever heard before.

Who's to have a Statue? The English, at present, answer this question in a very off-hand manner. So far as I can ascertain the method they have, it is somewhat as follows.

Of course, among the many idle persons to whom an unfortunate world has given money and no work to do, there must be, with or without wisdom (without, for most part), a most brisk demand for work. Work to do is very desirable, for those that have only money and not work. "Alas, one cannot buy *sleep* in the market!" said the rich Farmer-general.

Alas, one cannot buy work there; work, which is still more indispensable. One of these unfortunates with money and no work, whose haunts lie in the dilettante line, among Artists' Studios, Picture-Sales, and the like regions,—an inane kingdom much frequented by the inane in these times,—him it strikes, in some inspired moment, that if a public subscription for a Statue to somebody could be started, good results would follow. Perhaps some Artist, to whom he is Mæcenas, might be got to do the Statue; at all events there would be extensive work and stir going on,—whereby the inspired dilettante, for his own share, might get upon committees, see himself named in the newspapers; might assist in innumerable consultations, open utterances of speech and balderdash; and, on the whole, be comfortably present, for years to come, at something of the nature of 'a house on fire': house innocuously, nay, beneficently on fire: a very Goshen to an idle man with money in his pocket.

This is the germ of the idea; now make your idea an action. Think of a proper Somebody. Almost anybody much heard of in the newspapers, and never yet convicted of felony; a conspicuous commander-in-chief, duke no matter whether of Wellington or of York; successful stump-orator, political intriguer; lawyer that has made two hundred thousand pounds; scrip-dealer that has made two thousand thousand: —anybody of a large class, we are not particular, he will be your proper Somebody. You are then to get a brother idler or two to unite his twenty-pound note to yours: the fire is kindled, smoke rises through the editorial columns; the fire, if you blow it, will break into flame, and become a comfortable house on fire for you; solacing the general idle soul, for years to come; and issuing in a big hulk of Corinthian brass, and a notable instance of hero-worship, by and by.

Such I take to be the origin of that extraordinary population of Brazen and other Images which at present dominate the market-places of towns, and solicit worship from the English people. The ugliest images, and to the strangest class of persons, ever set-up in this world. Do you call these demigods? England must be dreadfully off for demigods! My friend, I will not do the smallest stroke of worship to them. One in the thousand I will snatch out of bad company, if I ever can; the other nine hundred and ninety-nine I will with pious joy, in the like case, reduce to the state of broken metal again, and veil forever from all men. As warming-pans, as cheap brass-candlesticks, men will get good of this metal; as devotionary Images in such form, evil only. These are not heroes, gods, or demigods; and it is a horrible idolatry, if you knew it, to set them up as such!

Are these your Pattern Men? *Great* Men? They are your lucky (or unlucky) Gamblers swollen *big*. Paltry Adventurers for most part; worthy of no worship; and incapable forever of getting any, except from the soul consecrated to flunkyism. Will a man's soul worship that, think you? Never; if you fashioned him of solid gold, big as Benlomond, no heart of a man would ever look upon him except with sorrow and despair. To the flunky heart alone is he, was he or can he at any time be, a thing to look upon with upturned eyes of 'transcendent admiration,' worship or worthship so-called. He, you unfortunate fools, he is not the one we want to be kept in mind of; not he at all by any means! To him and his memory,—if you had not been unfortunate and blockheads,—you would have sunk a coal-shaft rather than raised a column. Deep coalshaft, there to *bury* him and his memory, that men might never speak or hear of him more; not a high column to admonish all men that they should try to resemble him!

Of the sculptural talent manifest in these Brazen Images I say nothing, though much were to be said. For indeed, if there is no talent displayed in them but a perverse one, are not we to consider it a happiness, in that strange case? This big swollen Gambler, and gluttonous hapless 'spiritual Daniel Lambert,' deserved a coalshaft from his brother mortals:

let at least his column be ugly!—Nevertheless ugly columns and images are, in themselves, a real evil. They too preach ugliness after their sort; and have a certain effect, the whole of which is bad. They sanction and consecrate artistic botching, pretentious futility, and the horrible doctrine that this Universe is a Cockney Nightmare,—which no creature ought for a moment to believe, or listen to! In brief, they encourage an already-ugly Population to become in a thousand ways uglier. They too, for their ugliness,—did not the infinitely deeper ugliness of the thing they commemorate absorb all consideration of that,—would deserve, and do in fact incessantly solicit, abolition from the sight of men.

What good in the æsthetic, the moral, social or any human point of view, we are ever to get of these Brazen Images now peopling our chief cities and their market-places, it is impossible to specify. Evil enough we, consciously or unconsciously, get of them; no soul looks upon them approvingly or even indifferently without damage, all the deadlier the less he knows of it. Simple souls they corrupt in the sources of their spiritual being: wise souls, obliged to look on them, look with some feeling of anger and just abhorrence; which is itself a mischief to a peaceable man. Good will never be got of these Brazen Images in their present form. Of what use, till once broken-up and melted into warming-pans, they can ever be to gods or men, I own I cannot see. Gods and men demand that this, which is their sure ultimate destiny, should so soon as possible be realised.

It is tragically evident to me, our first want, which includes all wants, is that of a new real Aristocracy of fact, instead of the extinct imaginary one of title, which the anarchic world is everywhere rebelling against: but if it is from Popular Suffrage that we are to look for such a blessing, is not this extraordinary populace of British Statues, which now dominates our market-places, one of the saddest omens that ever was?

Suffrage announces to us, nothing doubting: "Here are your real demigods and heroic men, ye famous British People; here are Brazen and other Images worthy once more of some worship; this is the New Aristocracy I have chosen, and would choose, for you!" That is Suffrage's opinion. To me this populace of British Statues rises aloft over the Chaos of our affairs like the living symbol and consummate flower of said Chaos, and silently speaks the mournfulest prophecy. Perhaps as strange a Pantheon of brass gods as was ever got together in this world. They stand there, poor wretches, gradually rusting in the sooty rain; black and dismal,—when one thinks of them in some haggard mood of the imagination,—like a set of grisly undertakers come to bury the dead spiritualisms of mankind. There stand they, in all weathers, indicating to the British Population such a Heaven and such an Earth as probably no Population ever had before. In the social, political, religious, artistic, and other provinces of our affairs, they point towards depths of prostrate abasement which no man's thought has yet sounded. Let us timidly glance thitherward a little; gaze, for moments, into those abysses of spiritual death,—which, if we cannot one day sound them, and subdue them, will engulf us all!—And first as to this recipe of Popular Election.

Hudson the railway king, if Popular Election be the rule, seems to me by far the most authentic king extant in this world. Hudson has been 'elected by the people' so as almost none other is or was. Hudson solicited no vote; his votes were silent voluntary ones, not liable to be false: he *did* a thing which men found, in their inarticulate hearts, to be worthy of paying money for; and they paid it. What the desire of every heart was, Hudson had or seemed to have produced: Scrip out of which profit could be made. They 'voted' for him by purchasing his scrip with a profit to him. Every vote was the spontaneous product of those men's deepest insights and most practical convictions, about Hudson and themselves and this Universe: I say, it was not a spoken vote, but a silently-acted one; a vote for once incapable of being insincere. What their appetites, intelligences, stupidities, and pruriences had taught these men, they authentically told you there. I beg you to mark that well. Not by all the ballot-boxes in Nature could you have hoped to get, with such exactness, from these men, what the deepest inarticulate voice of the gods and of the demons in them was, as by this their spontaneous purchase of scrip. It is the ultimate rectified quintessence of these men's 'votes': the distillation of their very souls; the sincerest sincerity that was in them. Without gratitude to Hudson, or even without thought of him, they raised Hudson to his bad eminence, not by their voice given once at some hustings under the influence of balderdash and beer, but by the thought of their heart, by the inarticulate, indisputable dictate of their whole being. Hudson inquired of England: "What precious thing can I do for you, O enlightened Countrymen; what may be the value to you, by popular election, of this stroke of work that lies in me?" Popular election, with universal, with household and other suffrage, free as air, deep as life and death, free and deep as *spoken* suffrage never was or could be, has answered: "Pounds sterling to such and such amount; that is the apparent value of thy stroke of work to *us*,—blockheads as we are." Real value differs from apparent to a frightful extent in this world, try it by what suffrage you will!

Hudson's value as a demigod being what it was, his value as a maker of railways shall hardly concern us here. What Hudson's real worth to mankind in the matter of railways might be I cannot pretend to say. Fact knows it to the uttermost fraction, and will pay it him yet; but men differ widely in opinion, and in general do not in the least know. From my own private observation and conjecture, I should say, Trifling if any worth.

Much as we love railways, there is one thing undeniable:

Railways are shifting all Towns of Britain into new places; no Town will stand where it did, and nobody can tell for a long while yet where it will stand. This is an unexpected, and indeed most disastrous result. I perceive, railways have set all the Towns of Britain a-dancing. Reading is coming up to London, Basingstoke is going down to Gosport or Southampton, Dumfries to Liverpool and Glasgow; while at Crewe, and other points, I see new ganglions of human population establishing themselves, and the prophecy of metallurgic cities which were not heard of before. Reading, Basingstoke and the rest, the unfortunate Towns, subscribed money to get railways; and it proves to be for cutting their own throats. Their business has gone elsewhither; and they —cannot stay behind their business! They are set a-dancing, as I said; confusedly waltzing, in a state of progressive dissolution, towards the four winds; and know not where the end of the death-dance will be for them, in what point of space they will be allowed to rebuild themselves. That is their sad case.

And what an affair it is in each of the shops and houses of those Towns, thus silently bleeding to death, or what we call dancing away to other points of the British territory: how Joplin of Reading, who had anchored himself in that pleasant place, and fondly hoping to live by upholstery and paperhanging, had wedded, and made friends there,—awakens some morning, and finds that his trade has flitted away! Here it is not any longer; it is gone to London, to Bristol: whither has it gone? Joplin knows not whither; knows and sees only that gone it is; and that he by preternatural sagacity must scent it out again, follow it over the world, and catch it again, or else die. Sad news for Joplin:—indeed I fear, should his sagacity be too inconsiderable, he is not unlikely to break his heart, or take to drinking, in these inextricable circumstances! And it is the history, more or less, in every town, house, shop and industrial dwelling-place of the British Empire at this moment;—and the cipher of afflicted Joplins; and the amount of private distress, uncertainty, discontent; and withal of 'revolutionary movement,' created hereby, is tragical to think of. This is 'revolutionary movement' with a witness; revolution brought home to everybody's hearth and moneysafe and heart and stomach.—Which miserable result, with so many others from the same source, what method was there of avoiding or indefinitely mitigating? This surely, as the beginning of all: that you had made your railways *not* in haste; that, at least, you had spread the huge process, sure to alter all men's mutual position and relations, over a reasonable breadth of time!

For all manner of reasons, how much could one have wished that the making of our British railways had gone on with deliberation; that these great works had made themselves not in five years but in fifty-and-five! Hudson's 'worth' to railways, I think, will mainly resolve itself into this, That he carried them to completion within the former short limit of time; that he got them made,—in extremely improper directions I am told, and surely with endless confusion to the innumerable passive Joplins, and likewise to the numerous active scrip-holders, a wide-spread class, once rich, now coinless,—hastily in five years, not deliberately in fifty-five. His worth to railways? His *worth*, I take it, to English railways, much more to English men, will turn out to be extremely inconsiderable; to be incalculable damage rather! Foolish railway people gave him two millions, and thought it not enough without a Statue to boot. But Fact thought, and is now audibly saying, far otherwise! Rhadamanthus, had you been able to consult him, would in nowise have given this man twenty-five thousand pounds for a Statue. What if Rhadamanthus doomed him rather, let us say, to ride in Express-trains, nowhither, for twenty-five æons, or to hang in Heaven as a Locomotive Constellation, and be a sign forever!

Fact and Suffrage: what a discrepancy! Fact decided for some coalshaft such as we describe. Suffrage decides for such a column. Suffrage having money in its pocket, carries it hollow, for the moment. And so there is Rayless Majesty exalted far above the chimney-pots, with a potential Copper Likeness, twenty-five thousand pounds worth of copper over and above; and a King properly belonging only to *this* epoch.—That there are greedy blockheads in huge majority, in all epochs, is certain; but that any sane mortal should think of counting *their* heads to ascertain who or what is to be King, this is a little peculiar. All Democratic men, and members of the Suffrage Movement, it appears to me, are called upon to think seriously, with a seriousness approaching to despair, of these things.

Jefferson Brick, the American Editor, twitted me with the multifarious patented anomalies of overgrown worthless Dukes, Bishops of Durham etc., which poor English Society at present labours under, and is made a solecism by. To which what answer could I make, except, that surely our patented anomalies were some of them extremely ugly, and yet, alas, that they were not the ugliest! I said: "Have not you also overgrown anomalous *Dukes* after a sort, appointed *not* by patent? Overgrown Monsters of Wealth, namely; who have made money by dealing in cotton, dealing in bacon, jobbing scrip, digging metal in California; who are become glittering man-mountains filled with gold and preciosities; revered by the surrounding flunkies; invested with the *real* powers of sovereignty; and placidly admitted by all men, as if Nature and Heaven had so appointed it, to be in a sense godlike, to be royal, and fit to shine in the firmament, though their real worth is—what? Brick, do you know where human creatures reach the supreme of ugliness in Idols? It were hard to know! We can say only, All Idols have to tumble, and the hugest of them with the heaviest fall: that is our chief comfort, in America as here.

"The Idol of Somnauth, a mere mass of coarse crockery not

worth five shillings of anybody's money, sat like a great staring god, with two diamonds for eyes; worshipped by the neighbouring black populations; a terror and divine mystery to all mortals, till its day came. Till at last, victorious in the name of Allah, the Commander of the Faithful, riding up with grim battle-axe and heart full of Moslem fire, took the liberty to smite once, with right force and rage, said ugly mass of idolatrous crockery; which thereupon shivered, with unmelodious crash and jingle, into a heap of ugly potsherds, yielding from its belly half a wagon-load of gold coins. You can read it in Gibbon,—probably, too, in Lord Ellenborough. The gold coins, the diamond eyes, and other valuable extrinsic parts were carefully picked-up by the Faithful; confused jingle of intrinsic potsherds was left lying;—and the Idol of Somnauth once showing what it *was*, had suddenly come to a conclusion! Thus end all Idols, and intrinsically worthless man-mountains never so illuminated with diamonds, and filled with precious metals, and tremulously worshipped by the neighbouring flunky populations black or white;—even thus, sooner or later, without fail; and are shot hastily, as a heap of potsherds, into the highway, to be crunched under wagon-wheels, and do Macadam a little service, being clearly abolished as *gods*, and hidden from man's recognition, in that or other capacities, forever and a day!

"You do not sufficiently bethink you, my republican friend. Our ugliest anomalies are done by universal suffrage, not by patent. The express nonsense of old Feudalism, even now, in its dotage, is as nothing to the involuntary nonsense of modern Anarchy called 'Freedom,' 'Republicanism,' and other fine names, which expresses itself by supply and demand! Consider it a little.

"The Bishop of our Diocese is to me an incredible man; and has, I will grant you, very much more money than you or I would now give him for his work. One does not even read those Charges of his; much preferring speech which is articulate. In fact, being intent on a quiet life, you generally keep on the other side of the hedge from him, and strictly leave him to his own fate. Not a credible man;—perhaps not quite a safe man to be concerned with? But what think you of the 'Bobus of Houndsditch' of our parts? He, Sausage-maker on the great scale, knows the art of cutting fat bacon, and exposing it seasoned with grey pepper to advantage. Better than any other man he knows this art; and I take the liberty to say it is a poor one. Well, the Bishop has an income of five thousand pounds appointed him for his work; and Bobus, to such a length has he now pushed the trade in sausages, gains from the universal suffrage of men's souls and stomachs *ten* thousand a year by it.

"A poor art, this of Bobus's, I say; and worth no such recompense. For it is not even good sausages he makes, but only extremely vendible ones; the cunning dog! Judges pronounce his sausages bad, and at the cheap price even dear; and finer palates, it is whispered, have detected alarming symptoms of horseflesh, or worse, under this cunningly-devised grey-pepper spice of his; so that for the world I would not eat one of his sausages, nor would you. You perceive he is not an excellent honest sausage-maker, but a dishonest cunning and scandalous sausage-maker; *worth*, if he could get his deserts, who shall say what? Probably certain shillings a week, say forty; possibly (one shudders to think) a long round in the treadmill, and stripes instead of shillings! And yet what he gets, I tell you, from universal suffrage and the unshackled *ne-plus-ultra* republican justice of mankind, is twice the income of that anomalous Bishop you were talking of!

"The Bishop I, for my part, do much prefer to Bobus. The Bishop has human sense and breeding of various kinds; considerable knowledge of Greek, if you should ever want the like of that; knowledge of many things; and speaks the English language in a grammatical manner. He is bred to courtesy, to dignified composure, as to a second nature; a gentleman every fibre of him; which of itself is something very considerable. The Bishop does really diffuse round him an influence of decorum, courteous patience, solid adherence to what is settled; teaches practically the necessity of 'burning one's own smoke'; and does practically in his own case burn said smoke, making lambent flame and mild illumination out of it, for the good of men in several particulars. While Bobus, for twice the annual money,—brings sausages, possibly of horseflesh, cheaper to market than another!—Brick, if you will reflect, it is not 'aristocratic England,' it is the united Posterity of Adam who are grown, in some essential respects, stupider than barbers' blocks. Barbers' blocks would at least say nothing, and *not* elevate, by their universal suffrages, an unfortunate Bobus to that bad height!"

Alas, if such, not in their loose tongues, but in their heart of hearts, is men's way of judging about social worth, what kind of 'new Aristocracy' will the inconceivablest perfection of spoken Suffrage ever yield us? Suffrage, I perceive well, has quite other things in store for us; we need not torment poor Suffrage for this thing! Our *Intermittent* Friend says once:

'Men do not seem to be aware that this their universal ousting of unjust, incapable and in fact imaginary Governors, is to issue in the attainment of Governors who have a right and a capacity to govern. Far different from that is the issue men contemplate in their present revolutionary operations. Their universal notion now is, that we shall henceforth do without Governors; that we have got to a new epoch in human progress, in which Governing is entirely a superfluity, and the attempt at doing it is an offence, think several. By that admirable invention of the Constitutional Parliament, first struck-out in England, and now at length hotly striven-for and zealously imitated in all European countries, the task of Government, any task there may still be, is done to our hand. Perfect your Parliament, cry all men: apply the

Ballot-box and Universal Suffrage! the admirablest method ever imagined of counting heads and gathering indubitable votes: you will thus gather the vote, *vox* or voice, of all the two-legged animals without feathers in your dominion; what they think is what the gods think,—is it not?—and this you shall go and do.

'Whereby, beyond dispute, your Governor's task is immensely simplified; and indeed the chief thing you can now require of your Governor is that he carefully preserve his good humour, and do in a handsome manner nothing, or some pleasant fugle-motions only. Is not this a "machine": marking new epochs in the progress of discovery? Machine for doing Government too, as we now do all things by "machinery." Only keep your free-presses, ballot-boxes, upright-shafts and cogwork in an oiled unobstructed condition; motive-power of popular wind will do the rest. Here verily is a mill that beats Birmingham hollow; and marks "new epochs" with a witness. What a hopper this! Reap from all fields whatsoever you find standing, thistle-downs, dockseed, hemlockseed, wheat, rye; tumble all into the hopper,—see, in soft blissful, continuous stream, meal shall daily issue for you, and the bread of life to mankind be sure!'—

The aim of all reformers, parliamentary and other, is still defined by them as 'just legislation,' just laws; with which definition who can quarrel? They will not have 'class legislation,' which is a dreadfully bad thing; but 'all-classes legislation,' I suppose, which is the right thing. Sure enough, just laws are an excellent attainment, the first condition of all prosperity for human creatures; but few reflect how extremely difficult such attainment is! Alas, could we once get laws which were *just*, that is to say, which were the clear transcript of the Divine Laws of the Universe itself; so that each man were incessantly admonished, under strict penalties, by all men, to walk as the Eternal Maker had prescribed; and he alone received honour whom the Maker had made honourable, and whom the Maker had made disgraceful, disgrace: alas, were not here the very 'Aristocracy' we seek? A new veritable Hierarchy of Heaven,—approximately such in very truth,—bringing Earth nearer and nearer to the blessed Law of Heaven. Heroic men, the Sent of Heaven, once more bore rule: and on the throne of kings there sat splendent, not King Hudson, or King Popinjay, but the Bravest of existing Men; and on the gibbet there swung as a tragic pendulum, admonitory to Earth in the name of Heaven,—not some insignificant, abject, necessitous outcast, who had violently, in his extreme misery and darkness, stolen a leg of mutton,—but veritably the Supreme Scoundrel of the Commonwealth, who in his insatiable greed and bottomless atrocity had long, hoodwinking the poor world, gone himself, and led multitudes to go, in the ways of gilded human baseness; seeking temporary profit (scrip, first-class claret, social honour, and the like small ware), where only eternal loss was possible; and who now, stripped of all his gildings and cunningly-devised speciosities, swung there an ignominious detected scoundrel; testifying aloud to all the earth: "Be not scoundrels, not even gilt scoundrels, any one of you; for God, and not the Devil, is verily king, and this is where it ends, if even this be the end of it!"

O Heaven, O Earth, what an 'attainment' were here, could we but hope to see it! Reformed Parliament, People's League, Hume-Cobden agitation, tremendous cheers, new Battles of Naseby, French Revolution, and Horrors of French Revolution,—all things were cheap and light to the attainment of this. For this were in fact the millennium; and indeed nothing less than this can be it.

But I say it is dreadfully difficult to attain! And though 'class legislation' is not it, yet, alas, neither is 'all-classes legislation' in the least certain to be it. All classes, if they happen not to be wise, heroic classes,—how, by the cunningest jumbling of them together, will you ever get a wisdom or heroism out of them? Once more let me remind you, it is impossible forever. Unwisdom, contradiction to the gods: how, from the mere vamping-together of hostile voracities and opacities, never so dextrously or copiously combined, can or could you expect anything else? Can any man bring a clean thing out of an unclean? No man. Voracities and opacities, blended together in never such cunningly-devised proportions, will not yield noblenesses and illuminations; they cannot do it. Parliamentary reform, extension of the suffrage? Good Heavens, how by the mere enlargement of your circle of ingredients, by the mere flinging-in of new opacities and voracities, will you have a better chance to distil a wisdom from that foul caldron, which is merely bigger, not by hypothesis better? You will have a better chance to distil *zero* from it; evil elements from all sides, now more completely extinguishing one another, so that mutual destruction, like that of the Kilkenny cats, a Parliament which produces parliamentary eloquence only, and no social guidance *either* bad or good will be the issue,—as we now in these years sorrowfully see.

Universal suffrage: what a scheme to substitute for the revelation of God's eternal Law, the official declaration of the account of heads! It is as if men had abdicated their right to attempt following the abovesaid Law, and with melancholy resignation had agreed to give it up, and take temporary peace and good agreement as a substitute. In all departments of our affairs it is so,—literary, moral, political, social; and in all of them it is and remains eternally wrong. In every department, literary, moral, political, social, the man that pretends to have what is angrily called a choice of his own, which will mean at least some remnant of a feeling in him that Nature and Fact do still claim a choice of their own, and are like to make it good yet,—such man is felt as a kind of interloper and dissocial person, who obstructs the harmony of affairs, and is out of keeping with the universal-suffrage arrangement that has been entered upon.

Why not decide it by dice? Universal suffrage for your oracle is equivalent to flat despair of answer. Set up such oracle, you proclaim to all men: "Friends, there is in Nature no answer to your question; and you don't believe in dice. Try to esteem this oracle a divine one, and be thankful that you can thereby keep the peace, and go with an answer from the shrine of chaotic Chance."

Peace is good; but woe to the cowardly caitiff of a man, or collection of cowardly caitiffs styling themselves Nation, that will have 'peace' on these terms! They will save their ignoble skin at the expense of their eternal loyalty to the highest God. Peace? Better war to the knife, war till we all die, than such a 'peace.' Reject it, my friend, I advise thee; silently swear by God above, that, on earth below, thou for thy part never wilt accept it. Be *it* forever far from us, my poor scattered friends. Let us fly to the rocks rather; and silently appealing to the Eternal Heaven, await an hour which is full surely coming, when we too shall have grown to a respectable 'company of poor men,' authorised to rally, and with celestial lightning, and with terrestrial steel and such good weapons as there may be, spend all our blood upon it!—— ——

After all, why was not the Hudson Testimonial completed? As Moses lifted up the Brazen Serpent in the wilderness, why was not Hudson's Statue lifted up? Once more I say, it might have done us good. Thither too, in a sense, poor poison-stricken mortals might have looked, and found some healing! For many reasons, this alarming populace of British Statues wanted to have its chief. The liveliest type of Choice by Suffrage ever given. The consummate flower of universal Anarchy in the Commonwealth, and in the hearts of men: was not this Statue such a flower; or do we look for one more perfect and consummate?

Of social Hierarchies, and Religions the parent of these,

why speak, in presence of social Anarchy such as is here symbolised? The Apotheosis of Hudson beckons to still deeper gulfs on the religious side of our affairs; into which one shudders to look down. For the eye rests only on the blackness of darkness; and, shrunk to hissing whispers, inaudible except to the finer ear, come moanings of the ever-lasting tempest, and tones of *alti guai.* Nor is a certain vertigo quite absent from the strongest heads; a mad impulse to *take* the leap, then, and dwell with Eternal Death, since it seems to be the rule at present! One hurried glance or two,—holding well by what parapets there still are;—and then let us hasten to begone.

Worship, what we call human religion, has undergone various phases in the history of mankind. To the primitive man all Forces of Nature were divine: either for propitiation or for admiration, many things, and in a sense all things, demanded worship from him. But especially the Noble Human Soul was divine to him; and announced, as it ever does, with direct impressiveness, the Inspiration of the Highest; demanding worship from the primitive man. Whereby, as has been explained elsewhere, this latter form of worship, *Hero-worship* as we call it, did, among the ancient peoples, attract and subdue to itself all other forms of human worship; irradiating them all with its own perennial worth, which indeed is all the worth they had, or that any worship can have. Human worship everywhere, so far as there lay any worth in it, was of the nature of a Hero-worship; this Universe wholly, this temporary Flame-image of the Eternal, was one beautiful and terrible Energy of Heroisms, presided over by a Divine Nobleness or Infinite Hero. Divine Nobleness forever friendly to the noble, forever hostile to the ignoble: all manner of 'moral rules,' and well 'sanctioned' too, flowed naturally out of this primeval Intuition into Nature;—which, I believe, is still the true fountain of moral rules, though a much-forgotten one at present; and indeed it seems to be the one unchangeable, eternally *in*dubitable 'Intuition into Nature' we have yet heard of in these parts.

To the primitive man, whether he looked at moral rule, or even at physical fact, there was nothing not divine. Flame was the God Loki, etc.; this visible Universe was wholly the vesture of an Invisible Infinite; every event that occurred in it a symbol of the immediate presence of God. Which it intrinsically *is*, and forever will be, let poor stupid mortals remember or forget it! The difference is, not that God has withdrawn; but that men's minds have fallen hebetated, stupid, that their hearts are dead, awakening only to some life about meal-time and cookery-time; and their eyes are grown dim, blinkard, a kind of horn-eyes like those of owls, available chiefly for catching mice.

Most excellent Fitzsmithytrough, it is a long time since I have stopped short in admiring your stupendous railway miracles. I was obliged to strike work, and cease admiring in that direction. Very stupendous indeed; considerable improvement in old roadways and wheel-and-axle carriages; velocity unexpectedly great, distances attainable ditto ditto: all this is undeniable. But, alas, all this is still small deer for me, my excellent Fitzsmithytrough; truly nothing more than an unexpected take of mice for the *owlish* part of you and me. Distances, you unfortunate Fitz? The distances of London to Aberdeen, to Ostend, to Vienna, are still infinitely inadequate to me! Will you teach me the winged flight through Immensity, up to the Throne dark with excess of bright? You unfortunate, you grin as an ape would at such a question; you do not know that unless you *can* reach thither in some effectual, most veritable sense, you are a lost Fitzsmithytrough, doomed to Hela's death-realm and the Abyss where mere brutes are buried. I do not want cheaper cotton, swifter railways; I want what Novalis calls 'God, Freedom, Immortality': will swift railways, and sacrifices to Hudson, help me towards that?—

As propitiation or as admiration, 'worship' still continues

among men, will always continue; and the phase it has in any given epoch may be taken as the ruling phenomenon which determines all others in that epoch. If Odin, who 'invented runes,' or literatures, and rhythmic logical speech, and taught men to despise death, is worshipped in one epoch; and if Hudson, who conquered railway directors, and taught men to become suddenly rich by scrip, is worshipped in another,—the characters of these two epochs must differ a good deal! Nay, the worst of some epochs is, they have along with their real worship an imaginary, and are conscious only of the latter as worship. They keep a set of gods or fetishes, reckoned respectable, to which they mumble prayers, asking themselves and others triumphantly, "Are not these respectable gods?" and all the while their real worship, or heart's love and admiration, which alone is worship, concentrates itself on quite other gods and fetishes,—on Hudsons and scrips, for instance. Thus is the miserable epoch rendered twice and tenfold miserable, and in a manner lost beyond redemption; having superadded to its stupid Idolatries, and brutish forgettings of the true God, which are leading it down daily towards ruin, an immense Hypocrisy, which is the quintessence of all idolatries and misbeliefs and unbeliefs, and taken refuge under that, as under a thing safe! Europe generally has lain there a long time; England I think for about two hundred years, spinning certain cottons notably the while, and thinking it all right,—which it was very far from being. But the time of accounts, slowly advancing, has arrived at last for Europe, and is knocking at the door of England too; and it will be seen whether universal make-believe can be the rule in English or human things; whether respectable Hebrew and other fetishes, combined with real worship of Yorkshire and other scrip, will answer the purpose here below or not!

It is certain, whatever gods or fetishes a man may have about him, and pay tithes to, and mumble prayers to, the real 'religion' that is in him is his *practical Hero-worship.*

Whom or what do you in your very soul admire, and strive to imitate and emulate; is it God's servant or the Devil's? Clearly this is the whole question. There is no other religion in the man which can be of the slightest consequence in comparison. Theologies, doxologies, orthodoxies, heterodoxies, are not of moment except as subsidiary towards a good issue in this; if they help well in it, they are good; if not well or at all, they are nothing or bad.

This also is certain, Nations that do their Hero-worship well are blessed and victorious; Nations that do it ill are accursed, and in all fibres of their business grow daily more so, till their miserable afflictive and offensive situation becomes at last unendurable to Heaven and to Earth, and the so-called Nation, now an unhappy Populace of Misbelievers (*miscreants* was the old name), bursts into revolutionary tumult, and either reforms or else annihilates itself. How otherwise? Know whom to honour and emulate and follow; know whom to dishonour and avoid, and coerce under hatches, as a foul rebellious thing: this is all the Law and all the Prophets. All conceivable evangels, bibles, homiletics, liturgies and litanies, and temporal and spiritual lawbooks for a man or a people, issue practically there. Be right in that, essentially you are not wrong in anything; you read this Universe tolerably aright, and are in the way to interpret well what the will of its Maker is. Be wrong in that, had you liturgies the recommendablest in Nature, and bodies-of-divinity as big as an Indiaman, it helps you not a whit; you are wrong in all things.

How in anything can you be right? You read this Universe in the inmost meaning of it *wrong*: gross idolatrous Misbelief is what I have to recognise in you; and, superadded, such a faith in the saving virtue of that deadliest of vices, Hypocrisy, as no People ever had before! Beautiful recommendable liturgies? Your liturgies, the recommendablest in Nature, are to me alarming and distressing; a turning of the Calmuck Prayer-mill,—not my way of praying.

This immense asthmatic spiritual Hurdygurdy, issuing practically in a set of demigods like Hudson, what is the good of it; why will you keep grinding it under poor men's windows? Since Hudson *is* Vishnu, let the Shasters and Vedas be conformable to him. Why chant divine psalms which belonged to a different Dispensation, and are now become idle and far worse? Not melodious to me, such a chant, in such a time! The sound of it, if you are not yet quite *dead* to spiritual sounds, is frightful and bodeful. I say, this litany of yours, were the wretched populace and population never so unanimous and loud in it, is a thing no God *can* hear; your miserable 'religion,' as you call it, is an idolatry of the nature of Mumbojumbo, and I would advise you to discontinue it rather. You are Infidels, persons without faith; *not* believing what is true but what is untrue; Miscreants, as the old fathers well called you,—appointed too inevitably, unless you can repent and alter soon (of which I see no symptoms), to a fearful doom!

"It was always so," you indolently say? No, Friend Heavyside, it was not always so, and even till lately was never so; and I would much recommend you to sweep that foolish notion, which you often fling at me, and always keep about you as one of your main consolations, quite out of your head. Once the notion was my own too; I know the notion very well! And I will invite you to ask yourself in all ways, Whether it is not possibly a rather torpid and poisonous, and likewise an altogether incorrect and delusive notion? Capable, I assure you, of being quite swept out of a man's head; and greatly needing to be so, if the man would do any 'reform,' or other useful work, in this his day!

Till such notion go about its business, there cannot even be the attempt towards reform. Not so much as the pulling down, and melting into warming-pans, of those poor Brazen Representatives of Anarchy can be accomplished; but they will stand there prophesying as now, "*Here* is the 'New Aristocracy' you want; down on your knees, ye Christian souls!"—O my friend, and *after* Hudson and the other Idols have quite gone to warming-pans, have you computed what agonistic centuries await us, before any 'New Aristocracy' worth calling by the name of 'real,' can by likelihood prove attainable? From the stormful trampling-down of Sham Human Worth, and casting *it* with wrath and scorn into the meltingpot, onward to the silent sad repentant recognition of Real Human Worth, and the capability of again doing that some pious reverence, some reverence which were *not* practically worse than none: have you measured what an interval is there? Centuries of desperate wrestle against Earth and Hell, on the part of all the brave men that are born. Too true this, though figuratively spoken! Perilous tempestuous struggle and pilgrimage, continual marching battle with the mud-serpents of this Earth and the demons of the Pit—centuries of such a marching fight (continually along the edge of Red Republic too, and the Abyss) as brave men were not often called to in History before!—And the brave men will not yet so much as gird-on their harness? They sit indolently saying, "It is already all as it can be, as it was wont to be; and universal suffrage and tremendous cheers will manage it!"—

Collins's old Peerage-Book, a dreadfully dull production, fills one with unspeakable reflections. Beyond doubt a most dull production, one of the darkest in the book kind ever realised by Chaos and man's brain; and it is properly all we English have for a Biographical Dictionary;—nay, if you think farther of it, for a National Bible. Friend Heavyside is much astonished; but I see what I mean here, and have long seen. Clear away the dust from your eyes, and you will ask this question, What *is* the Bible of a Nation, the practically-credited God's-Message to a Nation? Is it not, beyond all else, the authentic Biography of its Heroic Souls? This is the real record of the Appearances of God in the History of a Nation; this, which all men to the very marrow of their bones can *believe*, and which teaches all men what the nature of the Universe, when you go to work in it, really *is*. What the Universe was thought to be in Judea and other places, this too may be very interesting to know: but what it is in England here where we live and have our work to do, that is the interesting point.—"The Universe?" M'Croudy answers. "It is a huge dull Cattle-stall and St. Catherine's Wharf; with a few pleasant apartments upstairs for those that can make money. Make money; and don't bother about the Universe!" That is M'Croudy's notion; reckoned a quiet, innocent and rather wholesome notion just now; yet clearly fitter for a reflective pig than for a man;—working continual damnation therefore, however quiet it be; and indeed I perceive it is one of the damnablest notions that ever came into the head of any *two*-legged animal without feathers in this world. That is M'Croudy's Bible; his Apology, poor fellow, for the *Want* of a Bible.

But how, among so many Shakspeares, and thinkers, and heroic singers, our National Bible should be in such a state; and how a poor dull Bookseller should have been left,—not to write in rhythmic coherency, worthy of a Poet and of all our Poets,—but to shovel together, or indicate, in huge rubbish mountains incondite as Chaos, the materials for writing such a Book of Books for England: this is abundantly amazing to me, and I wish much it could duly amaze us all. Literature has no nobler task;—in fact it has that one task, and except it be idle rope-dancing, no other. 'The highest problem of Literature,' says Novalis, very justly, 'is the Writing of a Bible.'

Nevertheless, among these dust-mountains, with their antiquarian excerpts and sepulchral brasses, it is astonishing what strange fragments you do turn up, miraculous talismans to a reader that will think,—windows through which an old sunk world, as yet all built upon veracity, and full of rugged nobleness, becomes visible; to the mute wonder of the modern mind. It struck me much, that of these ancient peerages a very great majority had visibly *had* authentic 'heroes' for their founders; noble men, of whose worth no clearsighted King could be in doubt; and that, in their descendants too, there did not cease a strain of heroism for some time,—the peership generally dying out, and disappearing, not long after that ceased. What a world, that old sunk one; Real Governors governing in it; Shams not yet anywhere recognised as tolerable in it! A world whose practical president was *not* Chaos with ballot-boxes, whose outcome was not Anarchy *plus* a street-constable. In how high and true a sense, the Almighty with continual enforcement of his Laws still presided there; and in all things as yet there was some degree of blessedness and nobleness there!

One's heart is sore to think how far, how very far all this has vanished from us; how the very tradition of it has disappeared; and it has ceased to be credible, to seem desirable. Till the like of it return,—yes, my constitutional friend, such is the sad fact, till the like of it, in new form, adapted to the new times, be again achieved by us; we are not properly a society at all; we are a lost gregarious horde, with Kings of Scrip on this hand, and Famishing Connaughts and Distressed Needlewomen on that—presided over by the Anarch Old. A lost horde,—who, in bitter feeling of the intolerable injustice that presses upon all men, will not long be able to continue even gregarious; but will have to split into street-barricades, and internecine battle with one another; and to fight, if wisdom for some new real *Peerage* be not granted us, till we all die, mutually butchered, and *so* rest,—so if not otherwise!

Till the time of James the First, I find that real heroic merit more or less was actually the origin of peerages; never, till towards the end of that bad reign, were peerages bargained for, or bestowed on men palpably of no worth except their money or connexion. But the evil practice, once begun, spread rapidly; and now the Peerage-Book is what we see;—a thing miraculous in the other extreme. A kind of Proteus' flock, very curious to meet upon the lofty mountains, so many of them being natives of the deep!—Our menagerie of live Peers in Parliament is like that of our Brazen Statues in the market-place; the selection seemingly is made much in the same way, and with the same degree of felicity, and successful accuracy in choice. Our one steady regulated supply is the class definable as Supreme Stump-Orators in the Lawyer department; the class called Chancellors flows by something like fixed conduits towards the Peerage; the rest, like our Brazen Statues, come by popular rule-of-thumb.

Stump-Orators, supreme or other, are not beautiful to me in these days: but the immense power of Lawyers among us is sufficiently intelligible. I perceive, it proceeds from two causes. First, they preside over the management and security of 'Property,' which is our God at present; they are thus properly our Pontiffs, the highest Priests we have. Then furthermore they possess the talent most valued, that of the Tongue; and seem to us the most gifted of our intelligences, thereby provoking a spontaneous loyalty and worship.

What think you of a country whose kings go by genealogy, and are the descendants of successful Lawyers? A poor weather-worn, tanned, curried, wind-dried human creature, called a Chancellor, all or almost all gone to horsehair and officiality; the whole existence of him tanned, by long maceration, public exposure, tugging and manipulation, to the toughness of Yorkshire leather,—meseems I have seen a beautifuler man! Not a leather man would I by preference appoint to beget my kings. Not lovely to me is the leather species of men; to whose tanned soul God's Universe has become a jangling logic-cockpit and little other. If indeed it have not become far less and worse: for the wretched tanned Chancellor, I am told, is usually acquainted with the art of *lying* too,—considerable part of his trade, as I have been informed, is the talent of lying in a way that cannot be laid hold of; a dreadful trick to learn! Out of such a man there cannot be expected much 'revelation of the Beautiful,' I should say.—O Bull, were I in your place, I would try either to get other Peers, or else to abolish the concern,—which latter indeed, by your acquiescence in such nominations, and by many other symptoms, I judge to be unconsciously your fixed intention.

You have seen many Chancellors made Peers in these late generations, Mr. Bull. And now tell me, which was the Chancellor you did really love or honour, to any remarkable degree? Alas, you never within authentic memory loved any of them; you couldn't, no man could! You lazily stared with some semblance of admiration at the big wig, huge purse, reputation for divine talent, and sublime proficiency in the art of tongue-fence: but to love him,—that, Mr. Bull, was, once for all, a thing you could not manage. Who of the seed of Adam could? From the time of Chancellor Bacon downwards (and beyond that your Chancellors are dark to you as the Muftis of Constantinople), I challenge you to show me one Chancellor for whom, had the wigs, purses, reputations etc., been peeled off him, who would have given his weight in Smithfield beef sinking offal. You unhappy Bull, governed by Kings you have not the smallest regard for; wandering in an extinct world of wearisome, oppressive and expensive shadows,—nothing real in it but the Smithfield beef, nothing preternatural in it but the Chartisms and threatened street-barricades, and this not celestial but infernal!

Sure enough, I find, O Heavyside, England once was a Hierarchy; as every Human Society, not either dead or else hastening towards death, always is: but it has long ceased to be so to any tolerable degree of perfection; and is now, by its Hudson and other Testimonials, testifying in a silent way to the thoughtful, what otherwise, by its thousandfold anarchic depravities, miseries, god-forgettings and open devil-worships, it has long loudly taught them to expect, that we are now wending towards the culmination in this particular. That to the modern English populations, Supreme Hero and Supreme Scoundrel are, perhaps as nearly as is possible to human creatures, indistinguishable. That it is totally uncertain, perhaps even the odds against you, whether the figure whom said population mount to the place of honour, is not in Nature and Fact *dis*honourable; whether the man to whom they raise a column does not deserve a coalshaft. And in fine, poor devils, that their universal suffrage, as spoken, as acted, meditated, and imagined; universal suffrage,—I do not say ballot-boxed and cunningly constitutionalised, but boiled, distilled, digested, quintessenced, till you get into the very heart's heart of it,—is, to the rational soul, except for stock-exchange, and the like very humble practical purposes, worth express *zero*, or nearly so. I think probably as near zero as the unassisted human faculties and destinies ever came, or are like to come.

Hierarchy? O Heaven! If Chaos himself sat umpire, what better could *he* do? Here are a set of human demigods, as if chosen to his hand. Hierarchy with a vengeance!—if instead of God, a vulpine beggarly Beelzebub or swollen Mammon were our Supreme *Hieros* or Holy, this would be a Hierarchy! I say, if you want Chaos for your master, adopt this;—if you don't, I beg you make haste to adopt some other; for this is the broad way to him! The Eternal Anarch, with his old waggling addlehead full of mere windy rumour, and his old insatiable paunch full of mere hunger and indigestion tragically blended, and the hissing discord of all the Four Elements persuasively pleading to him,—he, set to choose, would be very apt to vote for such a set of demigods to you.

As to the Statues, I know they are but symptoms of Anarchy; it is not they, it is the Anarchy, that one is anxious to see abated. Remedy for the Statues will be possible; and, as a small help, undoubtedly it too, in the mean time, is desirable. Every symptom you drive-in being a curtailment of the malady, by all means cure this Statue-building if you can! It will be one folly and misery less.

Government is loath to interfere with the pursuits of any class of citizens; and oftenest looks on in silence while follies are committed. But Government does interfere to prevent afflictive accumulations on the streets, malodorous or other unsanitary public procedures of an extensive sort; regulates gully-drains, cesspools; prohibits the piling-up of dungheaps; and is especially strict on the matter of indecent exposures. Wherever the health of the citizens is concerned, much more where their souls' health, and as it were their very salvation, is concerned, all Governments that are not chimerical make haste to interfere.

Now if dungheaps laid on the streets, afflictive to the mere nostrils, are a subject for interference, what, we ask, are high columns, raised by prurient stupidity and public delusion, to blockheads whose memory does in eternal fact deserve the sinking of a coalshaft rather? Give to every one what he deserves, what really is his: in all scenes and situations thou shalt do that,—or in very truth woe will betide thee, as sure as thou art living, and as thy Maker lives. Blockhead, this big Gambler swollen to the edge of bursting, he is not 'great' and honourable; he is huge and abominable! Thou shalt honour the right man, and not honour the wrong, under penalties of an alarming nature. Honour Barabbas the Robber, thou shalt sell old-clothes through the cities of the world; shalt accumulate sordid moneys, with a curse on every coin of them, and be spit upon for eighteen hundred years. Raise statues to the swollen Gambler as if he were great, sacrifice oblations to the King of Scrip,—unfortunate mortals, you will dearly pay for it yet. Quiet as Nature's counting-house and scrip-ledgers are, no faintest item is ever blotted out from them, for or against; and to the last doit that account too will have to be settled. Rigorous as Destiny;—she *is* Destiny. Chancery or Fetter-Lane is soft to her, when the day of settlement comes. With her, in the way of abatement, of oblivion, neither gods nor man prevail. "Abatement? That is not our way of doing business; the time has run out, the debt it appears is due." Will the law of gravitation 'abate' for you? Gravitation acts at the rate of sixteen feet per second, in spite of all prayers. Were it the crash of a Solar System, or the fall of a Yarmouth Herring, all one to gravitation.

Is the fall of a stone certain; and the fruit of an unwisdom doubtful? You unfortunate beings! Have you forgotten it; in this immense improvement of machinery, cheapening of cotton, and general astonishing progress of the species lately? With such extension of journals, human cultures, universities, periodic and other literatures, mechanics' institutes, reform of prison-discipline, abolition of capital punishment, enfranchisement by ballot, report of parliamentary speeches, and singing for the million? You did not know that the Universe had *laws* of right and wrong; you fancied the Universe was an oblivious greedy blockhead, like one of yourselves; attentive to scrip mainly; and willing, where there was no practical scrip, to forget and forgive? And so, amid such universal blossoming-forth of useful knowledges, miraculous to the thinking editor everywhere,—the soul of all 'knowledge,' not knowing which a man is dark and reduced to the condition of a beaver, has been omitted by you? You have omitted it, and you should have included it! The thinking editor never missed *it*, so busy wondering and worshipping elsewhere; but it is not here.

And alas, apart from editors, are there not men appointed specially to keep you in mind of it; solemnly set apart for that object, thousands of years ago? Crabbe, descanting 'on the so-called Christian *Clerus*,' has this wild passage: 'Legions of them, in their black or other gowns I still meet in every country; masquerading, in strange costume of body, and still stranger of soul; mumming, primming, grimacing,—poor devils, shamming, and endeavouring not to sham: that is the sad fact. Brave men many of them, after their sort; and in a position which we may admit to be wonderful and dreadful! On the outside of their heads some singular head-gear, tulip-mitre, felt coalscuttle, purple hat; and in the inside,—I must say, such a Theory of God Almighty's Universe as I, for my share, am right thankful to have no concern with at all! I think, on the whole, as broken-winged, self-strangled, monstrous a mass of incoherent incredibilities, as ever dwelt in the human brain before. O God, giver of Light, hater of Darkness, of Hypocrisy and Cowardice, how long, how long!

'For two centuries now it lasts. The men whom God has made, whole nations and generations of them, are steeped in Hypocrisy from their birth upwards; taught that external varnish is the chief duty of man,—that the vice which is the deepest in Gehenna is the virtue highest in Heaven. Out of which, do you ask what follows? Look round on a world all bristling with insurrectionary pikes; Kings and Papas flying like detected coiners; and in their stead Icaria, Red Republic, new religion of the Anti-Virgin, Literature of Desperation curiously conjoined with Phallus-Worship, too clearly heralding centuries of bottomless Anarchy: hitherto one in the million looking with mournful recognition on it, silently with sad thoughts too unutterable; and to help in healing it not one anywhere hitherto.'

But as to Statues, I really think the Woods-and-Forests ought to interfere. When a company of persons have determined to set-up a Brazen Image, there decidedly arises, —besides the question of their own five-pound subscriptions, which men of spirit and money-capital without employment, and with the prospect of seeing their names in the Newspapers at the cheap price of five pounds, are very prompt with,—

another question, not nearly so easy of solution. Namely, this quite preliminary question: Will it permanently profit mankind to have such a Hero as this of yours set-up for their admiration, for their imitation and emulation; or will it, so far as they do not reject and with success disregard it altogether, unspeakably tend to damage and disprofit them? In a word, does this Hero's memory deserve a high column; are you sure it does not deserve a deep coalshaft rather? This is an entirely fundamental question! Till this question be answered well in the affirmative, there ought to be a total stop of progress; the misguided citizens ought to be admonished, and even gently constrained, to take back their five-pound notes; to desist from their rash deleterious enterprise, and retire to their affairs, a repentant body of misguided citizens.

But farther still, and supposing the first question perfectly disposed of, there comes a second, grave too, though much less peremptory: Is this Statue of yours a worthy commemoration of a sacred man? Is it so excellent in point of Art that we can, with credit, set it up in our market-places as a respectable approach to the Ideal? Or, alas, is it not such an amorphous brazen sooterkin, bred of prurient heat and darkness, as falls, if well seen into, far below the Real? The Real, if you will stand by it, is respectable. The coarsest hob-nailed pair of shoes, if honestly made according to the laws of fact and leather, are not ugly; they are honest, and fit for their object; the highest eye may look on them without displeasure, nay, with a kind of satisfaction. This rude packing-case, it is faithfully made; square to the rule, and formed with rough-and-ready strength against injury;—fit for its use; not a pretentious *hypocrisy*, but a modest serviceable *fact*; whoever pleases to look upon it, will find the image of a humble manfulness in it, and will pass on with some infinitesimal impulse to thank the gods.

But this your 'Ideal,' my misguided fellow-citizens? Good Heavens, are you in the least aware what damage, in the very sources of their existence, men get from Cockney Sooterkins saluting them publicly as models of Beauty? I charitably feel you have not the smallest notion of it, or you would shriek at the proposal! Can you, my misguided friends, think it humane to set-up, in its present uncomfortable form, this blotch of mismolten copper and zinc, out of which good warming-pans might be made? That all men should see this; innocent young creatures, still in arms, be taught to think this beautiful;—and perhaps women in an interesting situation look up to it as they pass? I put it to your religious feeling, to your principles as men and fathrers of families!

These questions the Woods-and-Forests, or some other Public Tribunal constituted for the purpose, really ought to ask, in a deliberate speaking manner, on the part of the speechless suffering Populations: it is the preliminary of all useful Statue-building. Till both these questions are well answered, the Woods-and-Forests should refuse permission; advise the misguided citizens to go home and repent. Really, if this Statue-humour go on, and grow as it has lately done, there will be such a Public-Statue Board requisite; or the Woods-and-Forests will have to interfere, with such imperfect law as now is.

The Woods-and-Forests, or if not they, then the Commissioners of Sewers, Sanitary Board, Scavenger Board, Cleansing Committee, or whoever holds or can usurp a little of the ædile authority,—cannot some of them, in the name of sense and common decency, interfere at least thus far? Namely, to admonish the misguided citizens, subscribers to the next Brazen Monster, or sad sculptural solecism, the emblem of far sadder moral ones; and exhort them, three successive times, to make warming-pans of it and repent;—or failing that, finding them obstinate, to say with authority: "Well then, persist; set-up your Brazen Calf, ye misguided citizens, and worship it, you, since you will and can. But observe, let it be done in secret: not in public; we say, in secret, at your peril! You have pleased to create a new Monster into this world; but to make him patent to public view, we, for our part, beg not to please. Observe, therefore. Build a high-enough brick case or joss-house for your Brazen Calf; with undiaphanous walls, and lighted by sky-windows only: put your Monster into that, and keep him there. Thither go at your pleasure, there assemble yourselves, and worship your bellyful, you absurd idolaters; ruin your own souls only, and leave the poor Population alone; the poor speechless unconscious Population, whom we are bound to protect, and will!" To this extent, I think the Woods-and-Forests might reasonably interfere.

No. VIII

JESUITISM

[1st August 1850]

As in the history of human things, which needs above all to abridge itself, it happens usually that the chief actors in great events and great epochs give their name to the series, and are loosely reputed the causers and authors of them; as a German Reformation is called of Luther, and a French Reign of Terror passes for the work of Robespierre, and from the *Æneid* and earlier this has been the wont: so it may be said these current, and now happily moribund, times of ours are worthy to be called, in loose language, the Age of Jesuitism,—an epoch whose Palinurus is the wretched mortal known among men as Ignatius Loyola. For some two centuries the genius of mankind has been dominated by the gospel of Ignatius, perhaps the strangest and certainly among the fatalest ever preached hitherto under the sun. Some acquaintance, out of *Bartoli* and others, I have made with that individual, and from old years have studied the workings of him; and to me he seems historically definable, he more than another, as the poison-fountain from which these rivers of bitterness that now submerge the world have flowed.

Counting from the 'ever-blessed Restoration,' or the advent of that singular new Defender of the Faith called Charles Second, it is about two hundred years since we ourselves commenced that bad course; and deeply detesting the *name* of St. Ignatius, did nevertheless gradually adopt his gospel as the real revelation of God's will, and the solid rule of living in this world; rule long since grown perfectly accredited, complete in all its parts, and reigning supreme among us in all spiritual and social matters whatsoever. The singular gospel, or revelation of God's will! That to please the supreme Fountain of Truth your readiest method, now and then, was to persist in believing what your whole soul found to be doubtful or incredible. That poor human symbols were higher than the God Almighty's facts they symbolised; that formulas, with or without the facts symbolised by them, were sacred and salutary; that formulas, well persisted in, could still save us when the facts were all fled! A new revelation to mankind; not heard of in human experience, till Ignatius revealed it to us. That, in substance, was the contribution of Ignatius to the wellbeing of mankind. Under that thrice-stygian gospel we have all of us, Papist and at length Protestant too, this long while sat; a 'doctrine of devils,' I do think, if there ever was one;—and are now, ever since 1789, with endless misery and astonishment, confusedly awakening out of the same, uncertain whether towards swift agony of social death, or towards slow martyrdom of recovery into spiritual and social life.

Not that poor Loyola did all the feat himself,—any more than Luther, Robespierre, and other such did in the parallel cases. By no means. Not in his poor person shall the wretched Loyola bear the guilt of poisoning the world: the world was, as it were, in quest of poison; in the sure course of being poisoned; and would have got it done by some one: Loyola is the historical symbol to us of its being done. The most conspicuous and ostentatious of the world's poisoners; who, solemnly consecrating all the rest in the name of holiness or spiritual *Health*, has got the work of poisoning to go on with never-imagined completeness and acceleration in all quarters; and is worthy to have it called after him a *Jesuitism*, and be blamed by men (how judged by God, we know not) for doing it. That it is done, there is the sad fact for us; which infinitely concerns every living soul of us; what Ignatius got or is to get for doing it,—this shall not concern us at all.

And so, before dismissing busy English readers to their autumnal grouse-shooting,—the *ramadhan*, sacred fast, or month of meditative solitude and devout prayer, now in use among the English,—I have one sad thing to do: lead them a little to the survey of Ignatius and our universal Jesuitism; and ask them, in Heaven's name, if they will answer such a question, What they think of it, and of their share in it? For this is the central and parent phenomenon; the great Tartarean Deep, this, whence all our miseries, fatuities, futilities spring; the accursed Hela's realm, tenanted by foul creatures, ministers of Death Eternal, out of which poor mortals, each for himself, are called to escape if they can! Who is there that can escape; that can become alive to the terrible necessity of escaping? By way of finish to this offensive and alarming set of Pamphlets, I have still one crowning offence and alarm to try if I can give. The message, namely, That under all those Cannibal Connaughts, Distressed Needlewomen, and other woes nigh grown intolerable, there lies a still deeper Infinite of woe and guilt, chargeable on every one of us; and that till this abate, essentially those never will or can.

That our English solitaries, any noticeable number of them, in their grouse *ramadhan*, or elsewhere, will accept the message, and see this thing for my poor showing, is more than I expect. Not willingly or joyfully do men become conscious that they are afloat, they and their affairs, upon the Pool of Erebus, now nameless in polite speech; and that all their miseries, social and private, are fountains springing out of that, and like to spring perennially with ever more copiousness, till once you get away from that!——And yet who knows? Here and there a thinking English soul, the reflection, the devotion, not yet quite deafened out of him by perpetual noise and babble; such a soul,—left silent in the solitude of some Highland corry, waiting perhaps till the gillies drive his deer up to him,—may catch a glimpse of it, take a thought of it; may prosecute his thought; fling down, with terror, his Joe-Manton and percussion-caps, and fly to a better kind of *ramadhan*, towards another kind of life! Sure enough, if one in the thousand see at all, in this sad matter, what I see and have long seen in it, his life either suddenly or gradually will alter in several particulars; and his sorrow, apprehension and amazement will probably grow upon him, the longer he considers this affair; and his life, I think, will alter ever farther;—and he, this one in a thousand, will forgive me, and be thankful to the Heavens and me, while he continues in this world or in any world!—

The Spiritual, it is still often said, but is not now sufficiently considered, is the parent and first-cause of the Practical. The Spiritual everywhere originates the Practical, models it, makes it: so that the saddest external condition of affairs, among men, is but evidence of a still sadder internal one. For as thought is the life-fountain and motive-soul of action, so, in all regions of this human world, whatever outward thing offers itself to the eye, is merely the garment or body of a thing which already existed invisibly within; which, striving to give itself expression, has found, in the given circumstances, that it could and would express itself—so. This is everywhere true; and in these times when men's attention is directed outward rather, this deserves far more attention than it will receive.

Do you ask why misery abounds among us? I bid you look into the notion we have formed for ourselves of this Universe, and of our duties and destinies there. If it is a true notion, we shall strenuously reduce it to practice,—for who dare or can contradict his *faith*, whatever it may be, in the Eternal Fact that is around him?—and thereby blessings and success will attend us in said Universe, or Eternal Fact we live amidst: of that surely there is no doubt. All revelations and intimations, heavenly and earthly, assure us of that; only a Philosophy of Bedlam could throw a doubt on that! Blessings and success, most surely, if our notion of this Universe, and our battle in it be a true one; not curses and futilities, except it be not true. For battle, in any case, I think we shall not want; harsh wounds, and the heat of the day, we shall have to stand: but it will be a noble godlike and human battle, not an ignoble devil-like and brutal one; and our wounds, and sore toils (what we in our impatience call 'miseries'), will themselves be blessed to us.

But if, on the other hand, it were a false notion which we believed; alas, if it were even a false notion which we only pretended to believe? What battle can there be, in that latter fatal case! Our faith, or notion of this Universe, is not false only, but it is the father of falsity; a thing that destroys itself, and is equivalent to the death of all notion, all belief or motive to action, except what the appetites and the astucities may yield. We have then the thrice-baleful Universe of Cant, prophesied for these Latter Days; and no 'battle,' but a kind of bigger Donnybrook one, is possible for hapless mortals till that alter. Faith, Fact, Performance, in all high and gradually in all low departments, go about their business; Inanity well tailored and upholstered, mild-spoken Ambiguity, decorous Hypocrisy which is astonished you should think it hypocritical, taking their room and drawing their wages: from zenith to nadir, you have Cant, Cant,—a Universe of Incredibilities which are not even credited, which each man at best only tries to persuade himself that he credits. Do you expect a divine battle, with noble victories, out of this? I expect a Hudson's Statue from it, brisk trade in scrip, with Distressed Needlewomen, Cannibal Connaughts, and other the like phenomena, such as we now everywhere see!

Indisputably enough, what notion each forms of the Universe is the all-regulating fact with regard to him. The Universe makes no immediate objection to be conceived in any way; pictures itself as plainly in the seeing faculty of Newton's Dog Diamond, as of Newton; and yields to each a result accurately corresponding. To the Dog Diamond dogs'-meat, with its adjuncts, better or worse; to Newton discovery of the System of the Stars.—Not the Universe's affair at all; but the seeing party's affair very much, for the results to each correspond, with exact proportion, to his notion of it.

The saddest condition of human affairs, what ancient Prophets denounced as 'the Throne of Iniquity,' where men 'decree injustice by a law': all this, with its thousandfold outer miseries, is still but a symptom; all this points to a far sadder disease which lies invisible within! In new dialect, whatever modified interpretation we may put upon it, the same must be said as in old: 'God's judgments are abroad in the world'; and it would much behove many of us to know well that the essential fact lies there and not elsewhere. If we 'sin against God,' it is most certain 'God's judgments' will overtake us; and whether we recognise them as God's message like men, or merely rage and writhe under them like dogs, and in our blind agony, each imputing it to his neighbour, tear one another in pieces under them, it is certain they will continue upon us, till we either cease 'sinning,' or are all torn in pieces and annihilated.

Wide-spread suffering, mutiny and delirium; the hot rage of sansculottic Insurrections, the cold rage of resuscitated Tyrannies; the brutal degradation of the millions, the pampered frivolity of the units; that awful unheeded spectacle, 'the Throne of Iniquity decreeing injustice by a law,' as the just eye can see it everywhere doing:—certainly something must be wrong in the inner man of the world, since its outer man is so terribly out of square! The deliverer of the world, therefore, were not he who headed sansculottic insurrections never so successful, but he who pointed out to the world what nightmares were resting over its soul. Ignatius Loyola, and the innumerable company, Papist, Protestant, Sham-christian, Anti-christian, that have believed *his* revelation; universal prevalence, from pole to pole, of such a 'doctrine of devils'; reverent or quasi-reverent faith in the dead human formulas, and somnolent contempt of the divine ever-living facts, such as reigns now, consecrated and supreme, in all commonwealths and countries, and hearts of men; the Human Species, as it were, unconsciously or consciously, gone all to one Sodality of Jesuitism: who will deliver us from the body of this death! It is in truth like death-in-life; a living-criminal (as in the old Roman days) with a *corpse* lashed fast to him. What wretch could have deserved such a doom?

As to this Ignatius, I am aware he is admired, and even transcendently admired, or what we call worshipped, by multitudes of human creatures, who to this day expect, or endeavour to expect, some kind of salvation from him;—whom it is so painful to enrage against me, if I could avoid it! Undoubtedly Ignatius, centuries ago, gave satisfaction to the Devil's Advocate, the Pope and other parties interested; was canonised, named Saint, and raised duly into Heaven officially so-called; whereupon, with many, he passes, ever since, for a kind of God, or person who has much influence with the gods.—Alas, the admiration, and transcendent admiration, of mankind, goes a strange road in these times! Hudson too had his canonisation: and by *Vox Populi*, if not by Pope and Devil's Advocate, was raised to a kind of brass Olympus by mankind; and rode there for a year or two;—though he is already gone to warming-pans again. A poor man, in our day, has many gods foisted on him; and big voices bid him, "Worship, or be ——!" in a menacing and confusing manner. What shall he do? By far the greater part of said gods, current in the public, whether canonised by Pope or Populus, are mere dumb Apises and beatified Prize-oxen;—nay, some of them, who have articulate faculty, are devils instead of gods. A poor man that would save his soul alive is reduced to the sad necessity of sharply trying his gods whether they are divine or not; which is a terrible pass for mankind, and lays an awful problem upon each man. The man must do it, however. At his own peril he will have to do this problem too, which is one of the awfulest; and his neighbours, all but a most select portion of them, portion generally *not* clad in official tiaras, can be of next to no help to him in it, nay, rather will infinitely hinder him in it, as matters go. If Ignatius, worshipped by millions as a kind of god, is, in eternal fact, a kind of devil, or enemy of whatsoever is godlike in man's existence, surely it is pressingly expedient that men were made aware of it; that men, with whatever earnestness is yet in them, laid it awfully to heart!

Prim friend with the black serge gown, with the rosary, scapulary, and I know not what other spiritual block-and-tackle,—scowl not on me. If in thy poor heart, under its rosaries, there dwell any human piety, awestruck reverence towards the Supreme Maker, devout compassion towards this poor Earth and her sons,—scowl not anathema on me, listen to me; for I swear thou art my brother, in spite of rosaries and scapularies; and I recognise thee, though thou canst not me; and with love and pity know thee for a brother, though enchanted into the condition of a spiritual mummy. Hapless creature, curse me not; listen to me, and consider;—perhaps even thou wilt escape from mummyhood, and become once more a living soul!

Of Ignatius, then, I must take leave to say, there can this be recorded, that probably he has done more mischief in the Earth than any man born since. A scandalous mortal, O brethren of mankind who live by truth and not by falsity, I must call this man. Altogether,—here where I stand, looking on millions of poor pious brothers reduced to spiritual mummyhood, who curse me because I try to speak the truth to them, and on a whole world canting and grimacing from birth to death, and finding in their life two serious indubitabilities, Cookery and Scrip,—how, if he is the representative and chief fountain of all this, can I call him other than the superlative of scandals? A bad man, I think; not good by nature; and by destiny swollen into a very Ahriman of badness. Not good by nature, I perceive. A man born greedy; whose greatness in the beginning, and even in the end if we will look well, is indicated chiefly by the depth of his appetite: not the recommendable kind of man! A man full of prurient elements from the first; which at the last, through his long course, have developed themselves over the family of mankind into an expression altogether tremendous.

A young Spanish soldier and hidalgo with hot Biscayan blood, distinguished, as I understand, by his fierce appetites chiefly, by his audacities and sensualities, and loud unreasonable decision, That this Universe, in spite of rumours to the contrary, was a Cookery-shop and Bordel, wherein garlic, jamaica-pepper, unfortunate-females and other spicery and garnishing awaited the bold human appetite, and the rest of it was mere rumour and moonshine: with this life-theory and practice had Ignatius lived some thirty years, a hot human Papin's-digester and little other; when, on the walls of Pampeluna, the destined cannon-shot shattered both his legs,—leaving his head, hitting only his legs, so the Destinies would have it,—and he fell at once totally prostrate, a wrecked Papin's-digester; lay many weeks horizontal, and had in that tedious posture to commence a new series of reflections. He began to perceive now that 'the rest of it' was not mere rumour and moonshine; that the rest was, in fact, the whole secret of the matter. That the Cookery-shop and Bordel was a magical delusion, a sleight-of-hand of Satan, to lead Ignatius down, by garlic and finer temporal spiceries, to eternal Hell;—and that in short he, Ignatius, had lived hitherto as a degraded ferocious Human Pig, one of the most perfect scoundrels; and was, at that date, no other than a blot on Creation, and a scandal to mankind.

With which set of reflections who could quarrel? The reflections were true, were salutary; nay, there was something of sacred in them,—as in the repentance of man, in the discovery by erring man that wrong is not right, that wrong differs from right as deep Hell from high Heaven, there ever is. Ignatius's soul was in convulsions, in agonies of new birth; for which I honour Ignatius. Human sincerity could not but have told him: "Yes, in several respects, thou art a detestable Human Pig, and disgrace to the family of man; for which it behoves thee to be in nameless remorse, till thy life either mend or end. Consider, there as thou liest with thy two legs smashed, the peccant element that is in thee; discover it, rigorously tear it out; reflect what farther thou wilt do. A life yet remains; to be led, clearly, in some new manner: how wilt thou lead it? Sit silent for the rest of thy days? In some most modest seclusion, hide thyself from a humankind which has been dishonoured by thee? Thy sin being pruriency of appetite, give that at least no farther scope under any old or new form?"

I admit, the question was not easy. Think, in this his wrecked horizontal position, what could or should the poor individual called Inigo, Ignatius, or whatever the first name of him was, have done? Truly for Ignatius the question was very complicated. But, had he asked from Nature and the eternal Oracles a remedy for wrecked sensualism, here surely was one thing that would have suggested itself: To annihilate his pruriency. To cower, silent and ashamed, into some dim corner; and resolve to make henceforth as little noise as possible. That would have been modest, salutary; that might have led to many other virtues, and gradually to all. That, I think, is what the small still voices would have told Ignatius, could he have heard them amid the loud bullyings and liturgyings; but he couldn't, perhaps he never tried;—and *that*, accordingly, was not what Ignatius resolved upon.

In fact, Christian doctrine, backed by all the human wisdom I could ever hear of, inclines me to think that Ignatius, had he been a good and brave man, should have consented, at this point, to be damned,—as was clear to him that he deserved to be. Here would have been a healing solace to his conscience; one transcendent act of virtue which it still lay with him, the worst of sinners, to do. "To die forever, as I have deserved; let Eternal Justice triumph *so*, by means of me and my foul scandals, since otherwise it may not!" *Selbsttödtung*, Annihilation of Self, justly reckoned the beginning of all virtue: here is the highest form of it, still possible to the lowest man. The voice of Nature this, to a repentant outcast sinner turning again towards the realms of manhood;—and I understand it is the precept of all right Christianity too. But no, Ignatius could not, in his lowest abasement, consent to have justice done on him, not on *him*, ah no;—and there lay his crime and his misfortune, which has brought such penalty on him and us.

The truth is, it was not of Eternal Nature and her Oracles that Ignatius inquired, poor man; it was of Temporary Art and *hers*, and these sang not of self-annihilation, or Ignatius would not hear that part of their song. Not so did Ignatius read the omens. "My pruriency being terribly forbidden on one side, let it," thought Ignatius, deeply unconscious of such a thought, "have terrible course on another. Garlic-cookery and suchlike excitations are accursed to me forever; but cannot I achieve something that shall still assert my *Ego* I in a highly gratifying manner?" Alas, human sincerity, hard as his scourging had been, was not quite attainable by him. In his frantic just agonies, he flung himself before the shrine of Virgin Marys, Saints of the Romish Calendar, three-hatted Holy Fathers, and uncertain Thaumaturgic Entities; praying that he might be healed by miracle, not by course of nature; and that, for one most fatal item, his pruriency of appetite might, under new inverse forms,—continue with him. Which prayer, we may say, was granted.

In the depths of his despair, all Nature glooming veritable reprobation on him, and Eternal Justice whispering, "*Accept* what thou hast merited," there rose this altogether turbid semi-artificial glare of hope upon Ignatius, "The Virgin will save me, the Virgin has saved me;"—Well and good, I say; then be quiet, and let us see some temperance and modesty in you. Far otherwise did Ignatius resolve: temperance and true modesty were not among the gifts of this precious individual the Virgin had been at the pains to save. Many plans Ignatius tried to make his *Ego* I still available on Earth, and still keep Heaven open for him. His pilgrimings and battlings, his silent sufferings and wrestlings for that object, are enormous, and reach the highest pitch of the prurient-heroic. At length, after various failures and unsatisfactory half-successes, it struck him: "Has not there lately been a sort of revolt against the Virgin, and the Holy Father who takes care of her? Certain infernal Heresiarchs in Germany and elsewhere, I am told, have risen up against the Holy Father, arguing with terrible plausibility that he is an Unholy Phantasm: he;—and if so, what am I and my outlooks! A new light, presumably of Hell, has risen to that effect; which new light—why cannot I vow here, and consecrate myself, to battle against, and with my whole strength endeavour to extinguish?" That was the task Ignatius fixed upon as his; and at that he has been busy, he and an immense and ever-increasing sodality of mortals, these three hundred years; and, through various fortune, they have brought it thus far. Truly to one of the most singular predicaments the affairs of mankind ever stood in before.

If the new light is of Hell, O Ignatius, right: but if of Heaven, there is not, that I know of, any equally damnable sin as thine! No; thy late Pighood itself is trivial in comparison. Frantic mortal, wilt thou, at the bidding of any Papa, war against Almighty God? Is there no 'inspiration,' then, but an ancient Jewish, Greekish, Romish one, with big revenues, loud liturgies and red stockings? The Pope is old; but Eternity, thou shalt observe, is older. High-treason against all the Universe is dangerous to do. Quench not among us, I advise thee, the monitions of that thrice-sacred gospel, holier than all gospels, which dwells in each man direct from the Maker of him! Frightfully will it be avenged on thee, and on all that follow thee; to the sixth generation and farther, all men shall lie under this gigantic Upas-tree thou hast been planting; terribly will the gods avenge it on thee, and on all thy Father Adam's house!

Ignatius's black militia, armed with this precious message of salvation, have now been campaigning over all the world for about three hundred years; and openly or secretly have done a mighty work over all the world. Who can count what a work! Where you meet a man believing in the salutary nature of falsehoods, or the divine authority of things doubtful, and fancying that to serve the Good Cause he must call the Devil to his aid, there is a follower of Unsaint Ignatius; not till the last of these men has vanished from the Earth will our account with Ignatius be quite settled, and his black militia have got their mittimus to Chaos again. They have given a new substantive to modern languages. The word 'Jesuitism' now, in all countries, expresses an idea for which there was in Nature no prototype before. Not till these late centuries had the human soul generated that abomination, or needed to name it. Truly they have achieved great things in the world; and a general result which we may call stupendous. Not victory for Ignatius and the black militia,—no, till the Universe itself become a cunningly devised Fable, and God the Maker abdicate in favour of Beelzebub, I do not see how 'victory' can fall on that side! But they have done such deadly execution on the general soul of man; and have wrought such havoc on the terrestrial and supernal interests of this world, as insure to Jesuitism a long memory in human annals.

How many three-hatted Papas, and scandalous Consecrated Phantasms, cleric and laic, convicted or not yet suspected to be Phantasms and servants of the Devil and not of God, does it still retain in existence in all corners of this afflicted world! Germany had its War of Thirty Years, among other wars, on this subject; and had there not been elsewhere a nobler loyalty to God's Cause than was to be found in Germany at that date, Ignatius with his rosaries and gibbet-ropes, with his honey-mouthed Fathers Lämmerlein in black serge, and heavyfisted Fathers Wallenstein in chain armour, must have carried it; and that alarming Lutheran new-light would have been got extinguished again. The Continent once well quenched out, it was calculated England might soon be made to follow, and then the whole world were blessed with orthodoxy. So it had been computed. But Gustavus, a man prepared to die if needful, Gustavus with his Swedes appeared upon the scene; nay, shortly Oliver Cromwell with his Puritans appeared upon it; and the computation quite broke down. Beyond seas and within seas, the Wallensteins and Lämmerleins, the Hyacinths and Andreas Habernfelds, the Lauds and Charleses,—in fine, Ignatius and all that held of him,—had to cower into their holes again, and try it by new methods. Many were their methods, their fortune various; and ever and anon, to the hope or the terror of this and the other man of weak judgment, it has seemed that victory was just about to crown Ignatius. True, too true, the execution done upon the soul of mankind has been enormous and tremendous; but victory to Ignatius there has been none,—and will and can be none.

Nay, at last, ever since 1789 and '93, the figure of the quarrel has much altered; and the hope for Ignatius (except to here and there a man of weak judgment) has become a flat impossibility. For Luther and Protestantism Proper having, so to speak, withdrawn from the battlefield, as entities whose work was done, there then appeared on it Jean Jacques and French Sansculottism; to which all creatures have gradually joined themselves. Whereby now we have Protestantism *Im*proper,—a Protestantism universal and illimitable on the part of all men; the whole world risen into anarchic mutiny, with pike and paving-stone; swearing by Heaven above and also by Hell beneath, by the Eternal Yea and the Eternal No, that Ignatius and Imposture shall not rule them any more, neither in soul nor in body nor in breeches-pocket any more; but that they will go unruled rather,—as they hope it will be possible for them to do. This is Ignatius's 'destruction' of Protestantism: he has destroyed it into Sansculottism, such a form of all-embracing Protestantism as was never dreamt of by the human soul before. So that now, at last, there is hope of final death and rest to Ignatius and his labours. Ignatius, I perceive, is now sure to die, and be abolished before long; nay, is already dead, and will not even *galvanise* much farther; but, in fine, is hourly sinking towards the Abyss,—dragging much along with him thither. Whole worlds along with him: such continents of things, once living and beautiful, now dead and horrible; things once sacred, now not even commonly profane:—fearful and wonderful, to every thinking heart and seeing eye, in these days! That is the answer, slowly enunciated, but irrevocable and indubitable, which Ignatius gets in Heaven's High Court, when he appeals there, asking, "Am I a *Sanctus* or not, as the Papa and his Devil's-Advocate told me I was?"

The 'vivaciousness' of Jesuitism is much spoken of, as a thing creditable. And truly it is remarkable, though I think in the way of wonder even more than of admiration, what a quantity of killing it does require. To say nothing of the Cromwells and Gustavuses, and what they did, they and theirs,—it is near a century now since Pombal and Aranda, secular and not divine men, yet useful antiseptic products of their generation, felt called, if not consciously by Heaven, then by Earth which is unconsciously a bit of Heaven, to cut-down this scandal from the world, and make the earth rid of Jesuitism for one thing. What a wide-sweeping shear they gave it, as with the sudden scythe of universal death, is well known; and how, mown down from side to side of the world in one day, it had to lie sorrowfully slain and withering under the sun. After all which, nay, after 1793 itself, does not Jesuitism still pretend to be alive, and in this year 1850, still (by dint of steady galvanism) shows some quivering in its fingers and toes? Vivacious, sure enough; and I suppose there must be reasons for it, which it is well to note withal. But what if such vivaciousness were, in good part, like that of evil weeds; if the 'strength' of Jesuitism were like that of typhus-fever, not a recommendable kind of strength!

I hear much also of 'obedience,' how that and the kindred virtues are prescribed and exemplified by Jesuitism; the truth of which, and the merit of which, far be it from me to deny. Obedience, a virtue universally forgotten in these days, will have to become universally known again. Obedience is good, and indispensable: but if it be obedience to what is wrong and false,—good Heavens, there is no name for such a depth of human cowardice and calamity; spurned everlastingly by the gods. Loyalty? Will you be loyal to Beelzebub? Will you 'make a covenant with Death and Hell'? I will not be loyal to Beelzebub; I will become a nomadic Chactaw rather, a barricading Sansculotte, a Conciliation-Hall repealer; anything and everything is venial to that.

The virtues of Jesuitism, seasoned with that fatal condiment, are other than quite virtuous! To cherish pious thoughts, and assiduously keep your eye directed to a Heaven that is not real: will that yield divine life to you, or hideous galvanic life-in-death? To cherish many quasi-human virtues, really many possibilities of virtue; and wed them all to the principle that God can be served by believing what is not true: to put-out the sacred lamp of Intellect within you; to decide on maiming yourself of that higher godlike gift, which God himself has given you with a silent but awful charge in regard to it; to be bullied and bowowed out of your loyalty to the God of Light by big Phantasms and three-hatted Chimeras: can I call that by the name of nobleness or human courage?—"Could not help it," say you? If 'a man cannot help it,' a man must allow me to say he has unfortunately given the most conspicuous proof of caitiffhood that lay within his human possibility, and he must cease to brag to me about his 'virtues,' in that sad case!

But, in fact, the character of the poor creature named Ignatius, whether it be good or bad and worst, concerns us little; not even that of the specific Jesuit Body concerns us much. The Jesuits proper have long since got their final mittimus from England. Nor, in the seventeenth century,—with an ubiquitous alarming Toby Mathews, Andreas Habernfeld and Company; with there a Father Hyacinth, and here a William Laud and Charles First,—was this by any means so light a business as we now fancy. But it has been got accomplished. Long now have the English People understood that Jesuits proper, in so far as they are not Nothing (which is the commonest case), are servants of the Prince of Darkness: by Puritan Cromwelliads on the great scale, and on the small by diligent hunting, confinement in the Clink Prison, and judicial tribulation,—let us say, by earnest pious thought and fight, and the labours of the valiant born to us,—this country has been tolerably cleared of Jesuits proper; nor is there danger of their ever coming to a head here again. But, alas, the expulsion of the Jesuit Body avails us little, when the Jesuit *Soul* has so nestled itself in the life of mankind everywhere. What we have to complain of is, that all men are become Jesuits! That no man speaks the truth to you or to himself, but that every man lies,—with blasphemous audacity, and does not know that he is lying,—before God and man, in regard to almost all manner of things. This is the fell heritage bequeathed us by Ignatius; to this sad stage has our battle with him come.

Consider it, good reader;—and yet alas, if thou be not one

of a thousand, what is the use of bidding thee consider it! The deadliest essence of the curse we now labour under is that the light of our inner eyesight is gone out; that such things are not discernible by considering. 'Cant and even sincere Cant': O Heaven, when a man doing his sincerest is still but canting! For this is the sad condition of the insincere man: he is doomed all his days to deal with insincerities; to live, move, and have his being in traditions and conventionalities. If the traditions have grown old, the conventionalities will be mostly false; true in no sense can they be for him: never shall he behold the truth of any matter; formulas, theologic, economic and other, certain superficial readings of truth, required in the market-place, these he will take with him, these he will apply dextrously, and with these he will have to satisfy himself. Sincerity shall not exist for him; he shall think that he has found it, while it is yet far away. The deep, awful and indeed divine quality of truth that lies in every object, and in virtue of which the object exists,—from his poor eyes this is forever hidden. Not with austere divine realities which belong to the Universe and to Eternity, but with paltry ambiguous phantasms, comfortable and uncomfortable, which belong to his own parish, and to the current week or generation, shall he pass his days.

There had been liars in the world; alas, never since the Old Serpent tempted Eve, had the world been free of liars, neither will it be: but there was in this of Jesuit Ignatius an apotheosis of falsity, a kind of subtle quintessence and deadly virus of lying, the like of which had never been seen before. Measure it, if you can; prussic-acid and chloroform are poor to it! Men had served the Devil, and men had very imperfectly served God; but to think that God could be served more perfectly by taking the Devil into partnership,—this was a novelty of St. Ignatius. And this is now no novelty; to such extent has the Jesuit chloroform stupefied us all. This is the universal faith and practice, for several generations past, of the class called good men in this world. They are in general mutineers, sansculottes, angry disorderly persons, and a class rather worthy to be called bad, who hitherto assert the contrary of this. "Be careful how you believe truth," cries the good man everywhere: "Composure and a whole skin are very valuable. Truth,—who knows?—many things are not true; most things are uncertainties, very prosperous things are even open falsities that have been agreed upon. There is little certain truth going. If it isn't orthodox truth, it will play the very devil with you!"

Did the Human Species ever lie in such a soak of horrors, —sunk like steeping flax under the wide-spread fetid Hell-waters,—in all spiritual respects dead, dead; voiceless towards Heaven for centuries back; merely sending up, in the form of mute prayer, such an odour as the angels never smelt before! It has to lie there, till the worthless part has been rotted out; till much has been rotted out, I do perceive;— and perhaps the time has come when the precious *lint fibre* itself is in danger; and men, if they are not delivered, will cease to be men, or to be at all! O Heavens, with divine Hudson on this hand, and divine Ignatius on that, and the Gorham Controversy going on, and the Irish Tenant Agitation (which will soon become a Scotch and an English ditto) just about beginning, is not the hour now nearly come? Words fail us when we would speak of what Ignatius has done for men. Probably the most virulent form of sin which the Old Serpent has yet rejoiced in on our poor Earth. For me it is the deadliest high treason against God our Maker which the soul of man could commit.

And this, then, is the horrible conclusion we have arrived at, in England as in all countries; and with *less* protest against it hitherto, and not with more, in England than in other countries? That the great body of orderly considerate men; men affecting the name of good and pious, and who, in fact, excluding certain silent exceptionary individuals one to the million, such as the Almighty Beneficence never quite withholds, are accounted our best men,—have unconsciously abnegated the sacred privilege and duty of acting or speaking the truth; and fancy that it is not truth that is to be acted, but that an amalgam of truth and falsity is the safe thing. In parliament and pulpit, in book and speech, in whatever spiritual thing men have to commune of, or to do together, this is the rule they have lapsed into, this is the pass they have arrived at. We have to report that Human Speech is not true! That it is false to a degree never witnessed in this world till lately. Such a subtle virus of falsity in the very essence of it, as far excels all open lying, or prior kinds of falsity; false with consciousness of being sincere! The heart of the world is corrupted to the core; a detestable devil's-poison circulates in the life-blood of mankind; taints with abominable deadly malady all that mankind do. Such a curse never fell on men before.

For the falsity of speech rests on a far deeper falsity. False speech, as is inevitable when men long practise it, falsifies all things; the very thoughts, or fountains of speech and action become false. Ere long, by the appointed curse of Heaven, a man's intellect ceases to be capable of distinguishing truth, when he permits himself to deal in speaking or acting what is false. Watch well the tongue, for out of it are the issues of life! O, the foul leprosy that heaps itself in monstrous accumulation over Human Life, and obliterates all the divine features of it into one hideous mountain of purulent disease, when Human Life parts company with truth; and fancies, taught by Ignatius or another, that lies will be the salvation of it! We of these late centuries have suffered as the sons of Adam never did before; hebetated, sunk under mountains of torpid leprosy; and studying to persuade ourselves that this is health.

And if we have awakened from the sleep of death into the Sorcerer's Sabbath of Anarchy, is it not the chief of blessings that we are awake at all? Thanks to Transcendent Sansculottism and the long-memorable French Revolution, the one veritable and tremendous Gospel of these bad ages, divine Gospel such as we deserved, and merciful too, though preached in thunder and terror! Napoleon Campaignings, September Massacres, Reigns of Terror, Anacharsis Clootz and Pontiff Robespierre, and still more beggarly tragicalities that we have since seen, and are still to see: what frightful thing were not a little less frightful than the thing we had? Peremptory was our necessity of putting Jesuitism away, of awakening to the consciousness of Jesuitism. 'Horrible,' yes: how could it be other than horrible? Like the valley of Jehoshaphat, it lies round us, one nightmare wilderness, and wreck of dead-men's bones, this false modern world; and no rapt Ezekiel in prophetic vision imaged to himself things sadder, more horrible and terrible, than the eyes of men, if they *are* awake, may now deliberately see. Many yet sleep; but the sleep of all, as we judge by their maundering and jargoning, their Gorham Controversies, street-barricadings, and uneasy tossings and somnambulisms, is not far from ending. Novalis says, 'We are near awakening when we *dream that we are dreaming*.'

A man's 'religion' consists not of the many things he is in doubt of and tries to believe, but of the few he is assured of, and has no need of effort for believing. His religion, whatever it may be, is a discerned fact, and coherent system of discerned facts to him; he stands fronting the worlds and the eternities upon it: to *doubt* of it is not permissible at all! He must verify or expel his doubts, convert them into certainty of Yes or No; or they will be the death of his religion.—But, on the other hand, convert them into certainty of Yes *and* No; or even of Yes *though* No, as the Ignatian method is, what will become of your religion? Let us glance a little at this strange aspect of our affairs.

What a man's or nation's available religion at any time is,

may sometimes, especially if he abound in Bishops, Gorham Controversies, and richly endowed Churches and Church-practices, be difficult to say. For a Nation which, under very peculiar circumstances, closed its Bible about two hundred years ago, hanged the dead body of its Cromwell, and accepted one Charles Second for Defender of its *Faith* so-called; for such a Nation, which has closed its Bible, and decided that the sufficient and much handier practice would be to kiss the outside of said Bible, and in all senses swear zealously, by the same without opening it again,—the question what its 'religion' is, may naturally be involved in obscurities! Such dramaturgic fugle-worship going on everywhere, and kissing of the closed Bible, what real worship *religion*, or recognition of a Divine Necessity in Nature and Life, there may be—Or, in fact, is there any left at all? Very little, I should say.

The religion of a man in these strange circumstances, what living conviction he has about his Destiny in this Universe, falls into a most strange condition;—and, in truth, I have observed, is apt to take refuge in the stomach mainly. The man goes through his prescribed fugle-motions at church and elsewhere, keeping his conscience and sense of decency at ease thereby; and in some empty part of his brain, if he have fancy left, or brain other than a beaver's, there goes on occasionally some dance of dreamy hypotheses, sentimental echoes, shadows, and other inane make-believes,—which I think are quite the contrary of a possession to him; leading to no clear Faith, or divine life-and-death Certainty of any kind; but to a torpid species of *delirium somnians* and *delirium stertens* rather. In his head or in his heart this man has of available religion none. But descend into his stomach, purse and the adjacent regions, you then do awaken, even in the very last extremity, a set of divine beliefs, were it only belief in the multiplication-table, and certain coarser outward forms of *meum* and *tuum*. He believes in the inalienable nature of purchased beef, in the duty of the

British citizen to fight for himself when injured, and other similar faiths:—an actual 'religion' of its sort, or revelation of what the Almighty Maker means with him in this Earth, and has irrefragably, as by direct inspiration, charged him to do. This is the man's religion; *this* poor scantling of 'divine convictions' which you find lying, mostly inarticulate, in deep sleep at the bottom of his stomach, and have such difficulty in raising into any kind of elocution or conscious wakefulness.

Alas, so much of him, his soul almost wholly, is not only asleep there, but gone drowned and dead. The 'religion' you awaken in him is often of a very singular quality; enough to make the observer pause in silence. Such a religion, issuing practically in Hudson Statues, and, alas, also in Distressed Needlewomen, Cannibal Connaughts, and 'remedial measures suited to the occasion,' was never seen among Adam's Posterity before. But it is this modern man's religion; all the religion you will get of him. And if you can winnow-out the fugle-motions, fantasies, sentimentalisms, make-believes, and other multitudinous chaff, so that his religion stands before you in its net condition, you may contemplate it with scientific astonishment, with innumerable reflections, and may perhaps draw wise inferences from it.

A singular piece of scribble, in Sauerteig's hand, bearing marks of haste and almost of rage (for the words, abbreviated to the bone, tumble about as if in battle on the paper), occurs to me at this moment, entitled *Schwein'sche Weltansicht*; and I will try to decipher and translate it.

'*Pig Philosophy*

'If the inestimable talent of Literature should, in these swift days of progress, be extended to the brute creation, having fairly taken-in all the human, so that swine and oxen could communicate to us on paper what they thought of the Universe, there might curious results, not uninstructive to some of us, ensue. Supposing swine (I mean fourfooted swine), of sensibility and superior logical parts, had attained such culture; and could, after survey and reflection, jot-down for us their notion of the Universe, and of their interests and duties there,—might it not well interest a discerning public, perhaps in unexpected ways, and give a stimulus to the languishing book-trade? The votes of all creatures, it is understood at present, ought to be had; that you may "legislate" for them with better insight. "How can you govern a thing," say many, "without first asking its vote?" Unless, indeed, you already chance to know its vote,—and even something more, namely, what you are to think of its vote; what *it* wants by its vote; and still more important, what Nature wants, which latter, at the end of the account, is the only thing that will be got!— —Pig Propositions, in a rough form, are somewhat as follows:

'1. The Universe, so far as sane conjecture can go, is an immeasurable Swine's-trough, consisting of solid and liquid, and of other contrasts and kinds;—especially consisting of attainable and unattainable, the latter in immensely greater quantities for most pigs.

'2. Moral evil is unattainability of Pig's-wash; moral good, attainability of ditto.

'3. "What is Paradise, or the State of Innocence?" Paradise, called also State of Innocence, Age of Gold, and other names, *was* (according to Pigs of weak judgment) unlimited attainability of Pig's-wash; perfect fulfilment of one's wishes, so that the Pig's imagination could not outrun reality: a fable and an impossibility, as Pigs of sense now see.

'4. "Define the Whole Duty of Pigs." It is the mission of universal Pighood, and the duty of all Pigs, at all times, to diminish the quantity of unattainable and increase that of attainable. All knowledge and device and effort ought to be directed thither and thither only; Pig Science, Pig

Enthusiasm and Devotion have this one aim. It is the Whole Duty of Pigs.

'5. Pig Poetry ought to consist of universal recognition of the excellence of Pig's-wash and ground barley, and the felicity of Pigs whose trough is in order, and who have had enough: Hrumph!

'6. The Pig knows the weather; he ought to look out what kind of weather it will be.

'7. "Who made the Pig?" Unknown;—perhaps the Pork-butcher?

'8. "Have you Law and Justice in Pigdom?" Pigs of observation have discerned that there is, or was once supposed to be, a thing called justice. Undeniably at least there is a sentiment in Pig-nature called indignation, revenge, etc., which, if one Pig provoke another, comes out in a more or less destructive manner: hence laws are necessary, amazing quantities of laws. For quarrelling is attended with loss of blood, of life, at any rate with frightful effusion of the general stock of Hog's-wash, and ruin (temporary ruin) to large sections of the universal Swine's-trough: wherefore let justice be observed, that so quarrelling be avoided.

'9. "What is justice?" Your own share of the general Swine's-trough, not any portion of my share.

'10. "But what is 'my' share?" Ah! there in fact lies the grand difficulty; upon which Pig science, meditating this long while, can settle absolutely nothing. My share—hrumph! —my share is, on the whole, whatever I can contrive to get without being hanged or sent to the hulks. For there are gibbets, treadmills, I need not tell you, and rules which Lawyers have prescribed.

'11. "Who are Lawyers?" Servants of God, appointed revealers of the oracles of God, who read-off to us from day to day what is the eternal Commandment of God in reference to the mutual claims of his creatures in this world.

'12. "Where do they find that written?" In Coke upon Lyttelton.

'13. "Who made Coke?" Unknown: the maker of Coke's wig is discoverable.—"What became of Coke?" Died.—"And then?" Went to the undertaker; went to the'——But we must pull up: Sauerteig's fierce humour, confounding ever farther in his haste the fourfooted with the twofooted animal, rushes into wilder and wilder forms of satirical torch-dancing, and threatens to end in a universal Rape of the Wigs, which in a person of his character looks ominous and dangerous. Here, for example, is his fifty-first 'Proposition,' as he calls it:

'51. "What are Bishops?" Overseers of souls.—"What is a soul?" The thing that keeps the body alive.—"How do they oversee that?" They tie on a kind of aprons, publish charges; I believe they pray dreadfully; macerate themselves nearly dead with continual grief that they cannot in the least oversee it.—"And are much honoured?" By the wise very much.

'52. "Define the Church." I had rather not.—"Do you believe in a Future state?" Yes, surely.—"What is it?" Heaven, so-called.—"To everybody?" I understand so; hope so!—"What is it thought to be?" Hrumph!—"No Hell, then, at all?"—Hrumph!'

The Fine Arts are by some thought to be a kind of religion; the chief religion this poor Europe is to have in time coming: and undoubtedly it is in Literature, Poetry and the other kindred Arts, where at least a certain manliness of temper, and liberty to follow truth, prevails or might prevail, that the world's chosen souls do now chiefly take refuge, and attempt what 'Worship of the Beautiful' may still be possible for them. The Poet in the Fine Arts, especially the Poet in Speech, what Fichte calls the 'Scholar' or the 'Literary Man,' is defined by Fichte as the 'Priest' of these Modern Epochs,—all the Priest they have. And indeed Nature herself will teach us that the man born with what we call 'genius,' which will mean, born with better and larger understanding than others; the man in whom 'the inspiration of the Almighty,' given to all men, has a higher potentiality;—that he, and properly he only, is the perpetual Priest of Men; ordained to the office by God himself, whether men can be so lucky as to get him ordained to it or not: nay, he does the office, too, after a sort, in this and in all epochs. Ever must the Fine Arts be if not religion, yet indissolubly united to it, dependent on it, vitally blended with it as body is with soul.

Why should I say, Ignatius Loyola ruined our Fine Arts? Ignatius thought not of the Fine Arts; nor is the guilt all his. Ignatius, intent on the heart of the matter, did but consecrate in the name of Heaven, and religiously welcome as life in God, the universal death in the Devil which of itself was preparing to come,—on the Fine Arts as on all things. The Fine Arts are not what I most regret in the catastrophe so frightfully accelerated and consummated by him! If men's practical faith have become a Pig Philosophy, and their divine worship have become a Mumbojumboism, soliciting in dumb agony either change to the very heart or else extinction and abolition, it matters little what their fine or other arts may be. All arts, industries and pursuits they have, are tainted to the heart with foul poison; carry not in them the inspiration of God, but (frightful to think of!) that of the Devil calling and thinking himself God; and are smitten with a curse forevermore. What judgment the Academy of Cognoscenti may pronounce on them, is unimportant to me; what splendour of upholstery and French cookery, and temporary bullion at the Bank, may be realised from them, is important to M'Croudy, not to me.

Such bullion, I perceive well, can but be temporary;—and if it were to be eternal, would bullion reconcile me to them? No, M'Croudy, never. Bullion, temporary bullion itself, awakens the hallelujah of flunkies; but even eternal bullion ought to make small impression upon men. To men I count it a human blessedness, and stern benignity of Heaven, that when their course is false and ignoble, their bullion begins to leave them; that ultimate bankruptcy, and flat universal ruin, published in the gazette, and palpable even to flunkies, follows step by step, at a longer or shorter interval, all solecisms under this sun. Certain as shadow follows substance; it is the oldest law of Fate:—and one good day, open ruin, bankruptcy and foul destruction, does overtake them all. Let us bless God for it. Were it otherwise, what end could there be of solecisms? The temporary paradise of quacks and flunkies were now an eternal paradise; how could the noble soul find harbour or patience in this world at all? This world were the inheritance of the ignoble;—a very Bedlam, as some sceptics have fancied it; made by malignant gods in their sport.

But as to Jesuitism in the Fine Arts, and how its unsuspected thrice-unblessed presence here too smites the genius of mankind with paralysis, there were much to be said. Sorrowful reflections lie in that, far beyond what a discerning public fancies in these days; reflections which cannot be entered upon, which can hardly be indicated afar off, at present. Here too, as elsewhere, the consummate flower of Consecrated Unveracity reigns supreme; and here as elsewhere peaceably presides over an enormous Life-in-Death!

"May the Devil fly away with the Fine Arts!" exclaimed confidentially once, in my hearing, one of our most distinguished public men; a sentiment that often recurs to me. I perceive too well how true it is, in our case. A public man, intent on any real business, does, I suppose, find the Fine Arts rather imaginary. The Fine Arts, wherever they turn-up as business, whatever Committee sit upon them, are sure to be the parent of much empty talk, laborious hypocrisy, dilettantism, futility; involving huge trouble and expense and babble, which end in no result, if not in worse than none.

The practical man, in his moments of sincerity, feels them to be a pretentious nothingness; a confused superfluity and nuisance, purchased with cost,—what he in brief language denominates a *bore*. It is truly so, in these degraded days: —and the Fine Arts, among other fine interests of ours, are really called to recognise it, and see what they will do in it. For they are become the Throne of Hypocrisy, I think the highest of her many thrones, these said Arts; which is very sad to consider! Nowhere, not even on a gala-day in the Pope's Church of St. Peter, is there such an explosion of intolerable hypocrisy, on the part of poor mankind, as when you admit them into their Royal Picture-gallery, Glyptothek, Museum, or other divine Temple of the Fine Arts. Hypocrisy doubly intolerable; because it is not here, as in St. Peter's and some other Churches, an obliged hypocrisy but a voluntary one. Nothing but your own vanity prompts you here to pretend worshipping; you are not bound to worship, and twaddle pretended raptures, criticisms and poetic recognitions, unless you like it;—and you do not the least know what a damnable practice it is, or you wouldn't! I make a rule, these many years back, to speak almost nothing, and encourage no speech in Picture-galleries; to avoid company, even that of familiar friends, in such situations; and perambulate the place in silence. You can thus worship or not worship, precisely as the gods bid you; and are at least under no obligation to do hypocrisies, if you cannot conveniently worship.

The fact is, though men are not in the least aware of it, the Fine Arts, divorced entirely from Truth this long while, and wedded almost professedly to Falsehood, Fiction and suchlike, are got into what we must call an insane condition: they walk abroad without keepers, nobody suspecting their sad state, and do fantastic tricks equal to any in Bedlam,—especially when admitted to work 'regardless of expense,' as we sometimes see them! What earnest soul passes that new St. Stephen's, and its wilderness of stone pepperboxes with their tin flags atop, worth two millions I am told, without mentally exclaiming *Apagè*, and cutting some pious cross in the air! If that be 'ideal beauty,' except for sugarwork, and the more elaborate kinds of gingerbread, what is real ugliness? To say merely (with an architectonic trumpet-blast that cost two-millions), "Good Christians, you observe well I am regardless of expense, and also of veracity, in every form?" Too truly these poor Fine Arts have fallen mad!

The Fine Arts once divorcing themselves from *truth*, are quite certain to fall mad, if they do not die, and get flown away with by the Devil, which latter is only the second-worst result for us. Truth, fact, is the life of all things; falsity, 'fiction' or whatever it may call itself, is certain to be death, and is already insanity, to whatever thing takes up with it. Fiction, even to the Fine Arts, is not a quite permissible thing. Sparingly permissible, within iron limits; or if you will reckon strictly, not permissible at all! The Fine Arts too, like the coarse and every art of Man's god-given Faculty, are to understand that they are sent hither not to fib and dance, but to speak and work; and, on the whole, that God Almighty's *Facts*, such as given us, are the one pabulum which will yield them any nourishment in this world. O Heavens, had they always well remembered that, what a world were it now!

This seems strange doctrine: but it is to me, this long while, too sorrowfully certain; and I invite all my artist friends, of the painting, sculpturing, speaking, writing, especially of the singing and rhyming department, to meditate upon it, till, with amazement, remorse, and determination to amend, they get to see what lies in it! Homer's Iliad, if you examine, is no Fiction but a Ballad *History*; the heart of it burning with enthusiastic ill-informed *belief*. It 'sings' itself, because its rude heart, rapt into transcendency of zeal and admiration, is too full for speaking. The 'valour of Tydides,' 'wrath of the divine Achilles': in old Greece, in Phthiotis and Ætolia, to earnest souls that could *believe* them, these things were likely to be interesting! Human speech was once wholly true; as transcendent human speech still is. The Hebrew Bible, is it not, before all things, *true*, as no other Book ever was or will be? All great Poems, all great Books, if you search the first foundation of their greatness, have been veridical, the truest they could get to be. Never will there be a great Poem more that is not veridical, that does not ground itself on the Interpreting of Fact; to the rigorous exclusion of all falsity, fiction, idle dross of every kind: never can a Poem truly interest human souls, except by, in the first place, taking with it the *belief* of said souls. Their belief; that is the whole basis, essence, and practical outcome, of human souls: leave that behind you, as 'Poets' everywhere have for a long time done, what is there left the Poets and you!

The early Nations of the world, all Nations so long as they continued simple and in earnest, knew without teaching that their History was an Epic and Bible, the clouded struggling Image of a God's Presence, the action of heroes and god-inspired men. The noble intellect that could disenthral such divine image, and present it to them clear, unclouded, in visible coherency comprehensible to human thought, was felt to be a *Vates* and the chief of intellects. No need to bid him sing it, make a Poem of it. Nature herself compelled him; except in Song or in Psalm, such an insight by human eyes into the divine was not utterable. These are the Bibles of Nations; to each its Believed History is its Bible. Not in Judea alone, or Hellas and Latium alone; but in all lands and all times. Nor, deeply as the fact is now forgotten, has it essentially in the smallest degree ceased to be the fact, nor will it cease. With every Nation it is so, and with every man;—for every Nation, I suppose, was made by God, and every man too? Only there are some Nations, like some men, who know it; and some who do not.

The great Nations are they that have known it well; the small and contemptible, both of men and Nations, are they that have either never known it, or soon forgotten it and never laid it to heart. Of these comes nothing. The measure of a Nation's greatness, of its worth under this sky to God and to men, is not the quantity of cotton it can spin, the quantity of bullion it has realised; but the quantity of heroisms it has achieved, of noble pieties and valiant wisdoms that were in it,—that still are in it.

Beyond doubt the Almighty Maker made this England too; and has been and forever is miraculously present here. The more is the pity for us if our eyes are grown owlish, and cannot see this fact of facts when it is before us! Once it was known that the Highest did of a surety dwell in this Nation, divinely avenging, and divinely saving and rewarding; leading, by steep and flaming paths, by heroisms, pieties and noble acts and thoughts, this Nation heavenward, if it would and dared. Known or not, this (or else the terrible *inverse* of this) is forevermore the fact! The History of England too, had the Fine or other Arts taught us to read it right, is the record of the Divine Appearances among us; of the brightnesses out of Heaven that have irradiated our terrestrial struggle; and spanned our wild deluges, and weltering seas of trouble, as with celestial rainbows, and symbols of eternal covenants. It is the *Bible* of the Nation: what part of it they have laid to heart, and do practically know for truth, is the available Bible they have.

Ask yourselves, What are the eternal covenants which you can believe, and dare not for your life's sake but go and observe? These are your Bible, *your* God's Word such as it may be: these you will continually struggle to obey; other than these, not continually, or authentically at all. Did the Maker of this Universe reveal himself, to your believing Intellect, in scrip mainly, in Cotton Trades, and profitable industries and gamblings? Here too you will see 'miracles': tubular bridges, gutta-percha telegraphs; not to speak of sudden Hudson cornucopias, scrip manna-showers, and pillar-of-cloud for all the flunkies,—miracles after a sort. Your Bible will be a Political Economy; your psalmist and evangelist will be M'Croudy; your practical worship the insatiable desire, and continual sacred effort, to make money. Bible, of one or the other sort, bible, evangelist, and worship you infallibly will have:—and some are God-worships, fruitful in human heroisms, in blessed arts, and deeds long-memorable, shining with a sacred splendour of the empyrean across all earthly darknesses and contradictions: and some again are, to a terrible extent, Devil-worships, fruitful in temporary bullion, in upholstery, gluttony and universal varnish and gold-leaf; and issuing, alas, at length in street-barricades, and a confused *return* of them to the Devil whose they are!—My friend, I have to speak in crude language, the wretched times being dumb and deaf: and if thou find no truth under this but the phantom of an extinct Hebrew one, I at present cannot help it.

Hengst Invasions, Norman Conquests, Battles of Brunanburg, Battles of Evesham, Towton; Plantagenets, Wars of Roses, Wars of Roundheads: does the fool in his heart believe that all this was a Donnybrook Bedlam, originating nowhere, proceeding nowhither? His beautifully cultivated intellect has given him such interpretation, and no better, of the Universe we live in? He discerns it to be an enormous sooty Weaving-shop, and turbid Manufactory of eatables and drinkables and wearables; sparingly supplied with provender by the industrious individuals, and much infested by the mad and idle. And he can consent to live here; he does not continually think of suicide as a remedy? The unhappy mortal: if a soul ever awaken in him again, his first thought will be of prussic-acid, I should say!—

All History, whether M'Croudy and his Fine Arts know the fact or not, is an inarticulate Bible; and in a dim intricate manner reveals the Divine Appearances in this lower world. For God did make this world, and does forever govern it; the loud-roaring Loom of Time, with all its French revolutions, Jewish revelations, 'weaves the vesture thou seest Him by.' There is no Biography of a man, much less any History, or Biography of a Nation, but wraps in it a message out of Heaven, addressed to the hearing ear or to the not-hearing. What this Universe is, what the Laws of God are, the Life of every man will a little teach it you; the Life of All Men and of All Things, only this could wholly teach it you,—and you are to be open to learn.

Who are they, gifted from above, that will convert voluminous Dryasdust into an Epic and even a Bible? Who will smelt, in the all-victorious fire of his soul, these scandalous bewildering rubbish-mountains of sleepy Dryasdust, till they give-up the golden ingot that lies imprisoned in them? The veritable 'revelation,' this, of the ways of God to England; how the Almighty Power, and his mysterious Providences, dealt heretofore with England; more and more what the Almighty's judgments with us, his chastisements and his beneficences, were; what the Supreme Will, since ushering this English People on the stage of things, has guided them to do and to become. Fine Arts, Literatures, Poetries? If they are Human Arts at all, where have they been wool-gathering, these centuries long;—wandering literally like creatures fallen mad!

It awakens graver thoughts than were in Marlborough, that saying of his, That he knew no English History but what he had learned from Shakspeare. In Shakspeare's grand intelligence the History of England, cursory as was his study of it, does model itself, for the first time, into something of rhythmic and poetic; there are scattered traits and tones of a National Epos in those Historical Plays of his. In Shakspeare, more than in another, lay that high *vates* talent of interpreting confused human Actualities, and unfolding what divine melodious Ideals, or Thoughts of the Supreme, were embodied in them: he, more than any other, might have done somewhat towards making History a Bible. But, alas, it was not in the Temple of the Nations, with all intelligences ministering to him and coöperating with him, that his workshop was laid; it was in the Bankside Playhouse that Shakspeare was set to work, and the sovereign populace had ware for their sixpence from him there!—

After all, I do not blame the poor Fine Arts for taking into fiction, and into all the deeper kinds of falsity which grow from that. Ignatius, and a world too ready to follow him, had discovered the divine virtues of *fiction* in far higher provinces; the road to fiction lay wide-open for all things! But Nature's eternal voice, inaudible at present or faintly audible, proclaims the contrary nevertheless; and will make it known again one day. Fiction, I think, or idle falsity of any kind, was never tolerable, except in a world which did itself abound in practical lies and solemn shams; and which had gradually impressed on its inhabitants the inane form of character tolerant of that kind of ware. A serious soul, can it wish, even in hours of relaxation, that you should fiddle empty nonsense to it? A serious soul would desire to be entertained, either with absolute silence, or with what was truth, and had fruit in it, and was made by the Maker of us all. With the idle soul I can fancy it far otherwise; but only with the idle.

Given an idle potentate, monster of opulence, gluttonous bloated Nawaub, of black colour or of white,—naturally he will have prating story-tellers to amuse his half-sleepy hours of rumination; if from his deep gross stomach, sinking overloaded as if towards its last torpor, they can elicit any transient glow of interest, tragic or comic, especially any wrinkle of momentary laughter, however idle, great shall be their reward. Wits, story-tellers, ballad-singers, especially dancing-girls who understand their trade, are in much request with such gluttonous half-sleeping, black or white Monster of Opulence. A bevy of supple dancing-girls who with the due mixture (mixture settled by custom), and with not more than the due mixture, of lascivious fire, will represent to him, brandishing their daggers, and rhythmically chanting and posturing, the Loves of Vishnu, Loves of Adonis, Death of Psyche, Barber of Seville, or whatever nonsense there may be, according to time or country: these are the kind of artists fit for such unfortunate stuffed stupefied Nawaub, in his hours of rumination; upon these his hot heavy-laden eye may rest without abhorrence; if with perceptible momentary satisfaction emerging from his bottomless ennui,—then victory and gold-purses to the artist; be such artist crowned with laurel or with parsley, and declared divine in presence of all men.

Luxurious Europe, in its reading publics, dilettanti, cognoscenti and other publics, is wholly one big ugly Nawaub of that kind; who has converted all the Fine Arts into after-dinner amusements; slave adjuncts to his cookeries, upholsteries, tailories, and other palpably Coarse Arts. The brutish monster has turned all the Nine Muses, who by birth are sacred Priestesses of Heaven, into scandalous Bayadères; and they dance with supple motions, to enlighten the vile darkness of his ennui for him. Too truly *mad*, these poor Fine Arts! The Coarse Arts too, if he had not an authentic stomach and skin, which always bring him a little right again in those departments, would go mad.

How all things hang together! Universal Jesuitism having once lodged itself in the heart, you will see it in the very finger-nails by and by. Calculate how far it is from Sophocles and Æschylus to Knowles and Scribe; how Homer has gradually changed into Sir Harris Nicolas; or what roads the human species must have travelled before a *Psalm of David* could become an *Opera at the Haymarket*, and men, with their divine gift of Music, instead of solemnly celebrating the highest fact, or 'singing to the praise of God,' consented to celebrate the lowest nonsense, and sing to the praise of Jenny Lind and the Gazza Ladra,—perhaps the step from Oliver

Cromwell to Lord John Russell will not seem so unconscionable! I find it within, and not without, the order of Nature; and that all things, like all men, are blood-relations to one another.

This accursed nightmare, which we name Jesuitism, will have to vanish; our comfort is, that life itself is not much longer possible otherwise. But I say, have you computed what a distance forwards it may be towards some *new* Psalm of David done with our new appliances, and much improved wind-instruments, grammatical and other? That is the distance of the new Golden Age, my friend; not less than that, I lament to say! And the centuries that intervene are a foul agonistic welter through the Stygian seas of mud: a long *Scavenger Age*, inevitable where the Mother of Abominations has long dwelt.

It is to be hoped one is not blind withal to the celebrated virtues that are in Jesuitism; to its missionary zeal, its contempt of danger, its scientific, heroic and other prowesses, of which there is such celebrating. I do not doubt that there are virtues in it; that we and it, along with this immeasurable sea of miseries which it has brought upon us, shall ultimately get the benefit of its virtues too. Peruvian bark, of use in human agues; tidings from the fabulous East by D'Herbelot, Du Halde, and others; examples of what human energy and faculty are equal to, even under the inspiration of Ignatius: nothing of this small residue of pearls from such a continent of putrid shellfish, shall be lost to the world. Nay, I see, across this black deluge of Consecrated Falsity, the world ripening towards glorious new developments, unimagined hitherto,—of which this abominable mud deluge itself, threatening to submerge us all, was the inevitable precursor, and the means decreed by the Eternal. If it please Heaven, we shall all yet make our *Exodus* from Houndsditch, and bid the sordid continents, of once rich apparel now grown poisonous *Ou'-clo'*, a mild farewell! Exodus into wider horizons, into God's daylight once more; where eternal skies, measuring *more* than three ells, shall again overarch us; and men, immeasurably richer for having dwelt among the Hebrews, shall pursue their *human* pilgrimage, St. Ignatius and much other saintship, and superstitious terror and lumber, lying safe behind us, like the nightmares of a sleep that is past!—

I said the virtue of obedience was not to be found except among the Jesuits: how, in fact, among the *Anti*-Jesuits, still in a revolutionary posture in this world, can you expect it? Sansculottism is a rebel; has its birth, and being, in open mutiny; and cannot give you examples of obedience. It is so with several other virtues and cardinal virtues; they seem to have vanished from the world;—and I often say to myself, Jesuitism and other Superstitious Scandals cannot go, till we have read and appropriated from them the tradition of these lost noblenesses, and once more under the new conditions made them ours. Jesuitism, the Papa with his three hats, and whole continents of chimerical lumber will then go; their errand being wholly done. We cannot make our Exodus from Houndsditch till we have got our own along with us! The Jew old-clothes having now grown fairly pestilential, a poisonous incumbrance in the path of men, burn them up with revolutionary fire, as you like and can: even so,—but you shall not quit the place till you have gathered from their ashes what of gold or other enduring metal was sewed upon them, or woven in the tissue of them. That is the appointed course of human things.

Here are two excerpts from the celebrated Gathercoal, a Yankee friend of mine; which flash strangely a kind of torch-gleam into the hidden depths; and indicate to us the grave and womb of Jesuitism, and of several other things:

'Moses and the Jews did not *make* God's Laws,' exclaims he; 'no, by no means; they did not even read them in a way that has been final, or is satisfactory to me! In several important respects I find said reading decidedly bad; and will not, in any wise, think of adopting it. How dare I, think you?—And yet, alas, if we forget to read these Laws at all; if we go along as if they were not there!

'My enlightened friends of this present supreme age, what shall I say to you? That Time does rest on Eternity; that he who has no vision of Eternity will never get a true hold of Time, or its affairs. Time is so constructed; that is the *fact* of the construction of this world. And no class of mortals who have not,—through Nazareth or otherwise,—come to get heartily acquainted with such fact, perpetually familiar with it in all the outs and ins of their existence, have ever found this Universe habitable long. Alas, no; their fraternities, equalities, free-trade philosophies, greatest-happiness principles, soon came to a conclusion; and the poor creatures had to go,—to the Devil, I fear! Generations such as ours play a curious part in World-History.

'They sit as Apes do round a fire in the woods, but know not how to feed it with fresh sticks. They have to quit it soon, and march—into Chaos, as I conjecture; into that land of which Bedlam is the Mount Zion. The world turns out *not* to be made of mere eatables and drinkables, of newspaper puffs, gilt carriages, conspicuous flunkies; no, but of something other than these! Old Suetonius Romans, corrupt babbling Greeks of the Lower Empire, examples more than one: consider them; be taught by them, add not to the number of them. Heroism, not the apery and traditions of Heroism; the feeling, spoken or silent, that in man's life there did lie a Godlike, and that his Time-history was verily but an emblem of some Eternal: without this there had been no Rome either; it was this that had made old Rome, old Greece, and old Judea. Apes, with their wretched blinking eyes, squatted round a fire which they cannot feed with new wood; which they say will last forever without new wood,—or, alas, which they say is going out forever: it is a sad sight!'

Elsewhere my eccentric friend, as some call him,—whose *centre*, however, I think I have got into,—has this passage:

'Church, do you say? Look eighteen hundred years ago, in the stable at Bethlehem: an infant laid in a manger! Look, thou ass, and behold it; it is a fact,—the most indubitable of facts: thou wilt thereby learn innumerable things. Jesus of Nazareth and the life he led, and the death he died, does it teach thee nothing? Through this, as through a miraculous window, the heaven of Martyr Heroism, the "divine depths of Sorrow," of noble Labour, and the unspeakable silent expanses of Eternity, first in man's history disclose themselves. The admiration of all nobleness, divine *worship* of godlike nobleness, how universal it is in the history of man!

'But mankind, that singular entity mankind, is like the fertilest, fluidest, most wondrous element, an element in which the strangest things crystallise themselves, and spread out in the most astounding growths. The event at Bethlehem was of the Year One; but all years since that, eighteen hundred of them now, have been contributing new growth to it,—and see, there it stands: the Church! Touching the earth with one small point; springing out of one small seedgrain, rising out therefrom, ever higher, ever broader, high as the Heaven itself, broad till it overshadow the whole visible Heaven and Earth, and no star can be seen but through *it*. From such a seedgrain so has it grown; planted in the reverences and sacred opulences of the soul of mankind; fed continually by all the noblenesses of some forty generations of men. The world-tree of the Nations for so long!

'Alas, if its roots are now dead, and it have lost hold of the firm earth, or clear belief of mankind,—what, great as it is, can by possibility become of it? Shaken to and fro, in Jesuitisms, Gorham Controversies, and the storms of inevitable Fate, it must sway hither and thither; nod ever farther from the perpendicular; nod at last too far; and,—sweeping the Eternal Heavens clear of its old brown foliage and multitudinous rooks'-nests,—come to the ground with much confused crashing, and *disclose* the diurnal and nocturnal Upper Lights again! The dead world-tree will have declared itself dead. It will lie there an imbroglio of torn boughs and ruined fragments, of bewildered splittings and wide-spread shivers: out of which the poor inhabitants must make what they can!'—Enough now of Gathercoal and his torch-gleams.

Simple souls still clamour occasionally for what they call 'a new religion.' My friends, you will not get this new religion of yours;—I perceive, you already have it, have always had it! All that is *true* is your 'religion,'—is it not? Commanded by the Eternal God to be *performed*, I should think, if it is true! Do you not already, in your dim heads, know truths by the thousand; and yet, in your dead hearts, will you perform them by the ten, by the unit? New religion! One last word with you on this rather contemptible subject.

You say, The old ages had a noble belief about the world, and *therefore* were capable of a noble activity in the world. My friends, it is partly true: your Scepticism and Jesuitism, your ignoble no-belief, except what belief a beaver or judicious pig were capable of, is too undeniable: observe, however, that in this your fatal misery, there is action and reaction; and do not confound the one with the other. Put the thing in its right posture; cart not *before* horse, if you would make an effort to stir from this fatal spot! It is your own falsity that makes the Universe incredible. I affirm to you, this Universe, in all times, and in your own poor time as well, is the express image and direct counterpart of the human souls, and their thoughts and activities, who dwell there. It is a true adage, 'As the fool thinks, the bell clinks.' 'This mad Universe,' says Novalis, 'is the waste picture of your own dream.' Be noble of mind, all Nature gives response to your heroic struggle for recognition by her; with her awful eternal voices answers to every mind, "Yea, I am divine; be thou." From the cloud-whirlwind speaks a God yet, my friend, to every man who has a human soul. To the inhuman brute-soul, indeed, she answers, "Yea, I am brutal; a big cattle-stall, rag-fair and St. Catherine's wharf: enter thou, and fat victual, if thou be faithful, shall not fail."

Not because Heaven existed, did men know Good from Evil; the 'because,' I invite you to consider, lay quite the other way. It was *because* men, having hearts as well as stomachs, felt there, and knew through all their being, the difference between Good and Evil, that Heaven and Hell first came to exist. That is the sequence; that and not the contrary. If you have now no Heaven to look to; if you now sprawl, lamed and lost, sunk to the chin in the pathless sloughs of this lower world without guidance from above, know that the fault is not Heaven's at all; but your own! Our poor friends 'the Apes by the Dead Sea' have now no Heaven either; they look into this Universe now, and find it tragically grown to *be* the Humbug they insisted on its being. Moses went his ways, and this enchantment fell upon them! Such 'enchantments' rhadamanthine Nature does yet daily execute on the rebellious; he that has eyes may still daily see them,—fearful and wonderful ever as of old.

How can you believe in a Heaven,—the like of you? What struggle in your mean existence ever pointed thitherward? None. The first heroic soul sent down into this world, he, looking up into the sea of stars, around into the moaning forests and big oceans, into life and death, love and hate, and joy and sorrow, and the illimitable loud-thundering Loom of Time,—was struck dumb by it (as the thought of every earnest soul still is); and fell on his face, and with his heart cried for salvation in the world-whirlpool: to him the 'open secret of this Universe' was no longer quite a secret, but he had caught a glimpse of it,—much hidden from the like of us in these times: "Do nobly, thou shalt resemble the Maker of all this; do ignobly, the Enemy of the Maker."

This is the 'divine sense of Right and Wrong in man'; true reading of his position in this Universe forevermore; the indisputable God's-message still legible in every created heart,—though speedily erased and painted over, under 'articles,' and cants and empty ceremonials, in so many hearts; making the 'open secret' a very shut one indeed!—

My friends, across these fogs of murky twaddle and philanthropism, in spite of sad decadent 'world-trees,' with their rookeries of foul creatures,—the silent stars, and all the eternal luminaries of the world, shine even now to him that has an eye. In this day as in all days, around and in every man, are voices from the gods, imperative to all, if obeyed by even none, which say audibly, "Arise, thou son of Adam, son of Time; make this thing more divine; and that thing,—and thyself, of all things; and work, and sleep not; for the Night cometh, wherein no man can work!" He that has an ear may still hear.

Surely, surely this ignoble sluggishness, sceptical torpor, indifference to all that does not bear on Mammon and his interests is not the natural state of human creatures; and is not doomed to be their final one! Other states once were, or there had never been a Society, or any noble thing, among us at all. Under this brutal stagnancy there lies painfully imprisoned some tendency which could become heroic.

The restless gnawing ennui which, like a dark dim ocean-flood, communicating with the Phlegethons and Stygian deeps, begirdles every human life so guided,—is it not the painful cry even of that imprisoned heroism? Imprisoned it will never rest; set forth at present, on these sad terms, it cannot be. You unfortunates, what is the use of your money-bags, of your territories, funded properties, your mountains of possessions, equipments and mechanic inventions, which the flunky pauses over, awestruck, and almost rises into epos and prophecy at sight of? No use, or less than none. Your skin is covered, and your digestive and other bodily apparatus is supplied; and you have but to wish in these respects, and more is ready; and—the Devils, I think, are quizzing you. You ask for 'happiness,' "O give me happiness!"—and they hand you ever new varieties of covering for the skin, ever new kinds of supply for the digestive apparatus, new and ever new, worse or not a whit better than the old; and—and—this is your 'happiness'? As if you were sick children; as if you were not men, but a kind of apes!

I rather say, be thankful for your ennui; it is your last mark of manhood; this at least is a perpetual admonition, and true sermon preached to you. From the chair of verity this, whatever chairs be chairs of *cant*ity. Happiness is *not* come, nor like to come; ennui, with its great waste ocean-voice, moans answer, Never, never. That ocean-voice, I tell you, is a great fact, it comes from Phlegethon and the gates of the Abyss; its bodeful never-resting inexorable moan is the voice of primeval Fate, and of the eternal necessity of things. Will you shake away your nightmare and arise; or must you lie writhing under it, till death relieve you? Unfortunate creatures! You are fed, clothed, lodged as men never were before; every day in new variety of magnificence are you equipped and attended to; such wealth of material means as is now yours was never dreamed of by man before:—and to do any noble thing, with all this mountain of implements, is forever denied you. Only ignoble, expensive and unfruitful things can you now do; nobleness has vanished from the sphere where you live. The way of it is lost, lost; the possibility of it has become incredible. We must try to do without it, I am told.—Well; rejoice in your upholsteries and cookeries, then, if so be they will make you 'happy.' Let the varieties of them be continual and innumerable. In all things let perpetual change, if that is a perpetual blessing to you, be your portion instead of mine; incur that Prophet's curse, and in all things in this sublunary world 'make yourselves like unto a wheel.' Mount into your railways; whirl from place to place, at the rate of fifty, or if you like of five hundred miles an hour: you cannot escape from that inexorable all-encircling ocean-moan of ennui. No: if you would mount to the stars, and do yacht-voyages under the belts of Jupiter, or stalk deer on the ring of Saturn, it would still begirdle you. You cannot escape from it, you can but change your place in it, without solacement except one moment's. That prophetic Sermon from the Deeps will continue with you, till you wisely interpret it and do it, or else till the Crack of Doom swallow it and you. *Adieu: Au revoir.*

SUMMARY

No. I. THE PRESENT TIME

THE Present ever a 'New Era' to the thinking man: To know *it,* and what it bids us do, the sum of knowledge for us all. Judicial blindness. Our own days: If not days of endless hope too, then are they days of utter despair (p. 1).—A Reforming Pope, and the huge *un*reformable Popedom. The Sicilians first to follow the poor Pope's example. French exasperation and emulation. European explosion, boundless, uncontrollable: All Kings conscious they are but Playactors. A weltering mob, presided over by M. de Lamartine. A changed time since the word *Senior* was first devised to signify Superior (2).—Universal *Democracy,* an inevitable fact of the days we live in: Whence comes it? whither goes it? What is the meaning of it?—High shouts of exultation from the universal foolish human throat; drowning for the moment all reflection whatsoever. Bankruptcy of Imposture: At all costs, it is to be prayed by all men that Shams may *cease.* Heavyside, and his quiet blasphemy. Democracy not a Government; nor Parliament a practical substitute for a King. Unanimity of 'voting' will do nothing for us, if the voting happen to be *wrong.* A divine message, or eternal regulation of the Universe, there verily is, in regard to every conceivable procedure of man. Universal Suffrage, and the Ballot-box (8).—The ancient Republics, now pretty well admitted to be nothing to our purpose. One modern instance of Democracy, 'nearly perfect': The Republic of the United States. America too will have to strain her energies, in quite other fashion than this: America's Battle is yet to fight. Mere Democracy forever impossible: The Universe itself a Monarchy and Hierarchy. God Almighty's Noble in the supreme place,—under penalties. Everlasting privilege of the Foolish, to be governed and guided by the Wise: Intrinsically, the harshest duty a wise man, if he be indeed wise, has laid to his hand (18).—The new Sacrament of *Divorce,* called 'enfranchisement,' 'emancipation.' West-Indian Blacks and Irish Whites: Horses and *half*-brothers: The fate of all emancipated Helplessness, sooner or later, tragically inevitable. British industrial existence fast becoming one huge poison-swamp of reeking pestilence: Thirty-thousand outcast, ungoverned, unguided Needlewomen. Constituted Anarchy: 'British Liberty,' and what is it doing for us (24).—England

and her Constitution, the model of the world: At once unattainable by the world, and not worth attaining. Called a 'second time' to show the Nations how to live. England's one hope: Many *Kings*, not needing 'election' to command: Poor England never so needed them as now. The true 'commander' and King: Not quite discoverable by riddling of the popular clamour. The fateful Hebrew Prophecy, sounding daily through our streets. In regard to choice of men, next to no capability on the part of universal suffrage. The few Wise will have, by one method or another, to take, and to keep, command of the innumerable Foolish (30).—Captains of Industry: Organisation of Labour, the new strange task which no Government can much longer escape. Speech of the British Prime Minister to his Pauper Populations and the Respectable Professors of the Dismal Science. Alas, there are things that should be *done*, not spoken; that till the doing of them is begun, *cannot* be spoken (35).

No. II. MODEL PRISONS

The deranged condition of our affairs: Two ways of proceeding in regard to them: Selfish indifference, and self-lauding philanthropy. Indiscriminate mashing-up of Right and Wrong, ending in a Fraternity like Cain's (p. 48).—A London Prison of the exemplary or model kind. Certain Chartist notabilities undergoing their term. The Captain of the place, a true *aristos* and commander of men. His problem, to drill twelve-hundred scoundrels to do nothing, by 'the method of kindness.' Happy Devil's regiments of the line, what soldier to any earthly or celestial Power has such lodging and attendance as you here! Certainly it should not be the Devil's regiments of the line that a servant of God would first of all concentrate his attention on. Precisely the *worst* investment for Benevolence that human ingenuity could select. The highest and *best* investment: Solemn Shams and Supreme Quacks, riding prosperously in every thoroughfare (52).—Howard the Philanthropist, a sort of beatified individual: A dull practical solid man, full of English accuracy and veracity. Not the only benefactor that has worked without money for us: The Destinies opulent. Milton, Kepler, Dante. Cholera Doctors; Soldiers: Human virtue, if we went down to the roots of it, not so rare. Woe to us, it is so seldom elaborated, and built into a result! The Benevolent-Platform Fever, and general morbid sympathy, instead of hearty hatred, for scoundrels. Brotherhood? Be the thought far from me. Beautiful Black Peasantry, fallen idle: Interesting White Felonry, *not* idle. What a reflection, that we cannot bestow on an unworthy man any particle of our 'benevolence,' without withdrawing it from one to whom it of right belongs!

One thing needful for the world; but that one indispensable: Give us Justice, and we live; give us only counterfeits or succedanea, and we die. Modern ghastly Phantasm of Christianity, which they sing litanies to at Exeter Hall and elsewhere. Poor old Genius of Reform, and his Program of a new Era (62).—Christian Religion, and its healthy hatred of Scoundrels: From the Christianity of Oliver Cromwell to that of Mr. Hesperus Fiddlestring, what a road have we travelled! Gospel according to the Platform; *Exeat* Fiddlestring. Poor creatures, making and unmaking 'Laws,' in whose souls is no image or thought of Heaven's Law: Human Statute-books, growing horrible to think of (70).—What to do with our criminals?—An official Law-dignitary's bland perplexity, and placid discomfiture. Wonderful to hear what account we give of the punishment of our criminals: No 'revenge'; O Heavens, no!—Cant moral, Cant religious, Cant political. Hunger-stricken asphyxied hearts, calling themselves 'Christian.' Woe to the People that no longer venerate, as the emblem of God himself, the aspect of Human Worth! The true ground on which to deliberately slay a disarmed fellow-man: 'Revenge,' and the ineradicable tendency to *revancher* oneself on the wrong-doer, to *pay* him what he has merited. How it shall be done? a vast question, involving immense considerations. Terrible penalties of neglecting to treat hero as hero, and scoundrel as scoundrel: Dim oblivion of Right and Wrong: World-wide maddening Misery: New astonishing Phallus-Worship, and universal Sacrament of Divorce (72). —The Ancient Germans, and their grim public executions. Scoundrel is scoundrel; and no soft blubbering and litanying over him can make him a friend of this Universe. A 'didactic sermon,' as no spoken sermon could be. Except upon a basis of just rigour, sorrowful, silent, inexorable, no true Pity possible (82).—A *worst* man in England,—curious to think of,—whom it would be inexpressibly advantageous to lay hold of, and hang, first of all: Alas, our supreme scoundrel, alike with our supreme hero, very far from being known. Parliament, in its lawmakings, must really try to obtain some vision again. Let us to the wellheads, to the Chief Fountains of these waters of bitterness; and there strike home and dig! (83).

No. III. DOWNING STREET

Ineffectuality of our Redtape Establishments. The Colonial Office, a world-wide jungle, inhabited by doleful creatures, deaf or nearly so to human reason and entreaty. Foreign Office and Home Office perhaps even more impracticable: Hercules-Harlequin, the Attorney Triumphant, the World's Busybody,—these not the parts this Nation has a turn for. Proposed curtailments, rectifications and reformations (p. 87).—England's forlorn hope in Sir Robert Peel: The one likely or possible man. A Reformed Executive in Downing Street: Not a better Talking-Apparatus, but an infinitely better Acting-Apparatus the thing wanted. The Irish Giant advancing unheeded upon London itself (91).—Two kinds of fundamental error in our Government Offices: The work *ill-done*; and, what is still fataler, the *wrong kind* of work. For such elaborated Idleness a stupid subaltern better than a gifted one. O for an eye that could see in those hideous mazes, and a heart that could dare and do! (94).—What the British Nation at this time really wants. If our Government is to be a No-Government, what matter *who* administers it? The *real* Nimrod of this era the rat-catcher. The mighty question, Who is to be our Premier, and take in hand the 'spigot of taxation'? Right Honourable Zero, on his Sleswick thunder-horse. Who made those Downing Street Offices? No edifice of State that stands long, but has had the wise and brave contributing their lives to it. William Conqueror's Home Office. An English Seventy-four, and the old Seakings and Saxon Pirates (98).—'Human Stupidity' the accursed parent of all our sorrows. Practical reverence for Human Worth the outcome and essence of all true 'religions' whatsoever. Human Intellect, the exact summary of Human *Worth*. Abler Men in Downing Street; that, sure enough, would gradually remedy whatsoever has gone wrong amongst us. The divinest, most Herculean Ten Men to be found among the English Twenty-seven Millions. Courage; let us strive all thitherward as towards a door of hope! One Intellect still really human, not to be dispensed with anywhere in the affairs of men: Only Wisdom, that can recognise wisdom, and attract it, as with divine magnetism, from the modest corners where it lies hid (105).—To increase the supply of human Intellect in Downing Street, what 'method' alas! One small Project of Improvement: Government Servants to be selected *without* reference to their power of getting into Parliament: The Crown to have power to elect a few members. Beneficent germs, which one truly wise man as Chief Minister might ripen into living practices, invaluable to us all. A population counting by Millions from which to choose, were a seat in Parliament not primary: Robert Burns. All true 'Democracy' in this, that the able man be chosen, in whatever rank he be found: A truer and truer 'Aristocracy,' or Government of the *Best* (112).—One true Reforming Statesman; he the preliminary of all good. A strange feeling, to be at the apex of English affairs. This world, solid as it looks, made all of aerial and even of spiritual stuff. This and the other Premier seems to take it with perfect coolness: Reflections, sufficient to annihilate any man, almost before starting! Ask well, who is your Chief Governor, for around him men like to him will infallibly gather. Time was when an incompetent Governor could not be permitted among men (121).

No. IV. THE NEW DOWNING STREET

How the European Governments came to wreck for want of Intellect. No evil, or solecism against Nature, ever yet wrought its own cure. Intellect *has* to govern, and will do it; if not in alliance, then in hostility: Every Government absolves or convicts itself, before God and man, according as it determines which (p. 126).—The old Catholic Church, in its terrestrial relations to the State: Everywhere a road upwards for human nobleness lay wide open to all men. Over Europe generally the State has died; incapable in these years of any but *galvanic* life. The kind of heroes that come mounted on the shoulders of universal suffrage. England called as no Nation ever was, to summon out its *Kings*, and set them to their work: A New Downing Street, inhabited by the gifted; directing all its energies upon real and living interests (131).—The notion that Government can do nothing but 'keep the peace.' To be governed by small men, profess subjection to phantasms, not only a misfortune, but a curse and sin. Indigent Millionaires, and their owl-dreams of Political Economy. Only the man of worth can recognise worth in men. How a New Downing Street might gradually come (136).—The Foreign Office, in its reformed state: Insignificance of recent European Wars. Our War-soldiers *Industrial*; doing nobler than Roman works, when fighting is not wanted of them. Ministers of Works, of Justice, of Education: Tomorrow morning they might all begin to be! (143).—Constitutions for the Colonies now on the anvil: 'So many as are for rebelling, hold up your hands!' Our brave fathers, by valiant blood and sweat, gained for us rich possessions in all zones; and we, wretched imbeciles, cannot do the function of administering them. Miserabler theory than that of money on the ledger for the primary rule of Empires, cannot well be propounded: England will not readily admit that her own children are worth nothing but to be flung out of doors. Canadian Parliaments, and Lumber-log Governors. Choose well your Governor; and having found him, keep him (149).—The Home Office, undoubtedly our grand primary concern. Were all men doing their duty, or even seriously trying to do it, there would be no Pauper: Pauperism, our Social Sin grown manifest. Our Public Life and our Private, our State and our Religion, a tissue of half-truths and whole-lies: Cicero's Roman Augurs and their divine chicken-bowels: Despicable amalgam of true and false. A complete course of *scavengerism*, the thing needed. The State, as it gets into the track of its real work, will find it expand into whole continents of new activity: The want of wants, more indispensable than any jewel in the crown, that of men *able to command men* in the ways of welldoing (156).—Waste-land Industrials succeeding, other kinds of Industry will be found capable of regimenting. He is a good man that can command and obey; he that cannot is a bad. Etons and Oxfords, with their broken crumbs of mere *speech*: Our next set of Souls' Overseers, perhaps *silent* very mainly. Who of living statesmen will begin the long steep journey of Reform? Sir Robert Peel at his 'eleventh hour.' Still fataler omens (166).

No. V. STUMP-ORATOR

Our deep-rooted habit of considering human talent as best of all evincing itself in eloquent speech: Such a test liable to become the very worst ever devised. Hard sayings for many a British reader: The talker established in the place of honour; and the Doer lost and lamed in the obscure crowd. Eloquence, and the part it now plays in our affairs, one of the gravest phenomena (p. 172).—Universities and Schools in the old healthy Ages: The Working Man; Priest; young Noble: The one sure method of learning anything, practical apprenticeship to it. Not that he may speak, but that he may have something to speak of, the first need of a man. Every word, either a note or a forged-note. Do you want a man *not* to practise what he believes, then encourage him to speak it often in words: The serviceable thing,—to *clip-off* a bit of his eloquent tongue. What the art of speech *should* be, and should *not* be (177).—Vital *lungs* of Society: Methods by which men rise; and the kind of men. The country that can offer no career, a doomed country; nay, already dead. Our English careers to born genius twofold: Silent or unlearned career of Industrialisms: Articulate or learned career of the three Professions. To the gifted soul, not of taciturn, *beaver* nature, the field in England narrow and surprising to an extreme: The solitary proof-feat of talk, getting rather monotonous. Medicine, and its frightful medusa-heads of quackery: The profession of Human Healer radically a sacred one. Law and Church: Ingenuous souls just now shudder at the threshold of both these careers. Parliament, and its unquestioned eligibility, if attainable. Crowded portal of Literature: Haven of expatriated spiritualisms, vanities and prurient imbecilities. Talk with tongue or pen; there is in our England of the Nineteenth Century, that one method of emergence and no other (183).—Not even in Parliament should the essential function by any means be talk. Wisdom intrinsically of silent nature. Politeness, and breeding to business: How politeness was *invented*: Johnson, Burns. Parliament, as a school of manners: Seeking salvation in 'appearances.' A parliamentary bagpipe, and your living man fled away without return (194).—Nature admits no *lie*: Most men profess to be aware of this, but few in any manner lay it to heart. Diagnosis of a Lie, and Liar. Fail, by any sin or misfortune, to discover what the truth of a fact is, you are lost so far as that fact goes: Unfortunate British Parliament. Nature's silent exact Savings'-bank, and official register, correct to the most evanescent item: Creditor, by the quantity of veracities we have done; Debtor, by the quantity of falsities and errors. The practice of modern Parliaments, with Reporters sitting among them (201).—A benevolent plan of reform for our benighted world: At least one generation to pass its life in silence. Good Heavens, if such a plan were practicable, how the chaff might be winnowed-out of every man and thing!—Eye-service, our saddest woe of all. 'Public-speaking,' 'parliamentary eloquence,' a Moloch before whom young souls are made to pass through the fire,—to come out spiritually *dead*. Be not a Public Orator, thou brave young British man; not a Stump-Orator, if thou canst help it: To speak, or to write, Nature did not peremptorily order thee; but to work she did (209).

No. VI. PARLIAMENTS

The present Editor not one of those who expect to see the Country saved by farther 'reforming' the reformed Parliament we have got. If the captains of the ship are of that scandalous class who refuse to be warned, what are the miserable crew to do? (p. 214).—The English Parliament, windy and empty as it has grown to be, at one time a quite solid serious actuality: King Rufus and his Barons: The time of the Edwards, when Parliament gradually split itself into Two Houses. The Long Parliament the first that declared itself Sovereign in the Nation. A sad gradual falling-off in modern Parliaments: A solemn Convocation of all the Stump-Orators in the Nation, to come and govern us, not seen in the earth until recently (216).—Two grand modern facts, which have altered from top to bottom the function and position of all Parliaments. An Unfettered Press: Not the discussion of questions, only the ultimate voting of them, requires to go on, or can veritably go on, in St. Stephen's now. Still more important the question, King present there, or no King? Not as a Sovereign Ruler of the Twenty-seven million British souls has the reformed Parliament distinguished itself as yet. Another most unfortunate condition, that your Parliamentary Assembly is *not* much in earnest to do even the best it can. Parliaments, admirable only as Advising Bodies. United States. Only Two Parliaments of any actual Sovereignty: The English Long Parliament, and the French Convention. The horoscope of Parliaments by no means cheering at present: The thing we vitally need, not a more and more perfectly elected Parliament, but some reality of a Ruling Sovereign to preside over Parliament (220).—Poor human beings, whose practical belief is, that if we 'vote' this or that, so this or that will thenceforth *be*. Blundering, impious, pretended 'laws': Is arithmetic a thing more fixed by the Eternal than the laws of justice are? Eternal Law, silently present everywhere and everywhen. 'Voting' a thing of little value at any time: If of ten men, nine are recognisable as fools, how will you ever get a ballot-box to grind-out a wisdom from their 'votes'? (233).—Under whatever Reformed Downing Street England be governed, its Parliament too will continue indispensable: We must set it to its real function; and, at our peril and its, restrict it to that. Necessary to the King or Governor to know what the mass of men think upon public questions: He may thus choose his path with prudence; and reach his aim surely, if more slowly. The Leming-rat, and its rigidly straight course nowhither. The mass of men consulted at the hustings upon any high matter, as ugly an exhibition of human stupidity as this world sees. The vulgarest vulgar, not those in ragged coats at this day; the more the pity. Of what use towards the finding-out what it is wise to do can the 'fool's vote' be? You have to apprise the unwise man of his road, even as you do the unwiser horse. Memorable minorities, and even small ones: Cromwell and his Puritans: Tancred of Hauteville's sons Unit of that class, against as many zeros as you like (238).—What is to become of Parliament, less a question than what is to become of Downing Street. Who is *slave*, and eternally appointed to be governed; who *free*, and eternally appointed to govern. Could we entirely exclude the slave's vote, and admit only the heroic free man's vote, the ultimate New Era, and best possible condition of human affairs, had actually come. New definitions of slavery, and of freedom. To the Free Man belongs eternally the government of the world (247).

No. VII. HUDSON'S STATUE

The question 'Shall Cromwell have a Statue?' A People worthy to build Statues to Cromwell; or worthy only of doing it to Hudson. Show the man you honour; and you show what your Ideal of Manhood is, what kind of man you long inexpressibly to be. Pity Hudson's Statue was not completed and set up, so that all the world might see it: The practical English mind has its own notions of the Supreme Excellence; and in this of Hudson there was more of real worship than is usual (p. 254).—If the world were not properly *anarchic*, this question of a Statue would be one of the greatest and most solemn for it: Not lightly will a man give his 'reverence,' if he be still a man. A Hierarchy of Beneficences; the noblest man at the summit of affairs, and in every place the due gradation of the fittest for the place: All hangs upon giving our approval *aright*. How Statues are now got up (258).—Dismal, symbolic population of British Statues: The kind of Aristocracy Popular Suffrage would choose for us. Hudson a King, 'elected by the people,' as none other is or was: His *value* as a demigod; as a maker of railways. Answer to Jefferson Brick, the American Editor, touching overgrown worthless Dukes, and undergrown incredible Bishops: Our ugliest anomalies, done by universal suffrage, not by patent: Bobus of Houndsditch. This universal ousting of imaginary Governors, to issue in the attainment of Governors who have a right and a capacity to govern. Ballot-box and suffrage 'machine.' Alas, could we once get Laws which were *just*: The Bravest of existing Men on the throne; and on the gibbet the veritable Supreme Scoundrel of the Commonwealth. Universal suffrage, equivalent to abject helplessness and flat despair. Peace? Better war to the knife, war till we all die, than such a 'peace'! (263).—Hero-worship: This Universe wholly, this temporary Flame-image of the Eternal, one beautiful and terrible Energy of Heroisms; presided over by a Divine Nobleness, or Infinite Hero. Hypocritical Idolatries: Sets of gods or fetishes, to which prayers are mumbled; while the real *worship*, or heart's love and admiration, is elsewhere. Whom do you in your very soul admire, and strive to imitate and emulate; is it God's servant, or the Devil's? There is no other 'religion' in the man, of the slightest moment compared with this: Immense asthmatic spiritual Hurdygurdy. It was *not* 'always so,' and even till lately was never so (276).—Collins's dull old Peerage-Book, properly all we English have for a National Bible: Of these ancient peerages, a very great majority visibly *had* authentic 'heroes' for their founders. One's heart is sore to think how far, how very far all this has vanished from us. Our one steady regulated supply, the class definable as Supreme Stump-Orators in the Lawyer department. England once a Hierarchy: To the English modern populations, Supreme Hero and Supreme Scoundrel, perhaps as nearly as is possible to human creatures, indistinguishable (281).—High columns, raised by prurient stupidity and public delusion to gamblers and blockheads. The so-called Christian *Clerus*: Brave men many of them, after their sort; and in a position which we may admit to be wonderful and dreadful. But as to Statues, and the mischief *they* are doing, the Woods-and-Forests really ought to interfere (286).

No. VIII. JESUITISM

For some two centuries past, the genius of mankind dominated by the gospel of Ignatius. What the English reader may think of it, and of his share in it. The Spiritual, the parent and first-cause of the Practical. Thrice-baleful Universe of Cant, prophesied for these Latter Days: The Universe makes no immediate objection to be conceived in *any* way. The saddest condition of human affairs, where men 'decree injustice by a law' (p. 293).—A poor man, in our days, has many gods foisted on him: If Ignatius, worshipped by millions as a kind of god, is in eternal fact a kind of devil, surely it is pressingly expedient that men laid it awfully to heart. Ignatius Loyola, a man born greedy; full of prurient elements from the first. On the walls of Pampeluna: A wrecked Papin's-digester. Reflections, true, salutary, and even somewhat of sacred: Agonies of newbirth. The true remedy for wrecked sensualism,—to annihilate one's pruriency. Let Eternal Justice triumph *on* me, since it cannot triumph *by* me: The voice of Nature to a repentant outcast sinner turning again towards the realms of manhood; and the precept of all right Christianity too. Not so did Ignatius read the omens: The Task he fixed upon as his. Wilt thou then, at the bidding of any Pope, war against Almighty God? Frantic mortal, thy late Pighood itself is trivial in comparison! (299).—Precious message of salvation: Salutary nature of falsehoods, and divine authority of things doubtful. Not 'victory' for Ignatius and his black militia. Luther and Protestantism Proper: Jean Jacques and Protestantism *Im*proper. 'Vivaciousness' of Jesuitism. Obedience good and indispensable: Loyalty to Beelzebub; most conspicuous proof of caitiffhood within a man's possibility. This country tolerably cleared of Jesuits: Expulsion of the Jesuit Body of little avail, with the Jesuit *Soul* so nestled in the life of mankind everywhere. 'Cant, and even sincere Cant': O Heaven, when a man doing his sincerest is still but canting! The coward solacement of composure and a whole skin. Deadly virus of lying; and such an odour as the angels never smelt before. Awakening from the sleep of death into the Sorcerer's Sabbath of Anarchy (305).—A man's 'religion,' not the many things he tries to believe, but the few things he cannot doubt. The modern man's 'religion'; what poor scantling of 'divine convictions' he has. A singular piece of scribble, in Sauerteig's hand, on Pig Philosophy: Pigs of sensibility and superior logical parts: Their 'religion,'—notion of the Universe, and of their interests and duties there (313).—The Fine Arts, by some thought to be a kind of religion: Here too the consummate flower of Consecrated Unveracity reigns supreme. The new St. Stephen's, with its wilderness of stone pepper-boxes. The Fine Arts, like the coarse and every art of Man's god-given Faculty, sent hither not to fib and dance, but to speak and work. Homer's Iliad, no Fiction but a Ballad *History*: The Hebrew Bible, before all things, *true*, as no other Book ever was or will be. The History of every Nation an Epic and Bible, the clouded struggling image of a God's Presence. Beyond doubt the Almighty Maker made this England too; and has been and forever is miraculously present here. What are the eternal covenants we can believe, and dare not for our life's sake but go and observe? *These* are our Bible, *our* God's

Word, such as it may be. 'Miracles,' 'worships,' after their kind. No rhythmic History of England, but what we find in Shakspeare. Luxurious Europe; with its wits, story-tellers, ballad-singers, dancing-girls: All the Fine Arts converted into after-dinner Amusements. How all things hang together! Universal Jesuitism once lodged in the heart, you will see it in the very finger-nails by and by (320).—Our *Exodus* from Houndsditch: Yankee Gathercoal, and his strange-flashing torch-gleams. How simple souls clamour occasionally for what they call 'a new religion.' This Universe, in all times, the express image of the human souls, and their thoughts and activities, who dwell there. The 'open secret,' in these dark days a very shut one indeed. Surely this ignoble sluggishness, sceptical torpor, is not doomed to be our final condition: Under this brutal stagnancy there does lie painfully imprisoned some tendency which could become heroic (329).

INDEX

THE END

Printed by T. and A. Constable, Printers to Her Majesty
at the Edinburgh University Press.

Printed in Dunstable, United Kingdom

64840103R00211